More praise for 'Cross Purposes'

It's rare to find a book on topics such as religion or politics that isn't motivated by us-vs.-them tribalism or political agenda, but Welch has found a way to bridge the divide to invite honest discussion and reflection in both areas.

Whether you're a lifelong conservative who is praying for Trump to run in 2024, or a never-Trumper who would see that as the final trumpet being sounded prior to the apocalypse, you're sure to find the heartfelt and honest conversations from Welch's boots-on-the-ground approach to unpacking the changes in American evangelicalism both helpful and thought-provoking.
—**Belt of Truth Ministries**

Bob Welch exemplifies the biblical wisdom of being quick to hear, slow to speak, and slow to anger. His carefully researched, cool-headed, and balanced treatment of several controversial issues dominating our day helps to restore integrity and credibility to what it means to be a follower of Jesus.

At a time when discouragement is at an all-time high among pastors, as they have watched their churches follow the world in political rancor, Welch's gospel-centered wisdom is a great encouragement to me. May his tribe—the tribe of Christ, not the Far Right—increase.
—**Dr. Ben Cross, Lead Teaching Pastor, First Baptist Church, Eugene, Oregon**

Experienced by a man of faith and a compassionate investigative journalist, Welch's thoughtful journey of healing will speak to many hearts as it is meant to: Not as an attack, but as encouragement.
Jane Kirkpatrick, New York Times best-selling author

As a person of Christian faith but not an evangelical, I've watched the last five years with amazement and anguish. Nothing I've read so thoroughly and thoughtfully captures what I saw, too, as a disconnect between faith and followers as does Welch's Cross Purposes. *It is a powerful, thought-provoking personal reflection regarding our quest to, as Bonhoeffer says, say "yes to God."*

Clarice Wilsey, author of *Letters from Dachau: A Father's Witness of War, a Daughter's Dream of Peace*

Evangelicalism is not my religion; it is not my fight. Reading this wonderful book, however, I came to realize that truth in American politics is everyone's business. Welch's book is deeply researched, brilliantly written, and fearless, taking evangelicals to task for chasing political gain at cost to their values. Acknowledging his own complicity in "going along" and "remaining silent," Welch hopes to shake, motivate, challenge, and inspire evangelicals to embrace change, to listen to a wider variety of voices, and to return to the heart and soul of their faith.

Faris Cassell, award-winning author of *The Unanswered Letter*

Cross Purposes

Other books by Bob Welch

Saving My Enemy
The Wizard of Foz
52 Little Lessons from A Christmas Story
Lessons on the Way to Heaven
My Oregon III
52 Little Lessons from Les Misérables
Cascade Summer
Resolve
52 Little Lessons from It's a Wonderful Life
My Oregon II
Pebble in the Water
My Oregon
American Nightingale
The Things That Matter Most
My Seasons
Where Roots Grow Deep
A Father for All Seasons
More to Life Than Having It All

Collaborative efforts

1972 (with Steve Bence)
Leave No Man Behind (with Dr. Tony Brooks)
Boy in the Mirror (with Jim Bartko)
Healing Wounds (with Diane Carlson Evans)
Letters from Dachau (with Clarice Wilsey)
i am n (with The Voice of the Martyrs)
Easy Company Soldier (with Don Malarkey)

Children's books

The Keyboard Kitten (Illustrated by Tom Penix)
The Keyboard Kitten Gets Oregonized (Illustrated by Tom Penix)

Cross Purposes

One believer's struggle to reconcile
the peace of Christ with the rage of the Far Right

A Memoir

Bob Welch

Ragamuffin
Books

New York London Paris Yachats

Copyright 2021 by Bob Welch

All rights reserved. No part of this book may be reproduced in any form without written permission from the author, except by reviewers or authors who may quote brief passages in support of their works.

Ragamuffin Books

New York London Paris Yachats

ISBN: 978-0-9772306-4-8

Printing 012422

Also available as an e-book and an audiobook (both available on amazon.com)

All Bible passages are from the New International Version except for a handful from the King James Version that are noted with "KJV."

Front- and back-cover designs by Bob Welch with the assistance of Tom Penix of penwaxdesign. Back cover photo by Welch of his family's sailboat, "At Last," at Cultus Lake, September 2020.

To contact the author:

Email
bobwelch@bobwelchwriter.com

Web
bobwelchwriter.com

Snail Mail
PO Box 70785
Springfield, OR 97475

Twitter
@bob_welch23

*For Sally Jean,
Never afraid to exit the freeway
to explore with me the squiggly roads beyond*

Table of Contents

Prologue   13

2016

1. The Prayer   29
2. The Past   39
   - *Hope for the future: Remember our mission*   50
3. Saving Grace   53
4. The Perfect Storm   69
   - *Hope for the future: Love one another*   82
5. Marley & Me   85
6. Trials & Triumph   93
   - *Hope for the future: Replace pride with humility*   106

2017

7. The New President   113
8. Lilies of the Field   127
   - *Hope for the future: Live without fear*   138
9. 'Fire the SOB!'   143

2018

10. 'One of Us'   153
    - *Hope for the future: Welcome in, don't wall off*   164

2019

11. Wise Men & Folly   171
12. Opposite Day   181

Hope for the future: Choose character over comfort	190
13. Flags & Crosses	195

2020

14. Death & Deception	209
15. COVID Nation	217
16. The Decision	233
Hope for the future: Dedicate ourselves to the truth	238
17. Choosing Sides	243
18. Consider the Source	251
Hope for the future: See ourselves not as victims	260
19. Line in the Sand	263
20. Denial	271
Hope for the future: Not bow to celebrity 'leaders'	282

2021

21. Capitol Offense	289
Hope for the future: Find the courage to change	300
Afterword	311
Epilogue	317
Further Exploration	321
Readers' Group Questions	325
Acknowledgments	329
Bibliography	333
Reference Notes	337
Index	355

Your "yes" to God demands your "no" to all injustice, to all evil, to all lies, to oppression and violation of the weak and the poor, to all godlessness and mocking of the holy.

—Dietrich Bonhoeffer

Prologue

The opposite of love, I have found, is not hate, but indifference.
—Eli Weisel

The Sunday School teacher gathered her munchkins for story time. "OK, kids," she said, "let's begin with a question. Raise your hand if you think you know the answer. Ready?"

Bobblehead nods all around.

"I'm thinking of a little animal. It's usually brown or gray, lives in a tree, has a big, furry tail, and collects nuts for the winter. Any ideas?"

Twelve arms shot into the air, hands fluttering back and forth like runaway windshield wipers. The teacher pointed to a boy in the back.

"Wyatt?"

"Well, Ms. Walters, I know the answer's *Jesus*," he said, "but it sure sounds like a squirrel to me!"

Since Donald Trump announced his intention to run for president in 2015, I've felt a lot like that little boy: As an evangelical Christian, I knew the answer had to be Trump, but it sure seemed like something else to me.

In more than a half century of attending church, I've sat through thousands of sermons. Read hundreds of books. Attended countless Bible studies, retreats, and small-group discussions. And what I've been taught is that, as Christians, we were to:

- Be honest.
- Show humility.
- Lead by serving others.
- Be generous, particularly to the "least of these."
- Treat others as we would want to be treated.
- Forgive our enemies.
- Love courageously.
- Seek first the kingdom of God.
- Flee from idols.
- Be faithful.

And then suddenly, it seemed as if some mythical czar of evangelicalism—I picture the face, if not the faith, of actor Jim Carrey—snapped on a toothy smile, widened his eyes, tilted his head, and said:

Just kidding!

By now, contrasting Trump's ways with Christ's ways has become the stuff of cliché. But I had come to believe that deeper things were at work, that our evangelical faith was not only at cross-purposes with him, but with the Far Right in general; at cross-purposes with a zeal for America that bordered on idolatry; indeed, at cross-purposes with the very essence of Christianity as defined by Scripture: how we treat our neighbors. Try as I might, I couldn't reconcile the peace of Christ with the hard-edged politics of the Far Right.

Thus my decision to write a book that I'd never tried so hard *not* to write, so fearful was I of wounding friends, most of whom voted for Trump. The result is a four-course meal: part personal memoir, part historical review, part political analysis, and, I hope, part spiritual encouragement.

Here's what it's *not*: a 360-page screed on Trump, patriotism, and conservatism. Nor is it a love letter to liberalism. It's simply the story of one believer's journey to try and understand this uneasy melding of Jesus followers with hard-right politics, the discord hitting home with an uncomfortable truth: for decades, I'd been quietly complicit in it.

Then, in June 2016, I prayed a prayer that triggered a major reconsideration of my beliefs. Until then, it was as if I'd assumed that wherever the motorcycle of faith ventured, the sidecar of "Far Right" had to come along.

I no longer believe that. I've changed. And Trump prompted that change. His rise to power forced me to decide what I really stood for—and the answer, it turned out, wasn't him or the Christian nationalism he promotes. Instead, I realized I needed to stand for the Christ who endorses neither Republicans nor Democrats but transcends both.

EARLY ON in my year-long research and writing process, I thought I'd arrived on the mountaintop of understanding—Trump alone needed to be my focus. But after more studying, praying, interviewing, and listening, I realized I'd reached a false summit. Trump, per se, wasn't the problem; he was an oversimplification of a deeper, wider, more insidious challenge for evangelicals. Our problem, I realized, was locking arms with any person, political party, or movement that doesn't square scripturally with the One we serve. That promotes tribalism instead of truth. Country over Christ. And hate for our enemy.

After putting my semifinal draft under the scrutiny of no fewer than eleven editors, a final epiphany emerged: the Far Right—The Tribe—wasn't the true summit either. We can blame people or parties or movements but, in the end, we are responsible for this and only this: ourselves. Our actions. Our *reactions*.

The bottom line, I concluded, had to go beyond Trump and beyond evangelicals' response to him; it had to go to myself as a believer. Had the Trump years emboldened me to glorify God or skewed me to think less "Christianly" and more politically? Concerning the Great Commandment (love God and others), was I more compassionate or less? And in terms of the Great Commission (share Christ with others), was evangelicalism's influence helping my efforts or hurting?

During Trump's rise to power, I discovered I'd lost a certain naïvety I had about America, politics, and my evangelical faith in general. On the flip side, I found something critical: *new perspective.*

What both fueled and frustrated this shift was my professional background. For most of my life I worked in the newspaper business as a reporter, editor, and columnist. My faith and my profession had long been at odds with each other, but Trump brought the simmering to a boil. As an evangelical, I was scorned by the very media of which I was part. As a journalist, I was maligned as an "enemy of the people." Thus, I had a unique perspective from which to watch the Trump parade: too left for the Right, and too right for the Left. I was the proverbial man without a country.

TRUMP'S PRESIDENCY, with an assist from COVID, unsettled our country like nothing I've seen in my lifetime. His influence didn't turn evangelicals into different people overnight; instead, like microwave popcorn, his influence empowered the seeds of self-protection that the Moral Majority had started sowing in evangelicals four decades earlier.

Trump didn't create this sub-culture, he super-sized it. He tempted evangelicals with the lure of power. Fanned the flames of our fears. Encouraged us to bully The Enemy—Democrats, liberals, "socialists." And, refusing to accept clear-cut election results in 2020, ultimately incited violence that a small group of his more radical followers delivered with an attack on the US Capitol.

As if part of an evangelical X ray, Trump exposed our inner-most loyalties, forcing us to decide if we were OK with those loyalties. I was not. I saw, in myself, someone who, though subtly, had played his own self-protection game for decades, but only now had awakened to it.

As an evangelical, I didn't like the idea of having to justify, rationalize, or pretend I didn't see Trump's un-Christian, me-first myopia. And I didn't like how some of my fellow evangelicals—mostly the influential higher-ups—supported, excused, and enabled the man. The limbo-bar of moral reprehension could never be set too low for him; whatever he did—bully, demean, lie—most evangelicals defended him with the consistency of an auto-reply message.

Not that I shared my quiet defiance with others. I didn't instigate, or join in, Facebook discussions about Trump, some of which had all the temerity of prison riots. For the most part, I stayed silent, though soon realized an emerging truth: I had become a never-Trump evangelical, the kind of person Franklin Graham called "almost demonic."[1]

And if I had not amortized daily in expressing my sense that politics were diluting our faith, I decided, in September 2020, to make a lump-sum payment. You're holding it in your hands—some of you, I'd imagine, with some unease. Frankly, I understand; if you've read me before, you'll soon realize this isn't the typical inspirational book I write. That said, I hope it's an honest book, a Scripture-based book, and an encouraging book motivated not by any desire on my part to demean but to help us, as believers, find higher ground.

WHY BOTHER? Why write it? Why not let this sleeping dog lie? Because the Trump influence is only a piece in a much bigger puzzle. After the 2020 election, it was clear that he was not a one-and-done experiment in American conservatism, but the harbinger of a new normal. And how evangelicals respond going forward is crucial, frankly, to whether our collective faith re-emerges as any sort of answer to a world with questions, or wobbles further into the folds of a political party less concerned about the Prince of Peace than about the pride of power.

My motives aren't to shame or blame, but to challenge long-held assumptions, encourage dialogue, and question evangelicals, myself included. Should we be OK with this "new normal?"

Frankly, most have avoided the question, even from the pulpit. As evangelicals, when it comes to how politics relates to faith, we seem to either stick our heads in the sand or beat each other to death on Facebook; I have to believe there's a better way to understand each other, grow in our faith, and glorify God.

This is not a book that castigates anyone who voted for Donald Trump; we are more nuanced than our presidential preferences. Instead, it's a book that goes far deeper, I hope, ultimately posing a question author Henri Nouwen so eloquently asks: "To whom do I belong? To God or to the world?"[2]

I could write an entire book about the good I've seen Christians do in my lifetime. About how small-minded some on The Left can be about evangelicals. Or about how "we all just need to get along." But if all are worthy topics, none is my focus. This is a book aimed specifically at white evangelical Christians like myself, encouraging us to sharpen perspectives that I fear have been blurred by politics.

AS SOON as I hesitatingly said yes to this book-writing test, my insecurities kicked in. Who was I to write such a thing? I'd spent my life working at *newspapers*; I was part of the "liberal media." What evangelical would want to listen to a fake-news guy like me?

And for a book whose theme would be thick with politics, I wasn't particularly political; I think we place far too much importance on flawed people like ourselves—politicians—and on their flawed policies to right a world that can't be legislated, or bullied, into "rightness."

Then it dawned on me: because of this rare blend of "journalist" and "Christian," maybe I was *exactly* the right person to write this book. Most people rush to The Left or The Right like people grabbing seats on a bus. I don't; I see virtues and villains in both.

As a journalist for forty years in the prickly briars of American culture, I'd been galled by people's unwillingness to try to really understand each other—and, frankly, themselves. Few people change their minds about anything. Instead, in the theater of life, we read the lines that our respective directors hand us and play our parts. But, as evangelicals, rarely do we wonder what, exactly, we're conveying to the audience, those to whom we're supposed to be reflecting Christ.

Most of us live in bubbles, seldom venturing beyond our comfort zones; ninety-one percent of evangelicals say their friends are "mostly similar," making them the most cloistered group in America, according to a 2018 survey.[3] It works both ways. "Mike, quick," I said to an agnostic friend, a Democrat, as we huddled in our socially distanced chairs in a parking lot, "how many evangelicals have you had a meaningful conversation with?" He nodded at me. "One."

Largely because of that, we're basically clueless about each other, like the ship-cruise passenger who asks the deck officer, "What religion are the people with the patches behind their ears?" Oh, we're "experts" on whatever stereotype we've slapped on another group, but we rarely allow ourselves to see the nuances beyond.

As something of a hybrid, I've spent four decades exploring such nuances. My journalism career granted me access to all sorts of people, places, and experiences others were not. I've reported on the Pope and pedophiles, Olympians and outcasts, high society and homeless men whose life's possessions fit in a shopping cart. I've interviewed saints, soldiers, pacifists, white supremacists, Buddhists, nudists—you name it. In Boston, I was the lone gentile at a Jewish barbecue and in Oregon's Blue Mountains, the lone non-hunter on a week-long elk-hunting trip on which I was bucked off a horse with the dude ranch name of "Rusty."

Now, be honest: some of you have already dismissed my train of thought because you're evangelicals and, at the mention of the phrase "newspaper columnist," you jumped the tracks. With an assist to Trump, you thought "fake news." "Lamestream media." "Don't trust."

OK, try this on: I've also written half a dozen Christian-themed books and done dozens of interviews on conservative Christian radio and TV stations in the United States and Canada. Been a guest on Pat Robertson's *700 Club*. Served as an elder for more than two decades in my non-denominational evangelical church. Preached in more than a dozen churches. And led Christian men's retreats from Port Townsend, Washington, to Tampa Bay, Florida.

At age sixty-seven, I think I can say I've lived more of a "dual existence"—and, because of it, may be more objective—than most evangelicals. I polished a story for *Focus on the Family* magazine the same day I covered a Grateful Dead concert for *The Register-Guard*. I've won two "best column" awards from the National Society of Newspaper Columnists and a Gold Medallion book award from the Evangelical Christian Publishers Association.

What's more, my family experience is diverse. In geopolitical terms, my extended family is farther left than Cape Alava, Washington; my wife's farther right than Quoddy Head, Maine.

My evangelical friends around the country, some of whom live in heavily Christian places such as Colorado Springs and Fort Worth, shake their heads at my decidedly un-evangelical environs. I live in Eugene, Oregon, the most liberal city in one of the least-churched states in the nation—and most recently worked in the editorial department of a left-leaning newspaper.[4]

On the other hand, many of my liberal friends think I was abducted by evangelical aliens and returned to earth as "one of them." My book editor in New York, as we were working on a manuscript about a heroic World War II nurse, dubbed me "Ward Cleaver in combat boots."[5]

Having lived in two disparate worlds doesn't make me better than anybody else, it simply makes me privileged to have seen a lot of different perspectives and to realize that the blacks and whites we so easily see are nuanced with far more grays than some may want to believe.

For example, if I were asked what individual most profoundly shaped *how I regard other human beings*—the essence of what, according to my understanding of Scripture, we Christians should value highly—I'd say my late, great, non-evangelical, liberal, Trump-despising mother, whose empathy for others ran deep. And if I were asked to name someone who profoundly modeled for me *unconditional love*—the essence of Jesus's love for us—I'd say my evangelical, Trump-supporting father-in-law, the agronomy professor who I met when his seventeen-year-old daughter brought me home. I was a recovering agnostic, had hair to my shoulders, was dressed in overalls, and attended the rival liberal-arts school down the road—but that man accepted me just as I was, believed in me, and for half a century, has been nothing but an encouragement to me.

IN THE BOOK of Matthew, one of the "teachers of the law" comes to Jesus and asks, "Of all the commandments, which is the most important?" It's the equivalent of a more-secularized question that Billy Crystal (Mitch) asks of Jack Palance (Curly) in *City Slickers*. What's the *one thing*? What matters above everything else?

Jesus answered: "Love the Lord your God with all your heart and with all your soul and with all your mind. This is the first and greatest commandment. And the second is like it: 'Love your neighbor as yourself.' *All the Law and the Prophets hang on these two commandments* (Matthew 22)." [Italics mine.]

Love. That, the Scripture says, is to be the hallmark of those who follow Jesus. The thing that identifies us, defines us, drives us. Love. Not control. Not hate for our enemies. Not personal rights. Love.

Then along came Trump. And, like my fellow evangelicals, there I was, instinctively compelled to think he, of course, was our answer when, deep down, all I saw was a squirrel. Or something more sinister. "Watch out for false prophets," says Matthew 7:15. "They come to you in sheep's clothing, but inwardly they are ferocious wolves."

One morning, a photo appeared on my computer of a rally featuring Trump, a man who seemed to have no moral compunction whatsoever about lying. In the background of the giddy throng was a sign: "Evangelicals for Truth." And I said to myself: What's wrong with this picture?"

IN SEPTEMBER 2020, amid COVID, I started interviewing masked people I knew in coffee-shop parking lots: pastors, friends, acquaintances, anyone who, regardless of their political or religious beliefs, I thought I could learn from. I peppered people with email questions, did Zoom interviews, and listened to podcasts involving faith and politics. I scoured the Bible and read or re-read more than a hundred books. As I hiked, I doubled down on sermons, listening not only to my church pastor's but a handful of others. I thumbed through Twitter, following some people who amplified my perspective and some who clashed with it.

I prayed and pondered—a lot. As the 2020 election neared, I disciplined myself to listen to both sides of the news; on treks to the top of Mt. Pisgah, I'd tune to Fox News—on the way down, I'd switch to CNN, a heady reminder of how two groups of people can look at the same set of facts so differently. (Full disclosure: Though I'm a man of faith, whose very nature precludes certainty, I believe in evidence-supported facts. And I also believe in science, even though I see it as a complement to, rather than a replacement of, God.)

I decided to write the book as a memoir because: (a) religion and politics are deeply personal; (b) mine was a story in progress, dealt out like a fly-fisher's line; and (c) most books about Trump and evangelicals have been sociological overviews—head driven, not heart driven. I wanted to keep it at eye level, though not involve family or close friends' perspectives; this wasn't their story, but mine, and it would be self-serving to assume they would want to be part of the book—and, frankly, would complicate our relationships in unnecessary ways.

Likewise, when quoting people I knew, I chose to not include names. Though that goes against the grain of my journalistic intuition, I was already stepping through enough land mines to write this book. I didn't want to put friends at risk for having to defend comments that they had made to me, not the world, even if they knew I was gathering fodder for a book.

I wanted to be both tour guide and Guy on the Bus. And, finally, I wanted to welcome non-evangelical readers along on the ride, perhaps broadening their perspective on a faith group that's too often viewed only through a political filter.

AS I DEEPENED my research, I found myself racked with an unfamiliar emotion when it came to book writing: *fear*. I was afraid that as I broke from the evangelical pack, I would come across as a holier-than-thou critic of the very friends I loved, respected, and enjoyed. You see, I think a lot of non-evangelicals paint us—as we often paint others—with a fairly broad brush. Evangelicals, the stereotype goes, are narrow-minded, bigoted, self-righteous, judgmental, humor-less, dour, finger-pointing losers. And, I'm ashamed to admit, some evangelicals like that exist. But here's what might surprise "outsiders": many of the finest, most ethical, trustworthy, honest, humble, fun, sensitive, giving, loving, upbeat, compassionate, and empathetic people I know are evangelicals. And nearly all voted for Donald Trump.

To me, this was the biggest head-scratcher: how could people who, in many ways, saw the world as I did, valued what I did, read the same Bible I did, and worshipped the same God I did support a man who I saw as a political conniver using evangelicals only for personal gain? Did these friends know something I did not?

Clearly, this was not going to be a simple swan dive, but a

reverse-one-and-a-half somersault—into a wading pool. Great potential to get hurt. And it gets worse. Besides Trump, the book would have to include a handful of other incendiary topics such as COVID, race, and immigration.

"Seriously," said a young friend who shares my concerns about evangelicals' undying loyalty to the Far Right. "People will *hate* you if you write that book. My father-in-law and I still aren't talking. He loves Trump. And I dared to tell him I don't."

That's possible, though I'm hoping my closer friends will see my effort as a well-intentioned struggle to reconcile my personal faith with a force that challenged that faith. But I can't lie: first and foremost, I feared wounding people I cared about deeply.

A second fear, given Trump's 2020 loss, was that some would think I was rubbing it in—as if to say to those who supported him: *Ha! I was right and you were wrong.* Nope, not my circus, not my monkeys. I committed to this project two months before the 2020 election—and was "all in," regardless of the results. What's more, I was never that person on the social-media soap box, letting everyone know where he stood in the first place—meaning a "told-ya-so" now would be like a one-handed clap.

Finally, I feared that some people would think I'd recalibrated my beliefs to make great sums of money with a book based on a controversial topic. Only in my dreams. When I bounced the idea off my agent, who works mainly with Christian publishing houses, he passed without hesitation. I understood. As one of the two in ten evangelicals who didn't support Trump, I would be like the guy in Ketchikan, Alaska, who had the sunblock concession. So, I chose to self-publish, knowing I could make more money dishing up kung pao chicken at Panda Express.

Ultimately, I decided I could live with pushback. However, if I stayed silent, I couldn't live with something else: myself. "There comes a time," Martin Luther King Jr. said, "when silence is betrayal."

We become what we tolerate. As Christians, the championing of Trump weakened our witness to the world, deepened the divide between us and non-believers, and tainted some evangelicals—repeat, *some*—with a Trump-inspired contempt for others that clashes with our biblical call to love our enemies.

For me, silence felt far more comfortable—and that's exactly why I had to speak: because I'd come to believe that comfort played a huge role in why evangelicals cozied up to Trump. In the bastion of tribalism, going with the flow is always easier than resisting.

I imagine some evangelical pastors want to resist—want to say certain things from the pulpit, but don't because they fear they'll lose members, money, maybe even their jobs. But with less to risk, perhaps I can say what some pastors might be afraid to say and what some of their parishioners might be afraid to admit: that in the eyes of the world—that is, the people we're supposed to be mirroring Jesus to—what's come to define evangelicals in 2021 has less to do with grace and God than with guns and the GOP; less to do with Good News than Fox News; and less to do with welcoming in than walling off.

Exceptions abound. For half a century, I've seen the good works of Christians, some of whose sacrifices and friendships have benefited me. I've seen women support women who've been abused. I've watched people serve on medical missions overseas. I've seen countless acts of compassion: folks taking in foster kids, building bridges to prisoners at the Oregon State Penitentiary, truly ministering to "the least of these." Still, an increasingly vocal subset of evangelicals is sounding a loud and dissonant tone, not the sweet music of selfless love but the clanging cymbals of self-righteousness.

In saying such things, I'm aware that some fellow believers will think I've somehow gone over to the dark side, working against "us." That's OK; as a follower of Jesus, I'm not called to be popular or successful, just faithful. But I can't hide a truth that is increasingly apparent to a world that's watching: As evangelicals, some of us are too busy defending ourselves to examine our hearts. The resistance I presume I'll get from some reading this book is part of the very problem I'm addressing.

We spend more time looking at the world through our own eyes than, with empathy, imagining what the world might look like to others. And we too easily embrace a Far Right political movement that pines for power despite our serving a savior who " … made himself nothing by taking the very nature of a servant … . (Philippians 2:7-9)."

A FINAL NOTE before beginning my story: For decades, surveys have shown that among numerous demographic groups, white evangelical Christians are the least likely to believe African Americans have been, and are currently being, discriminated against. In 2020, after the brutal killings of a handful of African Americans, including George Floyd, played out on TV and social media, a survey by the Barna Group revealed this: self-identifying white Christians were *nearly twice as likely* to say race is "not at all" a problem in the US than they were in 2019, the previous year.[6] In other words, the well-publicized killings didn't create more empathy toward blacks among white evangelicals, but created *less*.

That's not fake news. That's not, as Trump likes to call it, the "lamestream media." That's a survey done by the most reputable Christian survey firm on the planet. That's a reflection of tribal thinking, not Bible thinking. And that's why I can't keep silent any longer. When you connect the dots, there's a disturbing pattern that suggests the people who should care the most about others may care the least.

That's why I'm telling my story about how Donald Trump changed my life. Because if our goal as Christians is to love God and to love others—including people different from us—we must return to the roots of our faith. And if truth is an essential part of that process, it behooves us to face it.

2016

1.

The Prayer

**The day after I offer one, I get
an answer that casts me
into the eye of the hurricane.**

There is only one history of any importance, and it is the history of what you once believed in and the history of what you came to believe in.

—Kay Boyle

It began with a prayer—the story of Donald Trump and me. As a columnist at Oregon's second-largest newspaper, *The Register-Guard*, in Eugene, I'd long told myself that I never wanted to place my security in a workplace but, instead, in deeper things. God things.

Once the thrill was even remotely gone, I planned to leave—emotionally ready or not. As Los Angeles Dodgers owner Branch Rickey once said: "Trade a player a year too early rather than a year too late." At fifty-nine, I'd been privileged to write a three-times-a-week column for fourteen years, and though it was the best job I'd ever had—choosing my own ideas with, blessedly, no meetings!—I decided December 2013 would be the end of the line.

I had no idea what the future held, but that's why I loved hiking the 2,650-mile Pacific Crest Trail: wondering what you'd find around the next bend or beyond the next pass. That's the adventure—the *not knowing*. So, on a snowy Friday afternoon—rare for these parts—I said goodbye to my colleagues, some of whom I'd worked with for more than two decades. I left my dream job with plans to write on my own, teach at the University of Oregon, and have more flexibility for sailing, speaking, writing, browsing used-book stores, and watching grandchildren's baseball games.

Things went well—until they didn't. In 2016, with the promise of the largest book deal I'd ever had, my wife Sally and I stretched ourselves thin with a great-room addition we'd dreamed of for years; we had five young grandchildren within ten minutes of us, and the added space would be perfect for their rambunctious visits.

But from the get-go I'd struggled to get on the same page with my editor in New York. After taking over for an author who'd started the project but left, I'd come to feel like a contractor hired to remodel a house that had never been square in the first place. At one point, my orders shifted so bizarrely that the editor wanted me to bracket a nonfiction story with fictional bookends—and I gamely did so, disjointed though it felt.

When I finished, the editor emailed me. "Bob, you've done a fabulous job, and I think we have a terrific reading experience to offer."

The next week he fired me.

He liked the book, but the publisher did not. She called it "unsalvageable." *Ouch*. In a four-decade writing career, I'd never experienced such a painful rejection. And the loss of potential income was nearly six digits. But what could I do?

"I'm going to have to get a job," I told Sally one evening on our back deck. "Just something part-time so we at least have some steady income, but I still have time to write books."

I had no idea what that job might be. Teacher's aide? The tool department at Jerry's Home Improvement? Sales clerk at REI? I hadn't a clue—and nobody was knocking down my door with possibilities. I'd known I wanted to be a writer since my fifth-grade teacher in Corvallis, Mrs. Wirth, made my Career-Day wish come true: an interview with Oregon State basketball coach Paul Valenti. I wanted to be a reporter.

So, this was strange. This was a lifetime of knowing, at least workwise, what lay before me every day. And, suddenly, peering into the darkness.

Which led to that prayer I mentioned. Nothing fancy. No "thees" or "thous." But tinged with desperation, a minor league version of George Bailey's breakdown in Martini's Bar in *It's a Wonderful Life:* "Please, God, if you're there," he tearfully prays, "Show me the way!" Mine was more like: *God, I thank you for how You've blessed us. But I'm getting a little desperate here, so if there's a job out there, please let me know. And, not to get picky, but if it could be part-time, that'd be cool. Thanks. Amen.*

The next night, June 2, 2016, I was sitting at a grandson's baseball game when my phone buzzed. It was the editorial page editor of *The Register-Guard*, encouraging me to apply for a job that had opened in his department. His associate editor was leaving; the position involved choosing and editing letters to the editor, which, in our yeasty political community, arrived by the hundreds each week. And writing an occasional editorial.

"Hey, I think you'd be perfect," he said. "Any interest in coming back and working for us? Of course, it would only be part-time."

THREE WEEKS later, when I walked into my new office as an associate editor, I felt like a sailor being shown the control panel of an airplane. Yes, I was a journalist, but the editorial department was another animal altogether. As a general columnist my job had been to share my opinion, but this was politics, something I'd stayed away from because it was neither my passion nor expertise. I had told the editor as much when I'd gone in for an interview.

Although we didn't discuss it, he knew something else about me: in a newsroom of perhaps sixty people, at a paper whose editorial department leaned decidedly left, you could count the conservative-to-moderates on one hand—and I was one of them. You can't write nearly 2,000 personal columns and not let readers know who you are and what you stand for. When I had started the job in 1999, I reminded myself that I was given a column, not a pulpit, and decided to try and be a "peacekeeper" columnist, try to help The Left understand The Right, and The Right understand The Left. Help people "see bigger." That said, I alluded to my faith when appropriate. And when *The Register-Guard* did a story on Christians in the media, I agreed to be interviewed, even if I didn't see why it should be newsworthy that someone of faith might report the news—anymore than that he or she might be left-handed or like cold pizza.

Among Christians I knew, few lived in the discombobulated world I did. At *The Register-Guard*, I was the rare church-goer among liberals; at church, the rare journalist among conservatives.

Technically, I was an "evangelical Christian," an admission that immediately makes me suspect to those who feed on stereotypes. But evangelicals are not monolithic. Two-thirds of us live outside the United States. One-quarter of American evangelicals are people of color.[7] Half live in the South.[8] Among white evangelicals, a third are Democrats.[9]

To me, labels are, at best, necessary evils—necessary because they can help us define and understand something or someone, evil because in doing so we can exaggerate whatever stereotype we neatly confine that "something" or "someone" to. The very phrase "evangelical Christian" isn't a favorite of mine for that very reason; in the last half century, it has morphed from its original meaning of bearer of "good news," derived from the Greek word *euangelion,* to the more modern translation: "the bigoted wacko with the "He > I" symbol on his car who just cut me off." (For some time, evangelicals had been considered "friendlier fundamentalists," the latter of whom could express a legalistic devotion to doctrine at the expense of love—but, as of late, evangelicals were now being seen less for their other-orientedness than for their political devotion to the Hard Right.)

Though my allegiance had never been to, say, the National Association of Evangelicals, I think I'd pass its "four-way test": uphold the Bible as one's ultimate authority; confess the centrality of Christ's atonement; believe in a born-again conversion experience; and actively work to spread the good news and reform society.[10]

Politically, I saw party labels as the same double-edged sword, helping define and stereotype people at the same time. A Republican for much of my life, I had briefly become an Independent, then registered as a Democrat mainly because I respected Barack Obama and wanted to help him win the party's nomination. To some, the idea that someone in The Tribe—conservative evangelicals—could capriciously switch to the "enemy party" might strike them as blasphemous. But my identity was in Christ, not a political party, and to place undue faith in a man-made institute would be the stuff of idolatry that Scripture warns against. ("You shall have no other gods before me," says Exodus 20:3.)

In sum, I was a Democrat in law, an Independent in spirit, and a Republican in policy, a complicated political cocktail that spoke less of my indecisiveness or passion than of my attempt to hold lightly to "the world." But, to simplify, I was politically right of center, which, in Eugene at the time, made you Rush Limbaugh.

Indeed, many Eugene liberals were quick to pigeonhole Christians. A neighbor with an undergraduate degree from Stanford and a doctorate from the University of Oregon told me of a friend finding out that he was a Christian. "How can that be?" he said. "I *liked* you. You like *jazz!*"

A refreshing exception to such stereotyping from liberals was Nicholas Kristof, a progressive *New York Times* columnist who I'd always admired because: (a) he was truly open-minded, rare for national columnists on either side of the fence; (b) he had a heart for the world's underdogs, traveling extensively to uncover their stories; (c) he grew up in Yamhill, near my wife's grandparents' farm in Oregon's Willamette Valley; and (d) he and his daughter, like me, were PCT hikers. Wrote Kristof in 2016:

> Too many secular liberals have moved from denouncing religious intolerance to embracing an irreligious intolerance of their own. Too

often, liberals mock conservative Christians in ways that would outrage them if Jews, Muslims, or others were the target. It is too often acceptable on liberal campuses to create a climate hostile and contemptuous of evangelicals—and that, too, is bigotry.

It also misunderstands the faith. In my reporting around the world, I've been awed by evangelical and Catholic missionary doctors risking their lives to ease suffering. And remember that it was evangelical pressure that led President George W. Bush to adopt a massive program to fight AIDS around the world, saving millions of lives and turning the tide on the disease.[11]

Kristof peeved many in his tribe when, in another column, he'd written about how close-minded university types could be, constituting what he called "liberal arrogance." Four studies had found that the proportion of Republican professors—I was an adjunct in the University of Oregon's School of Journalism & Communication—ranged from only 6 and 11 percent in the humanities to 7 and 9 percent in social sciences. He called Republicans "an endangered species" on college campuses.

He interviewed black sociologist George Yancey, an evangelical Christian, who said, "Outside academia I face more problems as black. But inside academia I face more problems as a Christian, and it is not even close."[12]

In the newspaper world, I found a less chilly climate as a Christian, though I did experience a few eye-rolling incidents. Once, half a dozen *R-G* editors, including me, were waiting for a meeting to begin when an editor casually referenced a letter in that morning's paper from a conservative pastor in our community. The topic was the death penalty and the pastor's pro-death stance seemed, to me, spiteful, insensitive, and arrogant. I remember thinking: *Man, it's hard to believe we share the same faith.*

"That's a Christian for you," the editor said to anyone listening.

Whoa. I wanted to say something right then and there but to do so might unnecessarily wound her in front of others; returning "evil for evil" wasn't the right play. Later, I asked if she had a minute to chat and, in her office, I politely told her I thought her comment cast an unfairly wide net on what constitutes a Christian.

"My standard for living is Jesus, not a hard-edged pastor," I said. "I'm surprised at how you assume all Christians are like this guy."

She didn't respond, as if not knowing *how* to respond.

"Let me ask you this: Are you an environmentalist?"

"Of course," she said.

"Oh, well, then you're one of the folks who spikes trees with giant nails—with no regard for whether that might injure or kill a logger."

"Of course not," she said.

"But do you see my point? Nobody likes to be defined by the extremists that are part of our groups. And yet that's exactly what you did with your comment. And what so many people do. We don't get to know people. We label them."

All of which is to say: given the chasm between Christians and non-Christians, it was fairly amazing that I'd just been hired to be part of a left-leaning editorial department at *The R-G*.

Did I believe this new job was an answer to prayer? I can't say for sure; a major aspect of faith is its mystery. Faith is "assurance about what we do not see (Hebrews 11:1)." What I *can* say is that I asked God for a part-time job, and within twenty-four hours I was essentially offered one. The cynic might suggest it was only a coincidence that I'd left full-time employment at the paper 905 days earlier and hadn't had a single job offer—not one—and then, after praying for a job for the first time, had such an offer the very next day. Conversely, the close-minded evangelical might suggest the job couldn't possibly have been an answer to prayer; why would a loving God allow "one of His own" to return to work for The Left-Wing Media—The Enemy?

In the 1990s, the Christian publishing house I wrote books for had me do dozens of in-person interviews with Christian TV and radio stations, mainly in the South and Midwest. The hosts would often take calls from listeners after the interview. A common question was: "How can you call yourself a Christian and work at a newspaper?"

I'd tell the caller that Scripture calls us to be salt and light in the world—and you can't do that very well unless you interact with that world. Not that my answer seemed to convince him or others who objected.

"Man," said one guy, "that's crazy."

AS AN ASSOCIATE editor, my new job was culling through the dozens of letters-to-the-editor each morning, pick four to eight that seemed representative of what seemed to be on our readers' minds, edit them, and slap headlines on them. I'd copy-edit editorials and op-ed pieces. And, at times, write an editorial.

My boss, a Democrat, had more confidence in me than I had in myself. One morning, he said, "Hey, join me in the conference room, we're interviewing Kate Brown."

"Uh, no, you're the expert, I—."

"You got this."

And there I was, fifteen minutes later, bouncing questions off Oregon's governor.

As I settled into the new gig, I took a strange liking to it. I enjoyed mixing it up with people who looked at the world differently than I did. I enjoyed getting to know the regulars. Some letter-writers were totally laid-back; this was, after all, "Blue Jean, Oregon." And some were 150-word sticks of dynamite. One older reader wrote hand-scrawled letters each week—you could *feel* the guy's anger—telling us that, as minions of the "Evil Red Guard," we were all going to "burn in hell along with Hillary and all other libs." Once, I wrote him back, thanking him for the letters, and ending with a cheery "God bless you!"

MY RETURN to the paper in 2016 was sandwiched between the Republican National Convention in Cleveland and the Democratic National Convention in Philadelphia. Neither offered much suspense. It was going to be Republican Donald Trump against Democratic Sen. Hillary Clinton in November to replace Obama as president.

It had been a little over a year since Trump had descended the escalator at New York's Trump Tower to announce his intention to run for president. Few gave him much of a chance. Unlike Ronald Reagan, the movie star who'd at least been governor of California before his plunge into the 1980 presidential race, Trump had never even been on a city utility board. He was a TV personality (*The Apprentice*), a billionaire, a businessman, and a lightning rod for lawsuits, tabloid headlines, and general chaos. He'd been married three times, accused of sexually assaulting women a handful of times, and sued literally thousands of times.[13]

To me, it didn't seem like an appealing resume—particularly for Christians who traditionally valued character and integrity. When President Bill Clinton had an affair with a White House intern in the mid-'90s, for example, some evangelicals jostled each other to see who could cast the first stone. Though I was no Hillary Clinton fan, Trump concerned me.

Among other things, including well-documented reports that Trump never read—a prerequisite, I believe, for understanding any issue—I was bothered by his contempt for the media. Obviously, I was biased; like a police officer who bristles at being called a "pig," I'd already grown tired of Trump's continual "fake news" flip of his hand whenever a story broke that cast him in a bad light. He called the national media "absolute scum" and "totally dishonest people."[14]

More so than most of my newspaper colleagues, I *did* believe the media, in general, leaned left—not because of any concerted effort to thwart The Right but because of unconscious bias. In most newsrooms, liberals outnumbered conservatives by as much as 5:1; from story ideas to interview questions to writing to editing to headlines to story placement, the process of producing news lent itself to bias, regardless of how fair the journalists involved aspired to be. But that's different—and less problematic—than a news organization like Fox that unabashedly plays to its bias and, at times, ignores evidence-based facts. The former, more often than not, is a good-faith effort to be objective that can be skewed by hidden biases, the latter a full-on rush to promote a particular political agenda, with little interest in objective truth.

But here's something that transcends both: No freedom-respecting individual should want to live in a country that doesn't have a free press to, among other things, hold public officials accountable. For me, it had nothing to do with Right or Left. It had to do with democracy, freedom, and preventing power-hungry despots from ruling like "off-with-their-heads" kings. The media are to democracy what police officers are to the law. Shouldn't we *want* to hold public officials' feet to the fire? Shouldn't we *want* to know how our tax dollars are being spent? Shouldn't we *want* to know who's polluting our water and preying on our children?

Every president has clashed with the media—that's a healthy part of democracy—but not until now did we have a presidential candidate who not only questioned reporters, but thought they were "the enemy of the people." That's a line you'd expect from a dictator, not a respecter of democracy.

But I wasn't fretting. "There's no way he'll get the nomination," I told a friend. "No way."

As the months passed, however, I was surprised to learn that evangelical support for Trump was growing. "He's against abortion," some would say. So was I. But Republicans had nearly twenty pro-life candidates to choose from, and only one had emerged as a clear-cut favorite: Trump. It was something else—and, as it increased, I began hearing music from the movie *Jaws*.

What I saw as a *threat*, I soon realized, many of my fellow evangelicals saw as an *opportunity*. I feared the fish, a Great White shark, would swallow us whole, a sort of modern-day Jonah; others hoped they would ride the fish, a glorious and feared Orca, to a new political promised land, as if an empowering scene from a faith-based *Free Willy*.

In June 2016, I was with some evangelical friends at the beach when the discussion turned to politics, something that rarely happened among us. "We're not electing a pastor-in-chief but a commander-in-chief," a friend said, an inference suggesting Trump's moral lapses shouldn't be a problem. He mentioned that Trump had invited hundreds of evangelical pastors to New York, and they'd been impressed with how willing he had been to "give them a seat at the table."

"Trump said he'd undo Obama's law allowing transgender people to serve in the military," he said.

There were nods around the table and no dissent whatsoever, including from me—even if I thought that transgender people in the military seemed an odd priority. I watched from afar but kept quiet, wary of Trump but not knowledgeable enough—or, frankly courageous enough—to question the consensus.

But in that moment, I realized that in even having doubts about Trump, I was already the odd man out.

2.

The Past

I'd been increasingly uncomfortable with the Far Right, but it was easier to go with the flow than to resist it.

Well, it's been building up inside of me for, oh, I don't know how long.
—The Beach Boys, "Don't Worry Baby"

In 1966, when Mark Hatfield, a US Republican senator—and Christian—from my home state of Oregon came out against the war in Vietnam, there was talk of a walkout at a Conservative Baptist Men's retreat at which he traditionally spoke. Long before it would burst onto the scene in the 1970s, the "Christian Right" was quietly posturing—and the GOP, not GOD, often seemed like the priority.

"I was shocked, dismayed, depressed," he wrote in his memoir, *Between a Rock and a Hard Place.* "To this day I cannot understand how believing Christians who have their allegiance to the Prince of Peace could cheer on the nation in that despicable and inhumane war."[15]

It would be other concerns, not Vietnam, that ultimately galvanized the Christian Right as a political force. And it wasn't abortion, though that's long been the evangelical storyline. Instead, the influences were a post-World War II fear of Soviet-based communism—beginning in 1949, Billy Graham fanned these flames at his crusades—and, beginning in 1976, a fear of desegregation.

"The abortion myth ... collapses under closer scrutiny," wrote Randall Balmer, the John Phillips Chair in Religion at Dartmouth University—and an evangelical Christian. "Evangelicals considered abortion a 'Catholic issue' in the 1970s; the Southern Baptist Convention called for the legalization of abortions in 1971, and evangelical leaders applauded the [1973] *Roe v. Wade* decision."[16]

But in 1976, the U.S. Internal Revenue Service revoked the tax-exempt status of Bob Jones University. The conservative religious college in Greenville, South Carolina, didn't allow interracial dating, which constituted unlawful racial discrimination. Overnight, evangelicals—spearheaded by conservative activist Paul Weyrich, founder of the Heritage Foundation—had a cause to rally around.[17] It had been only thirteen years since Sonny Hereford IV's father walked his first-grader to school—amid death threats and more than a hundred screaming parents—to defy Alabama's "white-only" public school system.

"The catalyst for the emergence of the Religious Right was not abortion," said Balmer. "It was defense of tax exemptions for racially segregated schools."[18] More to the point, it was evangelicals' concern that their white children would be forced to go to school with black children.

Ronald Reagan played on these white fears when running for president in 1980 against Jimmy Carter, the incumbent. The spiritual assets of Carter, an avowed born-again Christian, were good enough for the faithful in 1976—he beat Jerry Ford in what *Newsweek* magazine called "The Year of the Evangelicals"—but his political liabilities pushed the same voters to Reagan in 1980. Carter was too left for The Right. And

Reagan was only too happy to cozy up to conservative Christians, the first Republican of the twentieth century to do so.[19]

In April 1980, the first "Washington for Jesus" rally was held in Washington, D.C., defining the Christian Right's stances against abortion, homosexuality, drug abuse, and women's liberation. The event is regarded as a forerunner to the rise of political activism among conservative Christians.

Not coincidentally, the event came just a year after Jerry Falwell—who had founded his own segregationist academy in 1967—launched the Moral Majority. It was 1979, four years after Sally and I had been married and the year the first of our two sons was born.

At age twenty-five, I wasn't overly concerned about this faith-politics merger. In fact, few evangelicals seemed to be, though Billy Graham shared concerns when Reagan took office in 1981: "It would disturb me if there was a wedding between the religious fundamentalists and the political right," he said. "The Hard Right has no interest in religion except to manipulate it."[20]

Graham had learned his lesson the hard way; he had enjoyed a "seat at the table" with a handful of presidents, but when the one he'd been closest to, Richard Nixon, was forced to resign in the wake of his Watergate lies in the 1970s, it shook Graham to his core. "It was naïve of me, I suppose, to think that such a close relationship would never be used to serve [Nixon's] political ends," he said.[21]

The Moral Majority had no such qualms. "We must never allow our children to forget that this is a Christian nation!" said Falwell, who wouldn't speak out against abortion until 1978. "We must take back what is rightfully ours!" He later called the 1964 Civil Rights Act a "terrible violation of human and private property rights."[22]

Such rhetoric helped galvanize Christian conservatives in an "us-vs.-them" division that sounded the siren of fear against liberalism. "War makes the world understandable, a black and white tableau of them and us," wrote Chris Hedges in *War Is a Force That Gives Us Meaning*. Even culture war. "It suspends thought, especially self-critical thought. All bow before the supreme effort. We are one."[23]

For me, the sudden declaration that evangelicals were "moral" smacked head-on with Scripture's idea that, as believers, we are all broken people saved by grace; "for all have sinned and fallen short of the glory of God," says Romans 3:23. The moment you started calling yourself "moral" was the moment that, intentionally or not, you started putting yourself above others. That meant ignoring Genesis 1:27, which says "… God created mankind in His own image … ."

But in the 1970s, white Protestants were fleeing the Democrat Party in droves over what would seem to be a moral position—indeed, a *biblically sound* position: civil rights for Americans of all colors, not just white.

Instead, the Moral Majority helped usher in what would become known as "identity politics," whereby people began favoring candidates based not on their character or ideas, but on what political tribe with which they identified. I started to wonder about this new church-state alliance. I'd always embraced the idea that, as a Christian, I was "just another beggar looking for a piece of bread," a thought that always reminded me of my utter dependence on Him. But suddenly, the priggish folks at "corporate" seemed to be saying: *We're building a bread franchise—to feed ourselves!*

In retrospect, I realize it was my own ignorance that enabled such self-righteousness to take root, my silence that allowed it to spread, my lack of courage that encouraged it to thrive. I was a nobody, sure, but the sea of complicity is fed by seemingly insignificant drops of water that create creeks that flow into streams that become rivers that empty into that sea.

In 1983, Focus on the Family Founder James Dobson created a political arm called the Family Research Council to lobby against abortion and other "family-friendly" issues. And although the Moral Majority collapsed after a decade, Pat Robertson started a knockoff, the Christian Coalition, in 1989.

He chose Ralph Reed, a slick thirty-eight-year-old political strategist, to run an organization that he promised would "change politics in America. The evangelicals and Roman Catholics have more grassroots supporters than anyone, but they need leadership and direction."[24] To help provide both, Reed played on two things: the lure of power and the specter of fear, both of which Scripture warns believers to avoid. As

Christians, Reed preached that we needed to *demand* respect; otherwise, we'd be left behind, exploited, trampled. *Demand* respect in a way that Jesus never personally did nor recommended His followers do.

Reed was bright, opportunistic, and bold, once using the concept of guerrilla warfare to explain how he dealt with The Left. "I paint my face and travel at night," he told *The Virginian-Pilot* in 1991. "You don't know it's over until you're in a body bag."[25]

In this new drama, Reed obviously wasn't playing the part of The Good Samaritan. At the time, I remember thinking Reed, and his approach, seemed an odd fit for Christians. Matthew 5:16 says we are to "… let your light shine before others, that they may see your good deeds and glorify your Father in heaven." Fear, night-stalking, and hating our enemies seemed like a contradiction to good deeds. But who was I—and what did I know? I kept quiet. In some ways, I, too, traveled at night, not to plot against others but to protect myself. To not be seen. To blend in with The Tribe.

Among big-name evangelicals, Focus on the Family's Dobson had become increasingly brittle with his vernacular; in years to come, he would degrade Democrats on a regular basis, and spin conspiracy theories to scare people into voting for Republicans.

In fairness, Dobson's organization was an encouragement to millions of Christians in those decades, myself included; while Sally and I never bought into Dobson's pro-spanking stance, he helped people like us navigate the maze-like paths of parenting. In years to come I would write cover articles for *Focus on the Family* magazine. What came to disturb me was Dobson's attitude, which seemed so protective of The Tribe and so intent on gaining political ground that Jesus's call to love others seemed to get lost in the process. "If I speak in the tongues of men and of angels, but have not love, I am only a resounding gong or clanging cymbal," says 1 Corinthians 13:1.

Alas, I had no idea how much louder that clanging was going to get—and how it wouldn't be reserved for the headline makers such as televangelist Jim Bakker, whose sex scandal and fraud convictions made headlines for years in the 1980s and '90s.

BY 1990, A once-fledging radio personality from Missouri, Rush Limbaugh, had captured a larger audience than anyone on the airwaves. Bold and bombastic, Limbaugh catered to The Right and gleefully, humorously, and viciously attacked The Left, using the Gulf War and Bill Clinton's rise to the presidency in 1992 to endear himself to evangelicals. His daily show was part vaudeville, part informational, and all hate for Democrats.

Conservative Fox News joined the cause in 1996. At the time, neither Limbaugh—who, late in life, would identify as a believer—nor Fox News offered opinions from a strictly Christian point of view; they were simply right-wing conservatives. But they treated evangelicals with "friends-of-the-court" favor and evangelicals reciprocated in kind.

Rather than being encouraged to mix it up with those different from us, as Jesus did, we evangelicals were being coached to thwart The Enemy. Taking a cue from Limbaugh—"with talent on loan from God"—evangelicals were being taught we were flat-out better than others, such thinking calcified with deep-seated fear.

Beyond helping create a yearly salary for Limbaugh that would reach $85 million,[26] "fear offers something in return—a sense of control and safety, placing our wants, our needs, our anxieties at the center of importance," wrote Dan White Jr. in *Love Over Fear*. "We sort of like fear … There is a concreteness and clarity to fear that comforts us—I know who to stay away from, I know who my enemies are, I know who to oppose, I know who to potentially hate."[27]

As the century neared its end, millions of evangelicals—20 million listeners a day would ultimately tune into Limbaugh—followed arguably the most influential broadcaster in history.[28] (I wasn't among them.) Instead of building bridges, we evangelicals cloistered ourselves away from The Enemy. We built our own media networks, music networks, and who-we-hung-out-with networks.

It wasn't as if conservative Christians had been hijacked by the likes of Limbaugh; most had come willingly. His contempt for The Left justified his listeners' own. In a biblical flip, *his ways were their ways.*

"White evangelicals were drawn to this brand of conservative media, and this media, in turn, shaped conservative evangelicalism," wrote

Kristen Kobes Du Mez in *Jesus and John Wayne*. "Rush Limbaugh undoubtedly influenced countless white evangelicals, many of them profoundly. But this was not the case of politics hijacking religion; the affinities ran deep."[29]

IN 1998, WHEN news broke of President Bill Clinton, forty-nine, having had a long affair with a twenty-two-year-old White House intern, it was red meat to sharks. Said Phyllis Schlafly, who led the fight to shoot down the Equal Rights Amendment: "Americans can look forward to a succession of TV charlatans and professional liars occupying the White House."[30] Dobson issued a lengthy letter to his followers, saying Clinton's dishonesty—he'd lied about having oral sex with Monica Lewinsky in the White House—was part of a long pattern. Clinton, Dobson said, had lied about another affair, with Gennifer Flowers. He'd lied about dodging the draft. He lied about lots of things.

"Character *does* matter," Dobson wrote. "You can't run a family, let alone a country, without it."[31]

Later, when thousands of Haitians died in a 2010 earthquake, televangelist Pat Robertson's "Christian" approach was to blame it on themselves, saying the Haitians had signed a "pact to the devil."[32] Having been to Haiti twice on Christian medical missions, gotten to know some Haitians, and seen their eyes when they begged for us to take their children home with us so they might survive, I couldn't imagine a less Christ-like comment.

Internally, I had always been quietly conflicted by how some evangelicals—especially highly visible evangelicals—"played out" their faith. Why would someone like Robertson say such an un-empathetic thing? And how could his viewers hear such stuff and keep watching his show?

My questions began to come fast and often. Why would evangelicals be more likely than any other faith group to see immigrants and refugees as dangerous? While following a "thou-shalt-not-kill" God, why would we be the least likely to even *consider* the slightest gun-law restrictions in the wake of mass shootings? Or to doubt that people of color were discriminated against? Or forgetting that little bit in Genesis about God creating the heavens and the Earth, to see environmentalism as nothing more than the misplaced passions of "tree-huggers?"

The answers seemed to lie not in scriptural values—or in facts—but in tribal values spun daily by the higher-ups in the media who peddled fear. As Christians, it seemed to me, we should be pro-life not because it was a Republican platform, but because it was a biblical platform. ("Before I formed you in the womb I knew you; before you were born. I set you apart," says Jeremiah 1:5.) So why, then, weren't we willing to let go of the party line to support equal concern for the environment, refugees, and people of color? Simple. Because even if the latter were biblical priorities, they weren't party priorities. As a religious faith and a political party, the two were at cross-purposes with each other, meaning one had to become subservient to the other. In short, the Republican Party wasn't becoming more like the Church; instead, the Church was becoming more like the Republican Party.

In 2009, the GOP-spun Tea Party emerged to further fan the fear of conservatives, particularly regarding race and immigration. Leader Newt Gingrich's approach was as simple as it was effective: get nasty. Many evangelicals, especially at the upper echelon levels, were happy to oblige, and most of the rest, like me, were content with being quietly complicit.

Meanwhile, whatever Christ-based evangelical song was playing in the background, the bass beat of the faithful wasn't what we were *for*—ostensibly, Jesus, love, grace, justice, and the like—but what we were *against*: gun restrictions, abortion, homosexuals, immigrants, environmentalism, liberalism, Democrats, and government in general. In pockets here and there, certainly, people were doing the other-oriented work of God, but on the national stage, evangelicals were becoming known for wanting to *get*, not *give*.

Gradually, my eyes began opening. I had come to believe that the difference between how people lived out their faith was related to the concept of grace, God's willingness to love us despite our sin. Philip Yancey's 1997 book *What's So Amazing About Grace?* revolutionized my understanding of God's mercy—and how we respond to it. I was particularly struck by Yancey's reference to counselor David Seamands, who said: "Many years ago I was driven to the conclusion that the two major causes of most emotional problems among evangelical Christians are these: the *failure to understand, receive, and live out* God's unconditional grace and forgiveness; and the *failure to give out* that unconditional love, forgiveness, and grace to other people …. [Italic mine.] We read, we hear, we believe a good theology of grace. But that's not the way we live. The good news of the Gospel of grace has not penetrated the level of our emotions."[33]

Said author Brennan Manning in *The Ragamuffin Gospel*: "The American Church today accepts grace in theory but denies it in practice. Too many Christians are living in the house of fear and not in the house of love."[34]

When it came to evangelicals, the "good news" to which Seamands referred was sometimes being misinterpreted or misapplied by believers. To some, the good news seemed to be about new life in Jesus, grace, freedom in Christ, and welcoming others into the fold; to others, it seemed to be about law and order, rules and regulations, and obedience. But not necessarily obedience to Christ—though few would realize it or, if they did, admit it—but to The Tribe, the evangelical faithful, the cultural ebbs and flows, often greased with the oily sheen of politics.

Two strands of evangelicalism, I realized, had emerged: love and fear. I remember seeing a guy quietly crying during a sermon on marriage—he'd recently been divorced—and a handful of people surrounding him afterward, praying for him, encouraging him. I remember watching a porn-addicted young man humble himself before God and make one of the most amazing life turnarounds I'd ever seen. I remember a guy showing up to a "Four Seasons" outreach event I was involved in at church and becoming a regular at church the next week. After accepting Christ, he stopped drinking—and is still a changed man two decades later.

But the evil twin was never far away—not so much in my church but in the news. On Limbaugh's show. In mailboxes. My otherwise level-headed Methodist grandfather, I learned, had been donating money to televangelist Jimmy Swaggart and received a concerning letter when he stopped.

"I tell ya what, Bob, it shook me up."

He showed it to me. "Brother Ben," it began, "we've so appreciated your donations over the years to support building the Lord's Kingdom.

However, with your giving having stopped, we are concerned. We are sending you a small candle as a symbol of our faith in you to shine brightly for us again. If it is broken, we can only assume that some sort of sin in your life has blinded you to the needs of the Lord. And we can only pray that you will *repent*, return to wholeness, and resume your giving as a way of returning, like the Prodigal Son, to Our Savior's loving arms."

The candle, of course, was broken in half.

"Now, Bob, do you think they're right?" he asked. "Do you think there's some sin in my life? The candle *was* broken."

"I think there's sin in all of our lives," I said, "maybe even in the lives of the people who broke those candles in two before sending out that threatening message. I'd suggest making your donations elsewhere."

Not that my remark was rooted in some new-found conviction that evangelicalism was flying off the rails. TV evangelists were in a class all by themselves; I didn't trust them in the least. What I couldn't see then was how thin the line was between "us" and "them."

My Hope for the Future

That we might remember our mission — and our Source

I WAS SPEAKING at a Kiwanis Club when a member told me the story of his church-going daughter. She was driving along when a guy in a truck behind her started madly honking his horn at her. She tried to ignore him. He honked more. She shook her head in exasperation. More wild honking.

"Finally, I'd had it, Dad," she said. "I barely know how to do it, but best I could, I flipped him the bird."

In her rearview mirror, she saw the guy respond with a "what-the-heck" look of confusion. It was only when she arrived home, got her mail, and was walking back up the driveway that she saw it: The "Honk-if-you-love-Jesus" bumper sticker on the back of her car.

Some evangelicals have forgotten what we once stood for. We've forgotten our mission. Our story. Our Source. Like the proverbial frog in the boiling water, the faith of some evangelicals has withered not because of cultural changes that grate against our Christian value systems; there's nothing new about the world's resistance to the things of God, the Bible says. No, some people's faith has withered because, without noticing, we've allowed our inspiration to be shaped by political partisanship and not by a passion for Jesus.

The most transformational thing we can do as believers

is making our faith, not our politics, the priority. Not worrying about the success of The Tribe but committing to the glory of God.

Our identity needs to be in Christ, not a political party or political leaders or political ideas whose essence and aims aren't always particularly godly. How can we expect the world to be attracted to Him if we, as his supposed image-bearers, don't reflect His love and grace to that world?

"Let us fix our eyes on Jesus, the author and perfecter of the faith," says Hebrews 12:2.

We need to begin anew at what the Scottish evangelist Oswald Chambers refers to as the "Source"—the spring from which Living Water bubbles. Jesus. He, not political power, needs to be the headwaters of our hearts.

"Pay attention to the Source," wrote Chambers, "and out of you will flow rivers of living water."[1]

My role as a believer is to glorify Him through words and action, to share His love with others, to help make disciples. If politics, not people, becomes my focus, such a goal is virtually impossible. Politics is the worst way to bring about change because it too often forces change instead of fostering a desire to change. Changed minds won't change the world; changed hearts will.

"If you are a Christian, you are an ambassador for Christ, not your political party," tweeted Pastor Raymond Chang, president of the Asian American Christian Collaborative. "As much as you want to squeeze the kingdom of God into your party, know it doesn't fit. If you think your party is God's party, know that your understanding of Christ and His kingdom is too small."

As I was writing this chapter in our family's Oregon Coast cabin, I saw a runner on the beach fighting his way through sideways rain. When I popped outside to encourage him, I realized he was a man I knew from Eugene, an evangelical Christian involved in prison ministry. Later, after I invited him to meet for coffee (hot chocolate for me), I was encouraged to hear how he'd joined with an attorney to fight for a reduced sentence for a prisoner who seemed to have been given an unfairly harsh one. I love seeing Christians fighting for justice—not for themselves, but for others.

But when politics becomes the priority, we can get distracted from that kind of thinking. First, we can lose our zeal for outreach to the lost—because we're preoccupied with winning political gains for us. Second, we can see non-believers as people to oppose rather than people to befriend. As long as the GOP—or any political party—becomes our passion as Christians, it's "game-over." Jesus transcends Right, Left, everything in between, and everything beyond.

The idea that, as Christians, we might find a political party whose values, goals, and methods align completely with God's is naive; "For my thoughts are not your thoughts, neither are your ways my ways," declares the Lord in Isaiah 55:8. The two have different aims, different strategies, different styles.

They're like old rural highways that were replaced by freeways; yes, at times the old runs parallel with the new but at other times, the two go wildly different directions.

Political gains will never satisfy a human soul aching for deeper things. Since the 1960s, the percentage of Americans who trust government has slid from more than 70 percent to less than 30 percent, according to the Pew Research Center.[2] But in the slow-boil rage accompanying this distrust, many still think re-arranging the political deck chairs will make the voyage on the Titanic spectacular.

Deeper things are at root in people's dissatisfaction: an over-reliance on money and things to bring us happiness, an under-appreciation of God's grace; and an over-dependence on politics as "the answer." No, our deepest longings have no political fix.

"Seek ye first the kingdom of God, and His righteousness," says Matthew 6:33 (KJV), "and all these things shall be added unto you."

3.

Saving Grace

**In my early years in the faith,
I am blessed by people who model
the Jesus I've chosen to follow.**

The people who influence us the most are not those who detain us with their continual talk, but those who live their lives like the stars in the sky and "the lilies of the field"— simply and unaffectedly. Those are the lives that mold and shape us.

—Oswald Chambers

Teenagers and the sacred may seem an odd fit but in the early 1970s I remember the two being entwined. The occasions were Young Life meetings in someone's living room wherein a bunch of high schoolers would be singing "They will know we are Christians by our love, by our love, they will know we are Christians by our love." There was this sense of single-minded purpose, this sense of holiness, this sense of sacredness that I've never forgotten.

At sixteen, I pledged my life to Christ during a Fellowship of Christian Athletes meeting that I didn't want to be at; I only came to get the buddy who invited me off my back.

As a family, we were lukewarm Episcopalians for whom God was neither friend nor foe. Church, in my eyes, was a poor alternative to watching the NFL on Sunday mornings; I slipped out a window once during Sunday school.

But in October 1970, when I was a high school junior, God suddenly became real to me. My conversion was not the result of a season spent in deep spiritual consternation, nor of having had fire-and-brimstone hurled at me. Instead, I was sitting in the Roberts's rec room, hearing about God-come-to-earth as Christ—and how he desired a relationship with *me*, a lowly cross-country runner in a sea of football players. God was no celestial cop out to punish the lawbreakers, I learned. Instead, He had come to guide, forgive, and offer everlasting life to those who believed. And, beginning that night, I did.

I was given a copy of *Good News for Modern Man,* a gray paperback Bible about the size of a brick. It introduced me to a wild new way of seeing life: as Christians, we were to serve others, sacrifice for others, even strangers, and love boldly, even our enemies. I was humbled to be part of this faith.

Before this new step, I'd partied hardy for a year, not so much because of the beer—OK, maybe a little because of the beer—but because, in hindsight, I liked the sense of belonging. I went with the flow. It was safe. Comfortable. Affirming. But after my commitment to Christ, that desire disappeared. In college, when I'd hear fellow students going on about how drunk they'd gotten the night before, my quiet response was never "Tsk-tsk, you loser." It was pity that downing a twelve-pack of beer and puking was their idea of a good time. I didn't get it. I thought there was more to life.

Not that, after my conversion, I was suddenly all about the "others" who were supposed to know we were Christians by our love. My father was a good man, faithful to my mother and committed to her, my older sister, and me, but after feeling blessed for surviving World War II, he seemed to have little use for God. On the other hand, Mom, an Episcopalian and a Democrat, seemed more concerned about people in need than I did. Each Wednesday in the summer she would head out to the farm fields outside of Corvallis to organize volleyball night for Hispanic migrant workers. She always invited me but I never went. Looking back, I had the name—*Christian*—but she had faith in action, caring for the poor.

Decades later, I was driving with her when we heard a siren. Her eyes started to mist.

"Mom, what's wrong?" I asked.

"Oh, whenever I hear a siren, I know some family is about to get tragic news," she said. "And I feel for them."

MY SAVING GRACE during evangelicalism's rise to political prominence in the '80s, and '90s was a manager's special of inspiration: churches, pastors, mentors, friends, travel, music, and authors—a lesson for me in every slice of my life-experience pizza. Together, they kept me focused on the biblical Jesus, not the "Gumby" version the political Right had started configuring to fit their agenda.

I was blessed to attend a handful of evangelical churches in the Northwest that steered clear of politics. In the mid-1980s—with my having just turned thirty—Sally and I got in on the ground floor of a Kirkland, Washington, non-denominational church that had been founded with a multicultural bent. Among the three pastors was an African American, a former NFL linebacker who had a vision to bridge the gap between Seattle's black community and the East Side's white suburbs.

We were asked to join the mission board—and did so. As a church, we packaged food and toys and took them to individual families in Seattle's African American neighborhoods at Christmas. We rejoiced when black families began venturing across Lake Washington's floating bridges to join our fellowship.

We built a relationship with Mendenhall Ministries in Mississippi, which was founded to help one of the poorest communities in the country pull itself out of decades of poverty, hopelessness, and racism. We started sending ten-person teams to help the ministry build new buildings and repair old ones.

In 1988, the board sensed our congregation needed a better understanding of what was going on in Mendenhall, so they came to me. With my reporting background, would I be willing to go to Mississippi, interview people, take photographs, and write about the experience for the church back home? I'm insatiably curious about people and places, so I was an easy sell.

Mendenhall was a blend of inspiration and anguish. It was a town just southeast of Jackson where a black person wasn't welcome in a white church. Where abject poverty blurred the vision of people to pull themselves out of the pit. And where the needle on the "misery index" was always on "high."

One afternoon, I was sitting with a handful of African American children when one asked me to tell him about my house back home. I described our ramshackle two-story, four-bedroom rental, including the pea-green carpet and entry way that included a refrigerator that wouldn't fit into the kitchen.

"Mister," he said, "you live in a mansion."

I've never forgotten those words. They humbled me. How many times had I seen houses in upscale Bellevue far nicer than our rental, and felt somehow underprivileged because of it? Sally and I had joked that the fire hydrants in Bellevue didn't spew water, but Perrier. But the little boy's comment changed my perspective.

That's the value of getting outside our bubbles and into someone else's world. *Perspective.* The realization that what you experience is not what everybody experiences.

WHEN WE MOVED to Eugene in 1989 after I took a features-writing job at *The Register-Guard,* the features editor who hired me was the most amazing encourager I'd ever had as a boss. Once a week, he'd post these wittily written opuses telling the staff that we rocked—amid, of course, a few "nits."

He had an irrepressibility to him, despite having a teenage son struggling with muscular dystrophy. And, if I recall, was the first male I'd known who wore an earring. Politically, he leaned hard left. Spiritually, we were on different flight paths. But I had many reasons to respect him, not the least of which was because our new managing editor had wanted to hire another writer and the features editor—despite the risk of peeving his new boss—had fought for me.

Though we lived in a rented house near the McKenzie River in Springfield, Sally and I found a non-denominational church in Eugene that was love at first sight. The pastor was faithful, humble, and full of integrity; the people genuine; the congregation infused with a "same-team" spirit and an amazing sense of humor. The men's ministry once put on a Valentine's Day Gala & Tractor Pull event that proved legendary—at least in our minds. Main course: boxed pizza. Dessert: Candy bars. Late in the evening, our pastor popped out dressed as Elvis, pulled his wife up on stage, and lip-synched "Can't Help Falling in Love." Every Thanksgiving we'd play our traditional Turkey Bowl football game. When friends' sons were going to get married, we'd gather as a group of men to offer laughs and "big-life" advice. And twice we put on extravagant Christmas programs at Eugene's Hult Center, one in which I, as the emcee, walked out on a lights-out stage with 250 Christmas bulbs wrapped around me, an extension cord duct-taped to one of my shoes.

Not that we didn't take God seriously. From time to time, we held 24-hour prayer vigils. And early on, I'd learned the backstory of our people's faithfulness, how the congregation had originally met in a leaky building at the county fairgrounds—a risky setup in rainy Oregon. When the county condemned the building, instead of panicking, people prayed. Hard. A piece of property soon became available. A handful of elders took out second mortgages to secure down payments for it and a building. Plans were made. But the city said the site was in a floodplain; the church could only build if it raised the foundation level with a considerable amount of dirt that was going to cost a considerable amount of money.

People prayed fervently. Soon, the church got a call from someone at our local Catholic hospital, which, three miles away, was putting in a new parking garage that involved digging a huge hole.

"Heard you need dirt," said the hospital's spokesman. "We got tons."

The hospital loved the idea of having to transport it only three miles instead of clear out of town. So, we soon became a Protestant church built on a Catholic foundation.

For nearly a decade, the church hummed along. When my *R-G* boss's son died at eighteen, his family needed a place for the service; they didn't attend church. I went to our pastor, who happily offered ours. We laughed that it must have been a world record for the most journalists in an evangelical church at a single time.

Four years later, the laughter died. Trust at the church leadership level had, over the years, broken down. Sides were taken. Rumors spun. Feelings hurt. Friendships broken. And suddenly—for different reasons—all three pastors were gone. Just like that, those of us who hadn't left—about a third of the congregation split—were trying to keep the church alive with baling wire, prayer, and good intentions.

Crisis brings out the worst in some people, the best in others. I was blessed to be part of a rag-tag elder board that represented the latter. They taught me the two most important leadership lessons I'd ever learned: the value of humility and the tenacity of trust.

The former came to light in a decision we reached to resist simply blundering forward, assuming that we were "all good." Instead, despite having precious little money in the church coffers, the temporary leaders hired an outside consultant to evaluate us, to help us answer a few questions: Were *we* part of the problem? Did we have blind spots we needed to recognize? In other words, were we *worthy* to lead the church? Finally, were we "good" with each other as leaders?

"I want you to look at the man on your right," our consultant said on a Friday night that I'll never forget. "Do you trust him?"

All quiet on the elder front.

"When you're done with that, look to the man on your left. Do you trust *him*?"

A few nervous glances. A clearing of a throat or two.

"We can't go forward unless all of you come in with two 'yeses.' In leadership, trust is everything. Honesty is everything."

When the final elder offered his "double-yes," making it nine-for-nine, there were smiles and a few misty eyes in the bunch, mine included. I felt an instinctive sense that, come hell or high water, this church was going to rise from the ashes. And rise it did, even if it would take more than two years for us to really find our equilibrium.

Without a pastor, we brought in guest speakers, preached ourselves, and otherwise improvised to keep afloat. We encouraged people to not stop giving, but to trust that God was going to rebuild the church.

Meanwhile, something nagged at me: the thought that, during the turmoil, I'd let my frustration get the better of me in letters I'd written to our board in a failed attempt to "right the ship." That I owed apologies to two of the three pastors who'd left. But we had a church to rebuild, I reasoned, and, besides, it wasn't like I hadn't been hurt, too.

I put my conscience on hold.

THE PASTOR we hired was everything we'd hoped for: Humble. Honest. Sincere. He had great vision for our community and beyond. We built a partnership with a local HIV Alliance; played music, served food, and cut hair for the homeless in a monthly "under-the-bridge" event; put in a garden to provide produce for the poor; started a preschool; worked closely with a foster agency; raised money—and sent people with hammers—to build a dormitory in Myanmar for kids in danger of being sex-trafficked; baptized people, sometimes in the chilly Willamette River; and adopted a nearby elementary school that we encouraged by helping with landscaping, buying gift cards for teachers, and giving books to students.

Our pastor never needed to be the hero, the one who got credit. He would see a talent in someone who hadn't even seen it themselves; he would help them find a way to use that gift to glorify God. He did that for me. He knew I'd written a lot about, and had an interest in, relationships so would have me occasionally preach on the subject. Christians and race, for example.

He'd show up for 6 a.m. men's ministry meetings—with doughnuts. When Sally and I hatched an idea to create a marriage-coaching program for the church, he found—seemingly overnight—$10,000 so we could hire a professional marriage counselor as a consultant.

Was he perfect? Nope. He made mistakes like we all did. But he was willing to learn from them. He asked me to evaluate his sermons and offer feedback on how they could be better—not so he could look more impressive but so the congregation could get more meaningful messages about God.

"Leadership is taking the initiative for the benefit of others," his predecessor—like the current pastor, a friend of mine—had told us. I'd never forgotten that phrase. *Leadership is taking responsibility for the benefit of others.*

IF, IN THE pre-Trump years, churches and pastors shaped my faith, travel opportunities deepened that faith. In 1999, having written a few books on Christian subjects, I was invited to speak at a writers' conference at Mt. Hermon, a Christian camp in the redwood-thick mountains above Santa Cruz, California. There I met Dick Foth, the keynote speaker and president of a small Christian college who, for some reason, treated me as if I were the keynote speaker and he were a nobody.

He taught me about perspective, humor, and humility. He asked me questions, complimented me on my writing, made everything about *me*. I was blown away. He was a bigwig; I was a nobody. Foth had brought one of his teenage daughters to the retreat and struck me as the kind of leader, writer, and father I wanted to be; over a handful of sessions, I soaked up every word he spoke.

He taught me about how much the life of faith is about *perspective*, telling a story about a son to illustrate how sometimes we limit ourselves with narrow points of view.

"What's three plus five?" he asked his four-year-old.

The little boy unfolded three fingers on his left hand, five on the right, and counted them.

"Eight."

"OK, how about four plus two?"

Fingers unfolded, left and right.

"Six."

"Great. How about four plus eight?"

The little boy unfolded four fingers on his left hand and—.

"I can't tell you the answer to that one, Dad."
"Why not?"
"I'd have to have twelve fingers and I only have ten."

BEYOND TRIPS to Mt. Hermon and to Mississippi, I went to Haiti twice to work with my brother-in-law and sister-in-law on medical teams; Sally not only volunteered in Haiti but took similar trips to the Dominican Republic and Guatemala. It was in Haiti that I learned servanthood, the lesson not taught in words but in the selfless actions of teammates. I remember a volunteer nurse on our team holding the hand of a Haitian woman in labor for hours while a missionary, Miss Maxine, drove a Jeep down twisting dirt roads and literally *through* a river to a hospital—at night. My knuckles were white and my eyes wide, but the woman safely delivered a baby boy. What a beautiful cry in the Haitian night that was.

A few days later, I remember my brother-in-law-the-doctor helping patch up nearly a dozen victims in a "top-top" (bus) accident in the afternoon; blood everywhere. Then, while the rest of us were eating dinner, I noticed he was quietly transforming the "ER" into a church for our evening worship service. What an example of sacrificial service.

Meanwhile, God brought other amazing people into my life. People from church. Colleagues at work. And "Mrs. A," a retired schoolteacher twenty years my senior who taught me the value of courage, curiosity, and the power of words. I'd gotten to know her after writing a column about how she'd inspired her 1967-68 sixth-grade class to pledge that they would gather for a reunion at the Eugene Hotel on January 1, 2000—more than thirty years into the future. And they did it! On that day, nearly three-quarters of the twenty-seven class members showed up—a testament to Mrs. A's impact on her students.

She was Irish, Catholic, feminist, hard-headed, soft-hearted, and grammar-sensitive. (Those last three hyphens are in honor of her, though grammarians might argue it either way.)

"Scribe, in Tuesday's column you referred to 'your sons,'" she'd say. "I think Sally had a little something to do with those sons. Make it *our* sons."

She wrote poetry and taught me that life was fleeting. "Take risks," she said. "The ride ends before you know it." In her mid-seventies, she was struggling with pain from the moment I met her. "Got an ailment for every feckin' letter of the alphabet," she'd say with her Irish lilt. "I'm on 'U' now."

One night before I was going to see her, she emailed me. "Scribe, we're going to need a few extra hours tomorrow. I'm dying. I wondered if you might drive me around so I can see every house our family lived in around here—and that's a lot of houses."

I took her on her sentimental journey. A few months later she was gone, taken by the letter "C"—cancer.

I LEARNED faithfulness from a pastor and his wife—a brother-in-law and sister-in-law—who lost a sixteen-year-old son but didn't give up on God. I was inspired about generosity by a sister and brother-in-law who, out of the blue, offered to help Sally and me pay some of a son's college tuition. And I came to understand thankfulness from a colleague at *The Register-Guard*.

"Man," he once said about his family's tiny house in the country, "the other day I was out mowing my lawn and I could smell the spring blossoms and I just started crying. I'm like, 'God, why have you blessed me like this?'" I'd never met a gentler soul and a better listener, anyone who was more content and less influenced by the culture around him.

Another spiritual inspiration was a guy almost my parents' ages who, at men's small group meeting one morning, took me under his wing with a nine-word statement that I've never forgotten. I had arrived having barely slept, so worried was I about finances. I was working two jobs—a features editor by day and an author by night. In taking trips to France, Boston, and Washington, D.C., I had invested tens of thousands of dollars into writing a book about a World War II nurse that, after we landed an appearance on ABC's "Good Morning America," seemed a lock to pay huge dividends. But because President Ronald Reagan died, we got knocked off every time zone but one, and the book never got any traction. With eight straight years of sons' college payments coming due, I found myself in financial quicksand: the harder I tried to get out of the muck, the deeper I seemed to sink.

One morning, when the group leader asked me to answer a question from a video we'd seen, I just shook my head "no thanks." Afterward, the older guy approached me. "What's up, Welch?"

Unlike the others, he seemed genuinely concerned. And safe. I told him about my struggles. About how I kept praying and the situation never seemed to get better. About my sense of hopelessness. Then came the nine words from him that triggered my closest mentorship ever.

"Sounds to me like you're pissed off at God."

They were words of comfort—because, with them, I knew he wasn't "guilting" me for my lack of faith, he was daring to get into the muck with me. In short, he was doing what Jesus would do.

"Yeah," I said, "that's exactly it. I'm pissed off at God."

He prayed for me, then said, "Come by my office this afternoon." When I got there, he asked me to write down individual amounts I owed utilities and such. After further review, I wondered if he was now going to guilt me, make me feel small. The total came to $750. He pulled out his checkbook and wrote me a check for $1,000.

"It's a loan," he said. "Pay it back when you can."

"But I only needed seven—."

"Guys are too proud to say what they really need. Take it."

THE MUSICIAN who inspired me the most during these decades was Rich Mullins. Oh, I had my secular singers and bands—Neil Young and Crosby, Stills & Nash topped that list—but no Christian singer inspired me more than Mullins. I liked his music; I *loved* his testimony.

On his insistence, the profits from his tours and the sale of each album were entrusted to his church, which divided up the money, paid Rich the average salary for a laborer in the US for that year—and gave the rest to charity. Mullins was a free-spirit Christian, a guy who'd synthesized his faith not from daily devotionals but from the readings of St. Francis of Assisi. Mullins had no patience for evangelical pastors who peddled what he called "cheap faith," the get-'em-saved, build-the-numbers, pat-yourself-on-the-back variety. Faith in Christ, he reminded me, wasn't something you went through the motions about, nor was it always comfortable. In fact, he suggested, if it's comfortable, it's probably only a facsimile of the real thing. His perspective:

> Jesus said whatever you do to the least of these my brothers you've done it to me. And this is what I've come to think: That if I want to identify fully with Jesus Christ, who I claim to be my Savior and Lord, the best way that I can do that is to identify with the poor. This I know will go against the teachings of all the popular evangelical preachers. But they're just wrong. They're not bad, they're just wrong. Christianity is not about building an absolutely secure little niche in the world where you can live with your perfect little wife and your perfect little children in a beautiful little house where you have no gays or minority groups anywhere near you. Christianity is about learning to love like Jesus loved—and Jesus loved the poor and Jesus loved the broken-hearted.[35]

In 1997, at forty-one, Mullins died following an automobile accident. I'd heard an array of Bible-based explanations why God allows bad things to happen to good people, but I've never heard one that really satisfies me. In fact, I have all sorts of questions about Christianity that bug me, but I still believe. Because it's in the uncertainties where your faith is steeled, where your belief is proved real. And it's in the brokenness that we see our seamier sides, which helps us reach higher for our Jesus sides.

It was Mullins's convictions that convinced me to turn down a lucrative offer to write a daily devotional for Joel Osteen, whose Lakewood Church in Houston was the largest in America; I couldn't justify promoting a preacher whose prosperity gospel clashed with "the-love-of-money-is-the-root-of-all-evil" truth of Scripture.

Mullins had written the foreword for a book that, along with Yancey's *What's So Amazing About Grace?*, inspired me more than any other in the 1990s: Brennan Manning's *The Ragamuffin Gospel*.

I'd been introduced to the author/speaker by a colleague at *The Register-Guard* whom I ran with at lunch. He loaned me a bunch of tapes of Manning's talks. A former Franciscan priest and recovering alcoholic, Manning had been the featured speaker at a Quaker conference my friend and his family had attended. In *Ragamuffin*, Manning explained God's grace like Michelangelo painted ceilings, in a way that left me staring up in wonder. In the intro, he wrote:

> This book is not for the super-spiritual.
> It is not for the muscular Christians who have made John Wayne and not Jesus their hero.
> It is not for noisy, feel-good folks who manipulate Christianity into a naked appeal to emotion.

Instead, he said, the book was "written for the bedraggled, beat-up, and burnt-out."

> It is for the wobbly and weak-kneed who know they don't have it altogether and are too proud to accept the handout of amazing grace.
> It is for the bent and bruised who feel that their lives are a grave disappointment to God.
> It is for smart people who know they are stupid and honest disciples who admit they are scalawags.[36]

The most powerful talk I heard by him began not with some subtle boast of his righteousness but with him waking up in a gutter one morning, hungover. He taught me that vulnerability is an asset, pride a pitfall, and power the refuge of those who miss life's deeper virtues. He decried believers who didn't walk the talk.

"The greatest single cause of atheism in the world today is Christians who acknowledge Jesus with their lips, then walk out the door and deny him in their lifestyle," he wrote. "That is what an unbelieving world simply finds unbelievable."[37]

At its deepest, faith was not about memorizing the Bible, he said. Or about theology. Or even about *belief*. No, it was about *brokenness*. Only when we're on our knees, he'd say, can we really understand and accept grace—and hope to pass it on to others.

IN 1993, MY first book, *More to Life Than Having It All,* was published. When my publisher shared plans to send me to dozens of Christian TV and radio outlets mainly in the Midwest and South, I was pumped to broaden my horizons. But as I took such trips, I found myself disappointed. With few exceptions, the people seemed bored with their faith but ballyhooed by a subtle sense of privilege. The pattern prompted in me a line from Ernest Gordon's *To End All Wars*: "They regarded themselves as God's anointed and were therefore critical of everyone else. As far as I could see, they managed to extract the bubbles from the champagne of life, leaving it insipid, flat, and tasteless."[38]

I noted little joy about what Scripture tells us should be an "abundant life." Little humor. Little imagination. Little risk-taking. Little curiosity about, say, Oregon. Or *me*. The red light on the camera went on, they'd ask me the same questions the other stations asked, and I'd leave. After a few years of this, the places and faces all blurred together in a certain sameness—as if I'd fallen into an evangelical version of *The Stepford Wives*.

"If you Christians want to make us agnostics inclined to look into your religion, you must try to be more comfortable in the possession of it yourselves," wrote Hannah Whitall Smith in *The God of All Comfort*. "The Christians I meet ... seem to carry their religion as a man carries a headache."[39] Not the Christians I hung around with—one of whom, during a snowstorm, pulled up at a Starbucks drive-through on his horse—but I'd seen plenty of the headache variety, too.

In 1998, after I wrote a father-son book called *A Father for All Seasons*, I started getting asked to lead men's retreats for churches. Compared to book tours, this was the more rewarding experience. The retreats, often held in some woodsy environ, involved real guys who rarely got to plumb the depths of their souls and were suddenly given permission to do so. Father wounds. Marriages in trouble. Wrestling with addictions.

This was the kind of stuff Manning and Mullins, I'm sure, would have enjoyed. But some evangelicals couldn't relate to these two ragamuffins in the least. Remember, this was the mid-1990s. The Christian Coalition—described by my favorite humorist, Garrison Keillor, as "a Republican front with about as much to do with the Christian faith as the Elks Club has to do with large, hoofed animals"—had just taken the baton from the Moral Majority.[40] The Coalition refused to hire an executive director because the candidate wanted global AIDS to be on the agenda. Apparently, the Coalition's brass decided it would be better to let millions of people die than give the false impression that evangelicals were pro-homosexual.[41]

Republicanism was fast becoming like a political arm of the church. Limbaugh kept pushing the buttons of fear and hate; in years to come, he would refer to Chelsea Clinton as the "White House dog," call a Georgetown University student who opposed his politics a "slut" and "prostitute," and offer a parody on President Obama called "Barack the Magic Negro."[42]

Had Limbaugh taken the path of a Mullins or a Manning—had he chosen to emphasize the take-up-your-cross stuff of Jesus instead of the fear-fueled counterfeit of far-right conservatism—he probably wouldn't have become a millionaire many times over.

Among many evangelicals, he was a rock star, but, no, he wasn't Jesus. He was, it would turn out, only the earthly equivalent of John the Baptist. Though Limbaugh had risen to greatness among The Tribe, there was one coming who was "greater than he."

4.

The Perfect Storm

**Just as Trump wins the nomination,
I begin writing editorials for The R-G—
and understanding who this "gladiator" really is.**

*Alice: "Would you tell me, please, which way I ought to go from here?"
Cheshire Cat: "That depends a good deal on where you want to get to."*

—Lewis Carroll, *Alice's Adventures in Wonderland*

After I returned to *The Register-Guard* in July 2016, my job in editorial required me to read deeply and widely about politics, something I'd paid little attention to in the past. But rather than pull me over to the "dark side," the experience widened my vision, something that can't happen when you only watch, listen to, or read sources who support your narrative. Sometimes such reading confirmed what I already believed, sometimes it caused me to question what I already believed.

Regarding Trump, I learned much. That he was, for example, quick to judge and slow to forgive. When asked what his favorite Bible verse was, he said "the eye-for-an-eye" part. In 1989, when five African Americans were arrested for raping a white woman in Central Park, the business tycoon had taken out a full-page ad in the *New York Times* to demand they be put to death. DNA evidence later proved all five to be innocent.

In 2015, Trump said of Republican Senator John McCain, who'd been a POW in Vietnam: "He's not a war hero. He was a war hero because he was captured. I like people who weren't captured."[43]

When announcing his candidacy in June of that year, he announced his intent to build a wall to keep illegal Mexican immigrants out.

"The US has become a dumping ground for everybody else's problems. When Mexico sends its people, they're not sending their best. They're sending people that have lots of problems, and they're bringing those problems with them. They're bringing drugs. They're bringing crime. They're rapists. And some, I assume, are good people."[44]

As the 2016 primaries began, I learned that, above all else, Trump hated to lose—at anything. In February, when he was beaten by Senator Ted Cruz in the Iowa Caucus, he tweeted a harbinger of things to come: "Based on the fraud committed by Senator Ted Cruz ... either a new election should take place or Cruz's results nullified." He had done no investigation, nor cited any evidence, to back up his claims. But he *knew* he'd won.

Politics, of course, has always been a nasty business, but most candidates drew a line to ensure some civility. Not Trump; he had no lines. When a woman in the audience called Obama an "Arab," McCain, Obama's opponent in 2008, corrected her and politely took the microphone away from her. But as I began listening to Trump, I realized his "cringe factor" was beyond any public figure I'd ever heard. He mimed a reporter who had physical disabilities.

On August 1, 2016, he made insensitive remarks to a Gold Star family, parents of a Muslim American soldier who had been killed in Iraq. A writer friend of mine, a Christian, recoiled in pain and anger. She'd lost her father in Vietnam. "From that moment on," she told me, "I did whatever I could to see he wouldn't become president."[45] And, she said, lost three-fourths of her longtime Christian friends because of it.

Trump didn't seem bothered by provoking violence; he encouraged people at his rallies to pummel detractors and send him the bill. And he obviously wasn't bothered by lying. As early as 2011, he had beat the "Obama-is-a-Muslim" drum—and influenced followers to buy in. Within three months of his announcing his presidential run, 54 percent of Trump supporters believed Obama was a Muslim, even if the claim was proven to be a blatant lie.[46]

In February 2016, a Republican debate quickly spun into a verbal brawl, with Trump as the catalyst. He poked and provoked, bullied and boasted. *Did he really just reference the size of his genitals?* Of candidate Carly Fiornia, he said, "Look at that face! Would anyone vote for *that*? Can you imagine *that*, the face of our next president?!"[47] I couldn't figure out which was worse—that he didn't realize he was showing so little regard for others, or that he *knew* he was showing so little regard for others but simply didn't care.

But the more most evangelicals saw and heard of Trump, the more they supported him. As a journalist, I had never seen anything so incongruous in my life—the bonding of evangelicals and Trump. Robert Jeffress, senior pastor at Dallas First Baptist Church, said, "I want the meanest, toughest son of a you-know-what I can find to protect us. And I think that's the feeling of a lot of evangelicals."

I agreed—that's what people did seem to want. But I was among the "one in five" who thought that was shortsighted. It wasn't just his style that repelled me, it was his arrogance—a bad character flaw for a true leader. Trump exalted himself and denigrated others.

"If you can't stand Donald Trump, you think Donald Trump is the worst, you're going to vote for me," he said at a 2016 rally. "You know why? Justices of the Supreme Court."[48]

It was "conditional love" at its finest: *you help me become president, I'll ensure you a conservative Supreme Court that will rule in Christians' favor on pro-life and religious liberty issues.* This wasn't a show of respect for the evangelicals whose support he needed; this was a salesman who knew he had a buyer almost in his pocket.

I disagreed that evangelicals had no choice but to go with Trump. My decades in the Church had taught me the flaws of ends-justify-the-means thinking; Trump's promise to help conservatize the Supreme Court didn't make everything else about the man *not matter*. Character still mattered. Competence still mattered. Conscience still mattered. This triad of virtues would influence each of the thousands of decisions any president would make, some, perhaps, with people's lives on the line. To ignore a glaring lack of character was to buy a pit bull and ignore its temperament, hoping that the dog would somehow just "play nice."

But what did I know? By now, evangelicals were flocking to Trump like Best Buy shoppers at a Black Friday sale. In the rare times when I'd raise my concerns about Trump to evangelical friends, the response was predictable: "Yeah, he's got some rough edges, but I'm betting he'll surround himself with good people who will help him with his decision-making."

"Rough edges" belong to guys with Skoal rings on the back of their jeans who don't put the toilet seat down; Trump was cruel, crude, and condescending.

But, in fairness, let me digress because my perspective of Trump was being processed through a far different filter than that of many fellow evangelicals, including GOP ringleader Ralph Reed, the author of a book on Trump, *For God and Country*. Here's how Reed described the man at a 2016 rally:

> Trump came on stage to an ovation that rolled from the back of the arena like a wave, bathing him in adoration. He paced the stage like a gladiator, his shoulders back, chin and chest jutting, unreeling his greatest hits to uproarious applause and cheering. He vowed to build the border wall ("Who's going to pay for it?" "Mexico!"), appoint conservative judges, move the US Embassy to Jerusalem, renegotiate the Iran nuclear deal ("the worst deal ever made in the history of our country"), and make sure Americans said "Merry Christmas" again. This Christmas line elicited a standing ovation that seemed to last two minutes. When the crowd chanted "USA, USA, USA," or "Trump! Trump! Trump!" he would step away from the podium, slow-clapping or patting his heart to show his gratitude. On

a purely anthropological level, it was amazing to witness, unlike anything I had seen in forty years of political campaigns, and the bond between Trump and his audience was undeniable and almost without precedent. Trump had tapped into a profound sense of grievance and alienation among people of faith about the marginalization of their faith that had been brought about by liberal judges and a media that trafficked in anti-Christian bigotry. He checked every box on the issues: life, religious freedom, Israel, Iran, and judges.[49]

Of all Trump said at the rally, for me the most telling line—and response—had nothing to do with policy or Reed's over-the-top gladiator remarks. Instead, it was the "Merry Christmas" promise and the subsequent two-minute standing ovation.

The moment was a microcosm of Trump's ability to play to people's fears—*the Grinchian Democrats want to steal Christmas!*—in order to win them over. It absolutely did not matter whether the fear he raised was justified, trivial, or even true; by now, it was already clear that truth not only wasn't driving the Trump bus or on the bus but had been thrown *under* the bus.

Trump's tactics were obvious:

First, instill fear by making his followers feel *uncomfortable*; to inflame the Democrats' supposed "War on Christmas," he suggested they wanted to rid "Merry Christmas" from the America lexicon.

Second, blame this injustice on The Enemy. This binds The Tribe with a sense of "how-dare-they!" victimhood. In starting World War II, Germany justified invading Poland by using a false-flag "attack" on a German radio station, carried out by Nazi soldiers dressed as Poles.[50]

Third, "save the day" by attacking the "injustice" so Trump, their fearless leader, comes off as the hero.

LEADER-FOLLOWER relationships such as this—and many evangelicals aren't this gullible—can feed off narcissism on both sides. "The leader relies on the adoration and respect of his followers," wrote Chuck DeGroat in *When Narcicissm Comes to Church*. "The follower is attracted to the omnipotence and charisma of the leader. The leaders use polarizing rhetoric that identifies an outside enemy, bringing together leader and followers on a grandiose mission. The followers feed off the leader's certainty in order to fill their own empty senses of self. Interestingly, both are prone to a form of narcissism."[51]

If the subject—Christmas greetings—was trivial, Trump's rhetoric was the stuff of war, albeit a culture war. "The goal of … nationalist rhetoric is to invoke pity for one's own," wrote Hedges. "The goal is to show the community that what they hold sacred is under threat."[52]

Once people pledge their loyalty to a charismatic leader, they aren't interested in the truth. They are only interested in strengthening The Tribe—i.e., themselves—against The Enemy. In this new culture war, the soldiers who follow the leader are infused with a sense of righteous indignation.

"The soldier, neglected and even shunned during peacetime, is suddenly held up as the exemplar of our highest ideals, the savior of the state," wrote Hedges.[53] And their leader, meanwhile, emerges from the self-created "chaos" as a hero; *Look what I've done for you—saved Christmas!* (Lest you think this is an overstatement, Franklin Graham's praising of Trump after his presidential reign would include the fact that he "stood against the secularists who wanted to take Christ out of Christmas and that he brought back the greeting 'Merry Christmas!'")[54]

Among the many lessons a book-writing client of mine taught me about workplace bullying was how bosses can create "artificial chaos" so they can benefit themselves, not the company. "My boss knew he was in over his head on the job, knew he didn't have the smarts to actually lead the team to triumphs, so he'd purposely create friction between people so he could ride to the rescue," she said. "He was pining for attention—so sets a spot fire, puts it out, then, when the media arrive, happily takes credit for saving the forest."

Victories mobilize The Tribe. So do defeats. After the 9/11 attacks on America, church attendance spiked—at least for a few months. Patriotism swelled. And revenge was on lots of people's minds. David Fitch, an Illinois pastor, tells of a Sunday night service, after he asked his congregation, "What do you think God would have us do as a church?"

"Go kick some ass and teach these people a lesson," said one man, triggering a smattering of "Amens."

Reflected Fitch: "This vengeance brought him, and others in the congregation, a sense of excitement, even enjoyment."[55]

From the moment he came down the escalator in 2015, Trump had spun the narrative that The Left had, in essence, slammed a couple of planes into "our way of life." And suddenly, many evangelicals—already feeling under siege by government, the media, and Hollywood—saw Trump as the one who could empower them. Thus, in computer lingo, what a few evangelicals saw in Trump as a "bug," most others saw as a "feature."

"I'm not going to lie," said one of my parking-lot interviewees, an evangelical. "Trump is the worst. But so what? He'll get the job done."

"And you'll vote for him, right?"

"Of course."

For me, the "so what" exception grated against everything the Bible had taught me about how we are to conduct ourselves. "So what" says: What matters isn't whether the behavior is God-approved; what matters is whether *it works*. Your teenage son, you learn, was hitting speeds up to 90 mph while en route to see his girlfriend in a neighboring town. You confront him; point out how wrong that is.

"So what?" he argues, "she was heading back to school soon. I *had* to get there fast. I *had* to spend some time with her." In other words, the end justified the means. Some evangelicals were, if even subconsciously, arguing that they had to speed, even if it endangered others. *We have to support Trump; otherwise, the Democrats win!*

The foundation of our faith, I'd been taught, is God's Word. Do what it says. Don't obsess about results; they're not up to us. Be faithful. Trust Him for the outcome.

But as 2016 deepened, I began fidgeting more in my seat. It was like I was seeing the same image on the screen that my fellow evangelicals were seeing, but most of them were nodding their approval. Me? I was wincing.

WHEN TRUMP invited hundreds of evangelical pastors to New York in June 2016, it was a seminal moment in his rise to power, a quid-pro-quo crossroads with those who could influence tens of millions of believers. The question remained: In the long run, was this in the best interest of evangelicals and Trump, or just in Trump?

Twenty years ago, when Focus on the Family's political arm, the Family Research Council, was just beginning, then-FRC President Gary Bauer expressed concern about the church-state union. "I am not afraid that we will take over the Republican Party," he said. "I'm afraid the Republican Party ... may take over us."

Two decades later, Trump's "seat-at-the-table" invitation to evangelicals was far more defined—and the chance of it far more possible. Trump was smart; he knew about one-fourth of the electorate consisted of evangelicals—and many were feeling disenfranchised, unheard, and dissed.[56] In January 2016, he had told evangelical leaders, "Christianity will have power." And later, "We will respect and defend Christian Americans."[57]

Shortly after Trump was nominated as the Republican candidate for president, Penny Nance, CEO and president of the conservative Concerned Women for America, said she tried to resist Trump, then gave up. "I did everything I could do to blow up the tracks in front of the Trump train," she said, "and it didn't work, and so at this point you either jump on, or stand on the sidelines and wave."[58]

I disagreed that there was no other choice. *Not jumping on* was a choice, regardless of whether that meant voting for Hillary Clinton (not my choice), not voting at all (few people's choice), or writing in a candidate (*my* choice). In other words, think outside the box and vote your conscience. So, there I stood, alone at the station, waving as the train chugged into the distance, full of all sorts of people I loved and admired.

"Trump's promises to evangelicals were similar to Satan's offer to Jesus," wrote Napp Nazworth, editor of the *Christian Post*. "While tempting Jesus in the desert, the Bible tells us, 'the devil took him to a very high mountain and showed him all the kingdoms of the world and their splendor; and he said to him, 'All this I will give you, if you will fall down and worship me.' I'm not saying Trump is the antichrist. It is Trump's and Satan's use of similar methods that should concern us."[59]

Melding politics with faith is like a chemist combining two incompatible elements; the result is always discord. Christ's goals of others-first selflessness clashes head-on with us-first power. In other words, politics plus religion always equals politics. But Trump made it easy for some to forget such certainties—and forget the past. Take Bauer. Twenty years after he worried about the church being gobbled up by Republicanism, he, like most big-wig evangelicals, was all-in for Trump.

He wasn't alone in his "about-face." A 2011 poll done by the Public Religion Research Institute found that 60 percent of white evangelicals believed that a public official who "commits an immoral act in their personal life" cannot still "behave ethically and fulfill their duties in their public and professional life." But in 2016, the year Trump was running for president, that plummeted to 20 percent.[60] The new evangelical sound bite was: "I'm voting for a platform, not a person; an administration, not an individual."

Meanwhile, like the candidate they were backing, some evangelicals were sporting a new get-tough look. Tony Perkins, head of Family Research Council, said evangelicals "were tired of being kicked around by Barack Obama and his leftists. And I think they are finally glad that there's somebody on the playground that is willing to punch the bully."[61]

"What about turning the other cheek?" a *Christianity Today* reporter asked him, referencing Matthew 5:38-39, which says "You have heard that it was said, 'Eye for eye, and tooth for tooth.' But I tell you, Do not resist an evil person. If someone strikes you on the right cheek, turn to him the other also.'"

"We only have two cheeks," Perkins said. "Look, Christianity is not about being a welcome mat which people can just stomp their feet on."[62]

CONVENTIONAL WISDOM suggested Trump's promise to fight abortion explained the evangelical love for Trump. Or did it? In a survey from Wheaton College's Billy Graham Center, when white evangelicals were asked what influenced their 2016 votes for Trump, fewer than half mentioned abortion or the Supreme Court. Instead, their top issues were the economy, health care, national security, and immigration.[63] But even that was deceptive; what really mattered to evangelicals—historians, surveys, and anecdotal evidence later suggested—was exactly what Trump was promising: power, with a side order of nostalgia for an America that was warm and fuzzy—but mainly for those who were welcome at the Woolworth's lunch counter (white) or the dominant faith (Christian) or the privileged gender (male).

Here and there, a few conservatives saw Trump for what he was: the playground bully, period. In March, Sen. Mitt Romney, R-Utah, said, "Donald Trump is a phony, a fraud. His promises are as worthless as a degree from Trump University. He's playing members of the American public for suckers. He gets a free ride to the White House, and all we get is a lousy hat."[64]

But among evangelical voters, Trump's approval rating had climbed to sixty-one percent.[65] I considered it a moot point because I continued to naively believe that, like that pivotal "when-he-came-to-his-senses" moment from the Prodigal Son story, evangelicals would wake up and retreat from Trump.

In the end, I underestimated how fearful many evangelicals were. Their fear of liberals in general, and Hillary Clinton in particular, explained how willing they were to look the other way regarding Trump's bullying demeanor. That, to me, explained their willingness to back him far more than issues such as abortion or religious freedom; the idea that being "pro-life" was Trump's Get-Out-of-Jail-Free card with evangelicals sounded logical but ignored the deeper fear of evangelicals. And ignored how shallow the "pro-life" waters could be.

Deborah Fikes, the former executive advisor to the World Evangelical Alliance, points out that evangelicals in other countries were bewildered by American evangelicals' narrow views on "pro-life." "They're surprised at our reluctance to oppose almost any kind of gun-control reform; at our views on capital punishment; and at our unwillingness to accept climate change and care more for the Earth."[66]

"We are the richest country on the planet with the worst poverty," says Professor Matthew Desmond, a Princeton University sociologist.[67] As Trump was taking the political stage, the child poverty rate in Japan was 2 percent; in Germany, Sweden, and Norway, 4 percent. But in the US it was 21 percent.[68] It seemed to me that a healthy church spoke for unborn babies *and* pregnant mothers, victims of abuse, the oppressed, the unfairly incarcerated, the poor, and others.

Trump spoke to none of these concerns but triggered roars at his rallies when he'd simply shout, "Build the wall!" or "Make America Great Again!" Which is why I had begun thinking that the guy could actually win. The bulk of evangelicals weren't interested in the nitty-gritty gospel issues like the poor or huddled masses yearning to breathe free. Most simply wanted to win!

Sen. Marco Rubio, R-Florida, said Trump could not only win but take down the country in the process. "The politics of resentment against other people will not just leave us a fractured party," said Rubio, who bowed out of the race in March 2016, "they will leave us a fractured nation ... . They are going to leave us as a nation where people literally hate each other because they have different political opinions."[69]

In January 2016, Peter Wehner, an evangelical Christian and, at the time, a Republican, had written an editorial for *The New York Times* op-ed page headlined, "Why I Will Never Vote for Donald Trump." In it, he wrote, "Mr. Trump's virulent combination of ignorance, emotional instability, demagogy, solipsism, and vindictiveness would do more than result in a failed presidency; it could very well lead to a national catastrophe."[70] But the voices of Wehner and Rubio were drowned out by the clack-clack of the Trump train, filled with evangelicals headed for what many seemed to see as a new promised land.

IN THE SUMMER of 2016, I didn't care if anyone would hear my voice above the din, I could no longer stay silent.

On a mid-July morning, my editor stuck his head in my office.

"We're short on editorials for late in the week. Wanna take a crack?"

"Sure. Any particular topic?"

"Fielder's choice. Just run it by me first."

I hesitated. These were uncharted waters. It was one thing to write columns about our community under my byline; I had done that for fourteen years. It would be quite another to write an unsigned editorial that, in essence, says: *This is how this paper stands on this issue.* (The editorial page editor of our three-person staff was acutely attuned to the publisher's political, social, and economic views, though would check with him if he or another editorial writer were taking a questionable stance on something.) But I'd asked for this adventure, right? Prayed for it.

"Well, I'm fairly stunned that Trump seems to be everything evangelical Christians *wouldn't* want," I said. "And yet the polls show they love him. Seems odd to me. How about if I look into that?"

"Go for it."

My piece was the lead editorial on Friday, July 22, 2016, headlined "Trump's evangelical flock: What happened to claims that 'character matters?'" A condensation of it:

> Only five lines into his opening prayer Monday at the Republican National Convention, televangelist Mark Burns said, "We are electing a man in Donald Trump who believes in the name of Jesus Christ"—making it clear that Trump was tying the knot with evangelical Christians, and they with him.
>
> Who could blame him? White evangelical Christians comprise roughly a quarter of the electorate. And Trump and evangelicals share a common foe in Hillary Clinton, whom both despise.
>
> More puzzling is why evangelicals seem willing to check their faith at the door to follow a man who oozes the very self-righteousness that the founder of their faith, Jesus, condemned in deference to humility, grace, and truth. Indeed, the relationship seems, at best, awkward, and at worst, hypocritical—for both.
>
> Faith, clearly, has never been a priority for Trump. And power and position were never priorities for Jesus. Yet Trump is only too happy to be the evangelicals' new pied piper—and many evangelicals are only too happy to let him lead.
>
> In politics, people routinely use others for leverage; that's how the game is played. What's disturbing about this marriage is that evangelicals not only ostensibly live for "higher things," but can be quick to remind others that they should, too.
>
> In 2015, evangelicals were five times more likely than the general public to say faith "is an important factor in choosing a candidate," according to a Barna Group poll. And yet since Trump successfully began wooing Liberty University president Jerry Falwell Jr.—most students refused to be wooed—evangelicals have fallen for his style-over-substance approach like puppy-love teens. Last week, a Pew Research Center survey showed nearly eight in 10 white evangelical Protestants back Trump over Clinton, who may not be a pillar of faith herself but won't open the Democratic National Convention with prayer suggesting she is God's Chosen One.
>
> Thus, for evangelicals to embrace Trump—even as a perceived

lesser of two evils—is to align with a man whose values appear diametrically opposed to those of Jesus: He's dishonest ("Let us not love with words or speech but with actions and in truth—1 John 3:8). He's demeaning toward others. ("As you did it to one of the least of these my brothers, you did it to me."—Matthew 25:40). And he's self-righteous. ("Clothe yourselves with compassion, kindness, humility, meekness and patience"—Colossians 3:12).

For good measure, you could puzzle about how Trump says he's never asked for forgiveness—a cornerstone of evangelical belief.

"Here's a man who holds up the Bible one day, and the next day calls a lady a 'bimbo,'" says Max Lucado, among a cluster of evangelical pastors refusing to join the Trump camp.

A man who, even as racism divides the country, happily accepts [the] endorsement of a former grand wizard of the Ku Klux Klan.

For people who purport to trust in a limitless God, the idea that their only hope is Donald Trump would seem to suggest theirs is a small faith, indeed—fueled not by a love for the truth, but by a hatred for Hillary Clinton.

The morning the editorial ran, I arrived at my office and punched my "messages" button, expecting the usual handful.

There were far more.

My Hope for the Future

That we might love one another as we're called to

IN A FORTY-year career as a journalist, I was privileged to interview more than an estimated ten thousand people. Some were mean, egotistical, selfish people who'd done things to hurt others. Some were caring, compassionate, selfless people who'd done things to help others. But the difference between the two, frankly, wasn't whether they followed Jesus; the difference was whether they placed others above themselves. Some Christians did, some didn't; some non-Christians did, some didn't.

As Christians, we need to choose love in a political climate where hate for The Enemy runs deep.

"On Sunday, contemporary Christians are eager to worship a crucified Savior who loved and forgave his enemies," wrote Skye Jethani in *What if Jesus Was Serious?* "But on Monday we want permission to behave like the schoolyard bully who uses fear and anger to get ahead."

If, as Scripture reminds us, God is love (1 John 4:8), shouldn't *that* be the question we ask in how we treat others? What would *love* have me do? Not: What would The Tribe have me do?

"Love as I have loved you," says 2 Peter 1:7.

In ancient Rome, though Christians were persecuted, Roman citizens held them in high-esteem because "of how life-giving they were as neighbors," wrote Scott Sauls in *A*

Gentle Answer. As Christians, is that our reputation today?

If we are sons and daughters of the Prince of Peace we need to refrain from the rancor of the Far Right—the bully tactics that Trump inspired.

"As a prisoner for the Lord, then, I urge you to live a life worthy of the calling you have received," wrote Paul in Ephesians 4:1-2. "Be completely humble and gentle; be patient, bearing with one another in love."

And love, as they say, is a verb. It's not some nebulous warm and fuzzy feeling, it's giving and forgiving. It's time, energy, resources. It's seeking reconciliation. It's listening. It's being curious about someone different from you. It's church stuff, overseas stuff, coffee-shop missions stuff.

Finally, it's "caring-about-the-least-of-these" stuff. To this end, the sooner the Church stops treating "social justice" like some sort of rat that needs trapping, the sooner it will align with the Jesus it ostensibly follows. Does everything done under the banner of "social justice" square with the gospel? Of course not. But as evangelicals we too easily throw out the baby with the bath water.

As Christians we need to rid ourselves of the rancor and resentment that we often reflect to the world. "Make every effort to live in peace with everyone and to be holy; without holiness no one will see the Lord (Hebrews 12:4)."

If we are pro-life, we need that to mean more than being anti-abortion. It needs to mean being pro-people, from womb to tomb.

"We weep at the unjustified destruction of the unborn," wrote Manning. "Did we also weep when the evening news reported from Arkansas that a black family had been shotgunned out of a white neighborhood?"

Jerushah Duford, a granddaughter of Billy Graham, said she was decidedly pro-life—and couldn't support Trump for that very reason. His "pro-life" stance, she reasoned, wasn't comprehensive enough.

"The Jesus we serve promotes kindness, dignity, humility,

and [he] doesn't represent our faith," she said. "I genuinely wish the Democratic Party would have a greater value for life inside the womb. Yet I equally wish the Republican Party would place a greater value on life outside the womb. You cannot choose just one and define yourself as pro-life."

What we need is to love full-out as Jesus commanded, not only when it serves our political purposes.

What we *don't* need is one more Bible study. Don't get me wrong, I'm totally pro-Bible, but I've seen people swirl endlessly in studying it as if caught in a river's eddy. God's Word is a means to an end, not an end unto itself. If the priority for us is to love God and to love others, the endgame isn't learning how or why to be loving; it's to apply what we've learned—to *be* loving. And we can't do that—we can't engage, encourage, and share with others—unless we have the courage to get out of the shallows and into the river itself.

"Get rid of all bitterness, rage, and anger, brawling and slander, along with every form of malice," says Ephesians 4:31-32. "Be kind and compassionate to one another, forgiving each other, just as in Christ God forgave you."

"Can we move beyond our initial reactions, automatic opinions, and perceived threats?" asks author Dan White Jr. in *Love Over Fear*. "The very soul of being a Jesus follower is at stake with how we answer this question."

It's time to connect the dots. "Love one another" is mentioned over a dozen times in the New Testament. This "love stuff" isn't a little parsley thrown on the evangelical plate for looks; it's to be our nutritional sustenance as believers—and it's gotten lost in the heaping servings of political pride.

"And now these three things remain: faith, hope, and love," says 1 Corinthians 13:13. "But the greatest of these is love."

5.

Marley & Me

I begin a spirited email relationship with a pro-Trump letter-writer who sharpens me as we ping-pong opinions back and forth.

Many can argue, not many converse.

—A. Bronson Alcott

Eugene, Oregon, grew up as a mill town in the largest timber-producing state in the union. But in the 1960s and '70s—when University of Oregon students rioted often against the War in Vietnam—it took a hard left and never looked back. If the city was decidedly liberal—it hadn't voted for a Republican president since 1984 (Reagan over Mondale)—the outnumbered conservatives could be loud and proud. And who could blame them? Liberals, even if clad in the softness of

Birkenstocks and hemp, were no strangers to ripping right-wingers in well-barbed letters to the editor. And they had "the numbers."

All of which is to say the backlash to my Trump editorial from The Right was swift, sharp, and not at all unexpected; nearly all those messages were critical of the editorial. Among those who took exception was a guy named Marley*. He was a self-described "God-believer" who I knew from his regular letters; we limited readers to one per month and Marley was as regular as my Verizon bill. He had also attended a writers' workshop of mine a few years back.

I liked Marley. He was polite, passionate, respectful, and curious. But if we were on the same page regarding Trump's lack of character, we disagreed about what that meant when our mail-in ballots would arrive in three months. I believed I had to vote my conscience and, trusting that God was in control, let the chips fall where they may. He believed God could do great things through Trump, flawed though he was. As usual, the paper published his letter to the editor soon after it arrived:

> The Editors (*Trump's evangelical flock, July 22*) questioned how Christians can reconcile their faith with supporting Trump. The idea of "voting for the lesser of two evils" didn't seem compatible.
>
> I'm not sure you can say that choosing the lesser of two evils is incompatible with Christianity. Nor is a vote for the least problems a tacit approval or shared unity with a person's character or ideas.
>
> The Editors found pro-Trump evangelicals to be an enigma, wondering if they were: checking their faith at the door, hypocrites regarding character, falling for style-over-substance, or putting their hopes in man instead of God.
>
> I like the editors. I know they mean well. In their own way, they flatter true Christians as being so far above the fray that they wouldn't countenance a person perceived as being vulgar. Thank you. However, a few interviews with devout Christians, whose votes differ, might reveal how faith and choice express themselves in complex, differing ways.
>
> Hillary's repeated dishonesty and Donald's endemic vulgarity equally disqualify both for public office, yet one will be President. What's left to differentiate them? Their policies and apologies.

---

* Not his real name.

> Trump's [nomination] speech aligns with many of my values and concerns; his family's love and admiration for him affects me. Hillary's policies largely don't agree with mine; her estranged marriage would be a sad overlay on the White House.
>
> Lastly, Trump has admitted his vulgarity and pledged to stop. Hillary hasn't admitted lying about Benghazi nor her emails. Trump repented, Hillary has not.

Marley hammered home his lesser-of-two-evils defense. "You keep inferring we are voting *for* someone, and you keep maligning us by doing so. You put up a false construct: that voting for the lesser of two evils is voting for someone you agree with." And he amplified his theme of Clinton as an unrepentant liar, Trump as merely "vulgar." "In my view, lying violates the Ten Commandments," he wrote. "Hillary has been pernicious at it to the public. She has been unrepentant. To elect a liar is incompatible with Christianity."

At the time, Marley apparently didn't realize that I—a "brother in the faith"—had written the editorial. When Marley wrote back, I told him I was working at *The R-G* now and had written it. Thus, began numerous emails back and forth in the coming months after I'd encouraged him to write to me on my personal account since we were going beyond the scope of my job.

"No one elected Samson but God," he wrote me one day. "God used him to do his people good, even though many of his actions were not what we would expect—and I do mean *not* what we would expect: revenge killings, and things of that nature."

I agreed that God uses flawed people to do His work, myself among them. But, I said, if you want to live by that argument you must die by it, too. Must allow a Democrat the same "out"—say Hillary Clinton lying about the emails, a decision that pointed to flawed character but could be easily overlooked, right, in that God uses imperfect people? Or was lack of character only forgivable for Republicans?

He countered with an end-justifies-the-means logic that I enjoyed but couldn't buy.

I see Trump as correct in this: as he gives up running his businesses and letting his children do it, he is going to change from using the laws in his favor, to enforcing the laws to everyone's benefit. He's going to use his experience in business to cut out the con men duping us.

This morning, I wrote an email to the man who was the subject of the movie *Catch Me If You Can*. [Leonardo DeCaprio plays Frank Abignale, a daring and deceitful young man who impersonates airline pilots and doctors, forges checks, gets caught by the FBI, then, after prison time, uses his knowledge of "thinking like a con man" to help the government protect its citizens from being conned.] ... He's [given] 40 years of service to us. He said that when businesses ask him to look at their operations, after he leaves, he gets a phone call later that afternoon telling [him] that they have implemented every last thing he said and it is now in operation. But when he gives these recommendations to government entities, the answer is, "Well, thanks for your suggestions"—but nothing of it is implemented. That shocks him.

So put Trump in this same position as Abignale. What if Trump is willing to do exactly what Abignale is doing? To this day, Frank Abignale is the foremost authority on cyber-security because he just thinks like a con-man. And the thing is, he uses that con-man sense to stop con-men from gaining access. So, what if Trump is just like Frank, going to use his skills to bless America?

I enjoyed Marley's *Catch Me If You Can* example; I'd liked the movie. But in getting to his happy ending for Trump, he was making three assumptions that I could not: (a) that Trump had the moral compass to find true north; (b) that he had the empathy to re-channel his business knowledge to benefit someone other than himself and his family; and (c) that his business knowledge was worthy of being re-channeled. Even a cursory read of his background showed Trump was given millions of dollars by his father, so he invested it in housing, casinos, hotels, and golf-course resorts, often followed by lawsuits from those with whom he'd worked. In June 2016, *USA Today* reported that Trump and his businesses had been involved in 3,500 legal cases in US federal and state courts. By contrast, wheeler-dealer billionaire Mark Cuban told author Rick Reilly in 2018 that he had been involved in exactly two.[71]

How, Marley asked, had I reached my conclusions about Trump?

My reply:

I look at this decision—or at least attempt to—from a nonpolitical point of view. I look at it as simply: What's the right thing to do for me as a Christ follower?

In the last 35 years, starting with the Moral Majority, Christians have entered the political fray with gusto. Nothing wrong with that—unless politics and winning and power and displacing fear become more important than Christ. And I think that's what's happening here. Christians are panicking about America (see "idol worship") instead of trusting the God of the universe.

As believers, we're called to make the right decisions *regardless of their consequence*. For example, you wouldn't agree to work for a boss whose values were clearly immoral—regardless of what that would mean to you. (Loss of potential income, prestige, power, whatever.)

Shadrach, Meshach and Abednego refused to bow down to [King] Nebuchadnezzar—regardless of what that would mean to them. (They were destined to be burned alive, until God intervened.)

Dietrich Bonhoeffer refused to stop defying Hitler, regardless of what that would mean to him. (Death.)

Jesus went to the cross with a clear conscience—regardless of what that would mean to him. (He was tortured, then killed.)

All these people simply made what they felt was the clear-conscience decision even though they knew it would cost them *their lives*.

And yet here's what I hear Christians saying: "We must vote for Donald Trump even though he has flaws—serious flaws—and is patently un-Christ-like in so many ways—because if we don't vote for him Hillary will win. And we won't have a chance to reconfigure the Supreme Court. And liberals will reign."

In other words, the sky is falling.

In other words, God saves us from sin, parts the seas, walks on water, but can't overcome a Hillary win.

In other words, our God isn't big enough. The thing that is driving people to vote for Trump is fear, plain and simple.

What does that say about our faith?

Why would anyone want *what we have* if what we have is what everybody else has: *nothing*, really. A faith that we purport to be "mighty" but actually cowers to the political winds. A faith that melts into fear.

You needn't be a biblical scholar to see that what Christ honors above all is conviction for the things of God—regardless of the cost.

Regardless of whether that means losing in the human sense.

"Jesus Christ's life was an absolute failure from every standpoint but God's," wrote Oswald Chambers.

Why are we so afraid to *lose* in a cultural sense, knowing that we've already won in a big-picture, God-is-in-control sense?

Why are we willing to embrace a man who is *clearly* so diametrically opposed to the values, spirit, and temperament of Christ? Fear, plain and simple. Which suggests ours is no faith at all. It's simply a habit. A calling card we've been pulling out so long we've forgotten what it's really all about. A so-called trust that wilts when the consequences aren't even close to the thing that so many others have been willing to put on the line for their faith: death.

Sorry, but, in a sense, you asked! :)

The Trump love from evangelicals suggested group-think-gone-wild. When you identify as part of a group, experts say, you're more likely to become angry about politics, to be less influenced by information, and to be less likely to support bipartisan politicians who reach out across the aisle to find compromise. You're less likely to want a solution for all. You just want to win—to maintain, or regain, a sense of grandeur for the group.

Chip Berlet, a senior analyst at Political Research Associates in Boston, says some people subconsciously bend their faith to fit their politics.

"When you decide that taking power in a political system is the most important thing, then you rewrite the sacred texts of the religion to justify what you're doing," he says. "So, in your mind you're still faithful, but the version of the faith you've created serves your political needs."[72]

Jesus and his disciples didn't rant against, or panic over, the secular, anti-religious, power-thirsty, and blood-thirsty Caesars of their day. And here's why: "Our struggle is not against flesh and blood," says Ephesians 6:12, "but against the rulers, against the authorities, against the powers of this dark world and against the spiritual forces of wickedness in the heavenly realms." That doesn't sound like *people* to me, the "not-against-flesh-and-blood" line a dead giveaway.

Instead, says Chicago evangelical pastor David Fitch, too many evangelicals are about what he calls the "enemy-making machine." "It plays on making an enemy. It extracts the enemy from a relationship and makes them into an object around which we gather fear and loathing. … And we have done this, ironically, with the aim of working for a Christian nation."[73]

Does The Left do things that grate against God's deepest values? Absolutely. But discordant political ideologies do not justify our hating those who see things differently than we do. Trump, I could see in the early goings, was fanning the flame of bitterness that the Moral Majority had ignited thirty-five years earlier.

As Christians, we are called to fight *for* people, not against, people. Our battle is against the "cosmic powers" that hold these people, and all people, in bondage. And the warrior mentality leads to what was freezing Americans on both sides of the fence in fear: "negative polarization."

"In plain English this means that a person belongs to their political party not so much because they like their own party but because they hate and fear the other side," wrote conservative attorney—and evangelical—David French.[74]

THE MORE pro-Trump evangelicals I talked to, the more I realized I needed to better understand "cognitive dissonance." It describes the discomfort people feel when two "cognitions"—the process of reaching a conclusion—conflict, creating discord between an opinion and behavior. "I like to smoke" clashes with—is dissonant with—the proven fact that smoking is unhealthy. To reduce the disharmony between the two, the smoker needs to either *quit* smoking or *justify* continuing to smoke. *What does science know?* Or: *I don't smoke* that *often.*

"Dissonance is most painful when evidence strikes at the heart of how we see ourselves—when it threatens our belief that we are kind, ethical, competent, and smart," write social psychologists Elliot Aronson and Carol Tavris. "The minute we make any decision—*I'll buy this car; I will vote for this candidate*—we will begin to justify the wisdom of our choice and find reason to dismiss the alternative.[74]

"Before long, any ambivalence we might have felt at the time of the original decision will have morphed into certainty. As people justify each step taken after the original decision, they will find it harder to admit they were wrong at the outset. Especially when the end-result proves self-defeating, wrongheaded, or harmful."[75]

I could relate. Earlier, I mentioned the implosion in our church in the late 1990s—and how my conscience was telling me, in relation to two of the three pastors: *You need to apologize and seek their forgiveness.* That's the message I was getting, sent as if a bullet train from my conscience, triggering thoughts from Matthew 5:23-24: "So, what if you are offering your gift at the altar and remember that someone has something against you? Leave your gift there and go make peace with that person. Then come and offer your gift."

But as soon as I entertained that thought, my own cognitive dissonance kicked in: *The two pastors probably weren't wounded ... If they were wounded, they're probably now just healing; why rip the Band-Aid off? ...* And, *Hey, it's not like people didn't say some hurtful things to me ...*

At the root of my dissonance, frankly, was pride. There were a lot of things I couldn't do well; I couldn't learn a foreign language, understand the most rudimentary board games, or spell *hors*—just a sec, let me hit Spell Check—*hors d'oeuvres*. But I had done OK at relationships. And to admit I needed to apologize regarding relationships was to rip a hole in that pride.

It also meant being uncomfortable. You had to sit across from someone who might not trust you, who might dislike you, who might have hurt you, and say: *I'm sorry for ——————. Will you forgive me?*

Finally, it meant *change*. Our default format is sameness, tradition, "the way things have always been done." (Conservatism.) And forgiveness is just the opposite. It's out of the ordinary, "the way things usually *aren't* done." (Christ.)

So, add it all up and my pride rationalized: *Nope, not going there.*
And I didn't.

6.

Trials & Triumph

As the 2016 presidential election nears, I'm forced to ask myself a question I never thought I would: Am I demonic?

There is something treacherous, delusive, and ambiguous in the temptation of power.

—Vaclav Havel

The summer of 2016 started slipping away. In August, despite unseasonal cold and fog, I relished hiking to the top of Oregon's 10,353-foot South Sister with my older son and my eleven-year-old grandson; took my eighty-nine-year-old, twice-widowed mother on a sentimental journey to Central Oregon; and, with my brother-in-law, added another few hundred miles in our quest to hike the 2,650-mile Pacific Crest Trail. Since beginning in 2011, we now had more than half the trail done.

Meanwhile, the election neared. In August, a Quinnipiac University poll showed that nearly two-thirds of those who said they were voting for Trump were motivated more by ensuring that Hillary Clinton *doesn't* win.[75]

"More than guns, abortion, gay rights, small government—the Red State Christians I spoke to across the country were unified more in their hatred of Hillary than in any other way," wrote Angela Denker, a Lutheran pastor, in *Red State Christians: Understanding the Voters Who Elected Donald Trump*. "More than the issues themselves, they were motivated by a hatred of Hillary that felt personal and, they assumed, mutual."[76]

The Hillary haters apparently assumed right on the "mutual" matter. On September 9, 2016, Clinton, at an LGBQT fundraising event in New York, said something that lit the fire of Trump supporters. "You know, to just be grossly generalistic, you could put half of Trump's supporters into what I call the basket of deplorables, right? The racist, sexist, homophobic, xenophobic, Islamophoboic—you name it. And unfortunately, there are people like that. And he has lifted them up."[77]

I cringed. Slapping a label on someone—however well you might think it fits—is *just the opposite* of what we'd want someone to do to you, right? Says Luke 6:31: "Do to others as you would have them do to you." Clinton deserved any boomerang action she got on that one. And she did. For many pro-Trumpers, it deepened their sense that the Democrats hated them and—as some right-wing talk show hosts had begun to say in their hate-filled hyperbole—"want you *dead!*"

WHAT MAGNIFIED the meanness of the Clinton remark was that while she rarely stooped so low, Trump did so routinely. In 2015, after Fox News's Megyn Kelly pointed out that he'd publicly called women "fat pigs," "dogs," "slobs," and "disgusting animals," he doubled down, insinuating that Kelly's tough line of question was because she had "blood coming out of her eyes, blood coming out of her wherever."[78] He called Miss Universe contestant Alicia Machado "Miss Piggy." And in

April 2016, said, "If Hillary Clinton were a man, I don't think she'd get 5 percent of the vote."[79]

On the subject of women, that was just Trump's warm-up band. In early October 2016, about a month before the election, the *Washington Post* published a 2005 video showing Trump and "Access Hollywood" host Billy Bush having a conversation on a bus. In it, Trump talked of his attempt to seduce a married woman and suggested he might start kissing the woman he and Bush were about to meet.

"I don't even wait," he said. "And when you're a star, they let you do it. You can do anything. ... Grab 'em by the pussy. You can do anything."[80]

To some, the remarks sounded like boys-will-be-boys stuff. To others, pointing to the implied lack of consent, it sounded like his actions amounted to sexual assault.

If Democrats were livid, Republican leaders weren't exactly forgiving, which both stunned and encouraged me. Republican National Committee (RNC) Chairman Reince Priebus said, "No woman should ever be described in these terms or talked about in this manner. Ever." The RNC suspended all support of Trump's campaign shortly thereafter. Many members of the Republican Party, including John McCain, rescinded their support for Trump.

But the big evangelical guns didn't even fire a warning shot across Trump's bow. Franklin Graham said he wasn't giving Trump a pass, then gave Trump a pass. "This election isn't about Donald's behavior from 11 years ago … This election is about the Supreme Court and the justices that the next president will nominate. My prayer is that Christians will not be deceived by the liberal media about what is at stake for future generations." So, another closet door opens on Donald Trump's skeletons and the "liberal media" was to blame? For Trump, it was another sorry excuse for a man who needed, instead of protection, accountability. Someone close to him to say: *Grow up.*

From the beginning of Trump's campaign, Graham had curiously emerged as among the man's chief defenders. Here was the son of the country's best-known and respected evangelical, Billy. Franklin Graham's Samaritan Purse organization had done much to ease human suffering worldwide; I'd had a one-on-one interview with him back in the

'80s when I worked at *The Journal-American* in Bellevue, Washington, and was impressed with the guy. But, decades later, his incessant defense of Trump consistently clashed with the lesson his father had learned from Nixon—that politicians will happily exploit those of faith for their own ends.

Ralph Reed said he was disappointed in Trump but "people of faith are voting on issues like who will protect unborn life, defend religious freedom … " As such, this was low on Reed's "hierarchy of concerns."[81] Translation: *Women being abused was apparently a trivial matter; Trump winning the presidency was not.*

Other prominent evangelicals such as Bauer, Falwell, and Dobson quickly joined the cowardly choir—yes, the same Dobson who, during the Bill Clinton debacle, had said, "Character does matter. You can't run a family, let alone a country, without it."[82] None dared call Trump on the carpet.

In my office at *The Register-Guard*, the hypocrisy rankled me: The Republicans—some with no professed Christian commitment at all—had swiftly taken action to castigate Trump, but most evangelicals had sloughed off his statement as much ado about nothing.

A few had the courage to buck the trend, among them Beth Moore, a fabulously popular Bible-study leader from Houston whose women's events drew thousands, whose books had sold millions, and whose Twitter followers numbered 900,000.

"I'm one among many women who have been sexually abused, misused, stared down, heckled, talked naughty to," she tweeted to her followers. "Like we liked it. We didn't. We're tired of it." In another tweet, which seemed to be directed at Trump's supporters, she wrote, "Wake up, Sleepers, to what women have dealt with all along in environments of gross entitlement & power."

Moore's message was dynamite in two tweets—but the majority reaction wasn't "you-go-girl" encouragement from her fellow evangelicals. Quite the opposite. Women's church groups that had booked Moore canceled. Attendance at her events plummeted. Male evangelical pastors pressured her to recant; she refused, other than to say her comments didn't represent a political endorsement.[83]

The fallout was uncanny. Amid a Christian community whose New Testament says even lusting after a woman is a sin, the anger was aimed not at Trump for his lewd comments but at the female Bible teacher who dared to question Our Guy. In short, the Trump Machine was now coming after its own.

"What happens when, in the political or the religious arena, the far right-wing-fundamentalist-'tens' denounce the 'eights' as liberals?" tweeted Moore. "It's just a matter of time before they go for the 'nines.' The same formula works at the opposite end. A society forced into extremism is in peril."

In the days that followed, as hate mail and vicious Twitter comments pummeled her, Moore said she "cried out to God." Meanwhile, Trump kept being Trump. In an October 9, 2016, debate with Clinton, he threatened, if he won, to have her "locked up"; complained half a dozen times that moderators were interrupting him and giving Clinton softball questions; denied ever inappropriately touching a woman; and said, "I have great respect for women. Nobody has more respect for women than I do."[84]

IT WAS NOT news to me that lots of evangelicals hated The Left, but as the Trump saga unfolded, I had underestimated the depths of that hatred. Though I'd never worn my politics on my sleeve, I was—*gulp*—a registered Democrat. Did they hate me? As Graham suggested, was I "almost demonic?"

A young friend of Sally's who'd grown up in the South told me her former pastor was stunned to learn that she wasn't voting for Trump. "He wanted to make sure I wasn't voting for the Democrats," she told me, "because Democrats are demonic since they reject Jesus. They believe the Democratic Party is evil." (Sixty-three percent of Democrats identify as Christians, according to a Pew Research Center study in 2014, including a former columnist colleague at *The Register-Guard* whose courage and integrity ran deep, particularly when she sounded off against abortion in a community that leaned left.)[85]

And yet there I was, hunkering down every day in this supposed den of iniquity at *The Register-Guard*. Frankly, it was interesting working in the editorial department. My boss was among the best I'd ever had. He loved what he did and was great at it, having built an award-winning section, among the best in the country among papers our size. He treated people with undying respect—even conservatives, the wiser of whom saw him as an ally, not an enemy.

Because our offices were side by side, I often heard him talking on the phone with readers. Eugene was a politically charged place where people could go ballistic. But I never heard my boss raise his voice to a caller. In other words, the image that some evangelicals have of newspapers—that they plot each day about how to stick it to conservatives—did not mirror my experience, be it my two-year stint in editorial or my thirty-eight years in other roles and on other papers.

I'm not denying that the media are overwhelmingly staffed by liberals, some of whom have their anti-Christian biases. I'm simply saying that the people I've worked with, for the most part, were amazing journalists who didn't exist to thwart The Right. What's more, newspapers aren't comprised of only "heathen lefties." My closest friend, a graphic designer, was a Christian; so was a guy I hiked with on Mt. Pisgah and another guy who introduced me to Manning's Gospel-rich talks. And, in 1999, when an icon of a columnist, unabashedly liberal, retired at *The Register-Guard*, the paper didn't replace him with another liberal. It replaced him with me, knowing full well my Christian world view—and hired me yet again for the job in editorial in June 2016. But when evangelicals, in general, looked at the media, many seemed to see nothing but a dangerous adversary, a "them" out to get "us."

THE TRUMP TRAIN rolled on. Ten days later, in the last of three debates, Trump refused to say whether he'd concede the election if he lost. "I'll keep you in suspense," he said, another one of those foreboding remarks that hinted at his unwillingness to lose—at any cost.

Back at *The Register-Guard*, Marley emailed me. He had just heard the perfect explanation of Trump's appeal from Chris Matthews, a former MSNBC commentator—and a Democrat. And he just had to tell me. Said Matthews:

A lot of this support for Trump, with all his flaws which he displays regularly, is about the country—patriotic feelings people have. They feel like the country has been let down. Our elite leaders on issues like immigration, they don't regulate any immigration it seems. They don't regulate trade to our advantage, to the working man or working woman's advantage. They take us into stupid wars. Their kids don't fight but our kids do.

It's patriotic. They believe in their country. ... [There is a] deep sense that the country is being taken away and betrayed. I think that is so deep with people that they're looking at a guy who's flawed as hell like Trump and at least it's a way of saying 'I am really angry about the way the elite has treated my country.' And it's so deep that it overwhelms all the bad stuff from Trump. It's that strong.

"Yes to literally all of that," Marley wrote.

I understood why many evangelicals felt that way; a friend told me exactly that when I asked about his views on Trump. I think the essence could be boiled down to this line from Matthews alone: "I am really angry about the way the elite has treated my country. And it's so deep that it overwhelms all the bad stuff from Trump."

But here's what I'd been taught in decades of listening to sermons: don't let feelings get in the way of faith. Faith isn't feelings; it's often trusting God *despite* feelings. As Christians, our hope is not in what we can see, touch, and feel, but in the promises of God. "... faith is being sure of what we hope for and certain of what we do not see," says Hebrews 11:1. In other words, God was, and is, bigger than Hillary Clinton.

"Trust in the Lord with all your heart, and do not lean on your own understanding," says Proverbs 3:5.

In a 1998 Southern Baptist Convention resolution regarding Bill Clinton, SBC's board said, "We implore our government to live by the highest standards of morality both in their private actions and in their public duties." Now, they were arm-in-arm with Trump, ignoring his desecration of any "standards," and were angered that Russell Moore, who headed up SBC's public-policy arm, refused to back the man.[86]

"This dramatic abandonment of the whole idea of 'value voters' is one of the most stunning reversals in recent American political history," wrote the Public Religion Research Institute's Robert P. Jones.[87]

Was anyone else uncomfortable with this blurred line between politics and religion, between the United States and the Kingdom of God, between patriotism and nationalism? Yes, my research started to show, even if it was like a sprinkling of flutes amid Trump's row of tubas. Most evangelicals, I think, defaulted to the security of being protected by the playground bully.

"[Trump] was the reincarnation of John Wayne, sitting tall in the saddle, a man who wasn't afraid to resort to violence to bring order, who protected those deemed worthy of protection, who wouldn't let political correctness get in the way of saying what had to be said … ." wrote Du Mez.[88]

And, frankly, some evangelicals' loyalty to him and America, at the expense of their witness to Christ, bordered on idolatry.

"To take healthy pride in one's place of origin is one thing," wrote Randall L. Frame and Alan Tharpe in *How Right is the Right?* "But for Christians to support their nation uncritically and unconditionally amounts to idolatry. The role of the church is to stand outside the nation in an effort to evaluate it based on scriptural principals."[89]

In 2016, former *Christianity Today* editor Andy Crouch wrote that idols "work less and less well and they actually demand more and more of you until eventually, when the idol has totally taken over your life, it's not giving you anything it promised at the beginning, and it's asking you to totally abdicate your image-bearing identity."[90] In the end, idols aren't innocent—because to appease them you must exploit others, which grates against God's very nature.

In some ways, Trump had come to emulate narcissistic pastors, whom psychologist Diane Langberg, a Christian, had studied intently. "It's a burdensome charade," she wrote. "They cannot feed the sheep. They feed *off* the sheep."[91] [Italics mine.]

The reason idolatry initially works is because it is insidious; like a counterfeit bill, it can look like the real thing.

"When our political affiliation becomes religious in nature, we'll swear we're doing God's work when we're really just serving partisan interests," tweeted author Justin Giboney, an evangelical, in 2020. "Our politics and our faith usually don't align as well as we pretend they do."

But wasn't idol worship just a bunch of Old Testament stuff involving golden calves and the like? No. It was only convenient for we evangelicals to think that. In his book, *The Great Reckoning*, Stephen Mattson encourages readers to consider Matthew 6:24: "No one can serve two masters, for either he will hate the one and love the other, or he will be devoted to the one and despise the other. You cannot serve God and money." Now, he suggested, "replace the word money with 'the Republican Party,' or 'the Democratic Party,' or 'the United States of America.'"[92] Or, for that matter, "Donald Trump."

"As saints, we are cursed, not blessed by patriotism," wrote Oswald Chambers. "The idea of our nation is man's, not God's."[93]

AS I DEEPENED my research on Trump, I sensed that many *Register-Guard* readers assumed that all evangelicals were supporting him. Not the case. So, two weeks before the November 8, 2016, election—with Hillary Clinton polling four points ahead of Trump—I wrote a second *Register-Guard* editorial: "No-Trump evangelicals: Not all conservative Christians riding his bandwagon." It said, in part:

> Not all evangelicals are drinking the Trump Kool-Aid—and some [who did] are spitting it out. Though you wonder why it took so long, Wayne Grudem, an evangelical theologian whose "why-Christians-must-vote-for-Trump" essay was initially a popular email forward in evangelical circles, bailed on Trump after the "groping" revelation. Andy Crouch, the *Christianity Today* executive editor who spoke at Northwest Christian University [in Eugene] earlier this year, wrote: "Enthusiasm for a candidate like Trump gives our neighbors reasons to doubt that we believe Jesus is Lord." Marvin Olasky, a former Oregonian who's now editor in chief of the conservative Christian magazine *WORLD*, recently called Trump "unfit for power."
>
> There's a growing sense among such believers that a candidate's character matters, a voter's integrity matters, and their God can handle the election's outcome, whatever it is.
>
> "Our evangelical brothers and sisters around the world cannot understand how or why the majority of American evangelicals support Donald Trump," wrote Deborah Fikes, a former board member of the National Association for Evangelicals.
>
> Fikes echoes the spirit of lots of in-the-shadows evangelicals

who—while trying to live "do-unto-others" lives—aren't climbing aboard any political bandwagons, particularly one that shames the very God they trust.

And isn't voting one's conscience a victory in itself?

ON THE EVE of the election, with the polls showing Trump having narrowed the gap, I remained puzzled that Pro-Trump evangelicals thought "this is who we are, this is how we've always done it, this is what we must now do."

Why? Simply refusing to vote for someone seemed like a painless act of resistance; all we had to do was *not* mark a ballot for a terribly flawed man who, like the Wizard of Oz, hid behind a curtain of insecurity—and trust that, with God in control, the sky wouldn't fall. In a world where many had given their lives for godly causes, how uncomfortable was that?

The Tribe's no-other-choice thinking brought to mind a summer camping trip Sally and I had taken with my parents, my sister, and my brother-in-law to Waldo Lake in our first year of marriage. Although Sally had been on a few backpack trips with our family, she didn't understand, until this day, how deeply set Welch traditions were. The plan was to sail across the lake, backpack into a smaller lake, and camp.

But there was no way we could sail; it was raining too hard. Not that anybody from my family was going to let that deter us. Dad cranked up the motor and we moved forward with The Plan.[94]

"Tradition!" my father shouted, mimicking Teviya in *Fiddler on the Roof*.

As we motored across the lake, the drizzle became a downpour.

"Just a squall," said my father, water dripping from his nose. "It'll pass in no time."

I'm guessing it passed sometime shortly before New Year's. Meanwhile, we were all getting chilled from the late-summer rain, huddled in a mass of the-show-must-go-on determination. That's when Sally, in all her innocence, said it, something that would live in family lore for decades.

"Uh, are we really going to do this?"

Quiet.

"It just seems a little crazy. I mean, look at this rain!"

I mentally gulped. What was she thinking? This was blasphemous. This was to question decades of family traditions. This could threaten our marriage. My cognitive dissonance had risen to the occasion.

All was quiet, save for the rain tattering on the boat, our jackets, our hats—and the hum of the motor. Then my mother said, "You know, maybe she's right. It is pretty wet."

Like a maul splitting a fresh chunk of pine, the crack widened.

"We do have a nice fire back at the camp," said my sister.

And then my father did something I'd never seen him do before: He pushed on the rudder to turn the boat around.

"Helms alee!" he shouted. "We're coming about!"

And we returned from whence we came, enjoying a weekend around a campfire, a tarp flapping overhead, while we talked and read old *Reader's Digests*. Smoky, a little cold, but safe and sound.

BUT DANGER be damned, the Trump boat wasn't about to turn around. My fear that evangelicals "were really going to do this" was confirmed. On November 8, 2016, in one of the biggest upsets in presidential-election history, Trump beat Clinton to become the forty-fifth president of the United States. Clinton won the popular vote (48.2 percent to 46.1 percent) but Trump won the electoral-college (304 delegates to 227).

Oregon favored Clinton 50.1 percent to 39.1 percent. I was one of 72,594 Oregonians whose choice fell into the "other" category. To vote for Trump, I'd determined, was to defend what I, as a Christian, couldn't defend and to excuse what I couldn't excuse. I wrote-in Evan McMullen, a conservative from Utah, a Trump critic, and a candidate who at least had a mathematical chance to reach the White House. I knew he wouldn't win, but just as friends would tell me they "only voted for Trump because I can't vote for Hillary," I only voted for McMullen because I couldn't vote for Trump.

Some writers, including Patrick Kahnke (*MAGA SEDUCTION*), say Trump "co-opted the conservative Christian movement."[95] No, as evangelicals we approved of this merger and, like a kayaker reveling in the white water, either couldn't hear—or chose to ignore—the sound of the impending waterfall beyond.

On election night 2016, Mary L. Trump, the President-elect's niece, felt a deep sense of fatalism. "It felt," she wrote, "as though 62,979,636 voters had chosen to turn this country into a macro version of my malignantly dysfunctional family."[96]

My Hope for the Future

That we might replace pride with humility

AS DIFFICULT as our church split was in the late '90s, I learned an important lesson about trust and humility after we brought in a consultant and asked him to investigate *us*, the leaders-by-default.

When you dare to have a light shone on you and are honestly searching for the truth, good things happen. Writers find the same thing when it comes to being edited; it's painful—the worst part of the process—but it's a pay-me-now-or-pay-me-later proposition that makes us better.

Humility widens your perspective, softens your heart, and illuminates the needs of others. Pride limits your perspective, hardens your heart, and obscures the needs of others.

As believers, we need to replace pride with humility.

Loving others, especially enemies, is impossible when pride supplants humility. I can't feel your pain when I'm wallowing in my self-pity. I can't lift you up when I'm obsessed with having others lift me up. I can't forgive you if I'm waiting for you to first forgive me.

"God opposes the proud but gives grace to the humble," says James 4:6.

When politics becomes our lifeblood, it's easy to overlook how pride-based the pursuit is. The Democratic and

Republican parties aren't looking for Gospel-based *reconciliation*; they're looking for political-based *domination*. There's no biblical foundation for such priorities; quite the opposite.

So, first, we need to keep our perspective on politics.

Second, we need to think beyond The Tribe. Some evangelical churches seem reluctant to let individuals in their congregations think for themselves; it is easier to control people when you dictate what they should think, a pastor/friend of mine told me.

"Honestly, I hope evangelicalism dies so we can start with something fresh, something more authentic," said a forty-something friend from Texas, an attorney, and a conservative Christian who left his church in search of just that. "Evangelicalism is built on *not* thinking. All that matters is that you pray the prayer to accept Jesus and get saved. That's what we teach. There's a lack of thought in all we do. It's more comfortable for me *not* to think."

My favorite part of Dave Burchett's book, *When Bad Christians Happen to Good People*, was the opening line: "I am a hypocrite." (Welcome to the club.) My favorite part of Don Miller's book, *Blue Like Jazz*, was when he wrote about a group of Christian students at ultra-liberal Reed College in Portland who had traditionally not involved themselves in the school's funky annual festival. This particular year, however, they decided that rather than cloister away from other students they would set up a confessional booth in which they would—wait for it—confess *how Christians had failed others*. By not being more loving, by killing people during the Crusades, by televangelists who lied and cheated money out of people, by how they had misrepresented Jesus. (Been there, done that.)

"When we Christians behave badly, or fail to behave well," said C.S. Lewis, "we are making Christianity unbelievable to the outside world."

Being humble doesn't mean bowing to the winds and whims of culture; at times, we *do* need to resist movements that defy God's ways. But even then, we need to do so not with haughty indifference but genuine humility.

"Always be prepared to give an answer to everyone who asks you to give the reason for the hope that you have," says 1 Peter 3:15-16. "But do this with gentleness and respect, keeping a clear conscience, so that those who speak maliciously against your good behavior in Christ may be ashamed of their slander."

Screaming at school boards and stalking public officials whose policies on COVID-thwarting masks we might disagree with are not the kind of things Jesus would do.

The real question is: In relation to Luke 18:9-14, are we the Pharisee who says, "Thank you, my God, that I am not like other men" or the tax collector who says, "God, be merciful to me, a sinner."

Without a willingness to humble ourselves, we will only see the "us" we think we are, not the "us" we *actually* are. And why would we expect repentance from the wider world if we're unwilling to repent ourselves?

EARLIER, I MENTIONED two pastors to whom I sensed I owed apologies. I mustered the courage to meet one man and his wife for lunch and apologize; if difficult, it was soul-cleansing for us all, I believe. But I rationalized that I would need to pass on coming clean with the guy who lived in Chicago. It needed to be done in person, I told myself, and he lived far, far away. (Code for: *My pride precluded me from being brave.*)

Several years later, I was doing book research in Boston. I told the travel agent—remember them?—that I needed to be back in Eugene by a particular time.

"There's only one connection we can use to make that

happen," she said after crunching about 1.3 billion keystrokes. "But I doubt you'll want it; you'd have a five-hour layover."

"Where?"

"Chicago."

What possibly could I do with five hours in Chi—?

After I phoned him, the pastor said he'd be happy to meet me at the airport, where I finally did what I should have done long before: humbled myself, apologized, and asked for his forgiveness.

We hugged each other goodbye.

2017

7.
The New President

**I entertain the idea that I
could have misjudged Trump,
so take a deep dive into his past.**

We don't see things as they are. We see them as we are.

—Anais Nin

The question hit me after I'd seen footage of Trump's post-election meeting with Barack Obama: Had I been wrong about the man? Maybe those who'd predicted his tough-guy act was just a ruse to fire up conservatives and help him win the presidency had been right.

When Trump met Obama two days after the election, he was cordial, restrained, almost humble. Like old-time pro wrestling, maybe, I thought, he'd played the bad-guy bully, knowing fear, panic, and emotionalism would rouse the crowd and help him get elected. Now that he'd succeeded, maybe he would rein himself in, listen to those who knew more than he did, and get to work leading the country.

It was "an honor" to meet Obama, Trump said afterward. "President Obama came away from the meeting with renewed confidence in the commitment of the president-elect to engage in an effective, smooth transition," said White House Spokesman Josh Earnest.

Whatever the answer to my could-I-have-misjudged-Trump? question was, I decided I needed to learn more about him so over the next few months I read or listened to a handful of books on him. I disciplined myself to choose books that I knew would be critical of him, including David Cay Johnston's *The Making of Donald Trump,* and those that would be kind to him, including *The Making of the President 2016,* written by his close friend Roger Stone. A far-right political lobbyist, Stone ultimately would be indicted for fraud but be pardoned by Trump. To broaden my perspective, I also read books about political leadership in America, including Jon Meacham's *The Soul of America* and Doris Kearns Goodwin's *Leadership.*

The Meacham and Goodwin books made me wistful for days when leaders, even if flawed, would take the moral high ground. Conversely, the more I read about Trump himself, the more I realized he wasn't likely to become one of them. From the time he bullied other students at the military academy Trump had attended in his teens, his life had a me-first consistency to it that, barring a miracle, wasn't likely to change. That was a lesson I learned in *Too Much and Never Enough,* which was particularly insightful in that its author, Trump's niece, Mary L. Trump, not only had perspective on his childhood but had a Ph.D. in psychology. These two excerpts—the first about the lack of respect Trump's father, Fred, had for Trump's brother, Freddy—were especially telling:

> The only reason Donald escaped the same fate is that his personality served his father's purpose. That's what sociopaths do: they co-opt others and use them toward their own ends—ruthlessly and efficiently, with no tolerance for dissent or resistance. Fred [the father] destroyed

Donald, too, but not by snuffing him out as he did Freddy; instead, he short-circuited Donald's ability to develop and experience the entire spectrum of human emotion. By limiting Donald's access to his own feelings and rendering many of them unacceptable, Fred perverted his son's perception of the world and damaged his ability to live in it. [Donald's] capacity to be his own person, rather than an extension of his father's ambitions, became severely limited.[97]

Ideally, the rules at home reflect the rules of society, so when children go out into the world, they generally know how to behave. When kids go to school, they're supposed to know that they shouldn't take other children's toys and they're not supposed to hit or tease other children. Donald didn't understand any of that because the rules in the house, at least as they applied to the boys—be tough at all costs, lying is okay, admitting you're wrong or apologizing is a weakness—clashed with the rules he encountered at school. Fred's fundamental belief about how the world worked—in life, there can be only one winner and everybody else is a loser (an idea that essentially precluded the ability to share) and kindness is weakness—[was] clear.[98]

The young Trump seemed eerily like the current version. But everywhere I looked, many evangelicals were only standing taller for Trump, now that he'd won.

"What I like about him," a longtime friend I interviewed told me, "is that, unlike most politicians, he says what he means. Too many others are one way in private and another way in public."

Granted, Trump spoke his mind and, frankly, never tried to come across as someone he wasn't; I was surprised, for example, that although some evangelical higher-ups—Dobson among them—suggested that Trump was a "baby Christian," Trump never really tried to play that card. Never tried to pretend he was particularly spiritual. But what worried me about the man *wasn't that he wasn't spiritual.* What worried me was his niece's observation that the man's operating system was corrupt, which I suspected could adversely influence virtually every decision he made. What worried me was that my fellow evangelicals either didn't care about Trump's demeanor or did, but with cognitive dissonance, had found ways to rationalize it.

In retrospect, once again, I was being naïve. "In 2016, many observers were stunned at evangelicals' apparent betrayal of their own values," Du Mez wrote. "In reality, evangelicals did not cast their vote despite their beliefs, *but because of them*."99 [Italics mine.] Trump, I'd come to realize, filled a need for many Christians that I clearly didn't have, this sense of something having been taken away from us and Trump stepping in to return it to its rightful owner.

Until now, I'd based most of my opinion of Trump on what he'd said or done in a few months' time—and reported quickly by the "history-in-a-hurry" media. But now that I'd taken a deeper dive with my reading of him, I realized how deeply the iceberg plunged beneath the surface.

I was the exception, not the rule, among evangelicals. To many people—including a Christian who told me he thought Trump was "more of a salesman than a liar" and whose "hyperboles," not lies, were exaggerated by the media to hide an otherwise "substantive man"—Trump represented their safe haven. And I couldn't argue that one of the reasons he'd become president was that the Democrats hadn't done much to appease The Right—but much to anger it.

"Donald Trump [was] the culmination of a long-term destructive trend: the public's utter contempt for politics," wrote Wehner, an evangelical who worked as a Republican commentator on politics and the media. "By *contempt* I don't mean merely extreme frustration or anger over what [was] happening politically ... Americans [had] crossed over a threshold from frustration to despair, from unhappiness to rage, from deep skepticism to corrosive cynicism."100

Here, though, was the difference between evangelicals like Wehner and the 81 percent who voted for Trump: while Wehner acknowledged the "corrosive cynicism" plaguing the country, he couldn't accept the idea that Trump was the antidote to it. He did not vote for the man and, later in the year, left the Republican Party. Others clung to their man. Like Wehner, I could not. As Maya Angelou said: "When someone shows you who they are, believe them the first time."

AS 2017 UNFOLDED, Trump's victory wracked some churches with division. "I witnessed churches, my own included, that were rife with division and heartbroken over politics," wrote Denker, the *Red State*

Christian author.[101]

Ours did not appear to be among them. I can't recall a single awkward conversation, much less an argument, involving Trump. In retrospect, I think that was good—and bad. Good because we valued unity and our silence preserved it; bad because none of us seemed willing, able, or encouraged to discuss what was emerging as an elephant in the evangelical room: whether our faith was benefitting from, or being exploited by, what some were calling "Christian nationalism," a Trump-pumped blending of church and country.

A friend of mine who pastors an evangelical church in our community—not the church I attended—was stunned at how fervently people in his congregation had backed Trump.

"After he won, I realized I didn't know the people in the body very well, so I began having coffee with folks just to hear where they were coming from," said my friend, who'd reluctantly voted for Trump in 2016. "At the same time, I realized it was unfair to only listen to the pro-Trump people, so I started meeting with people who I knew didn't see the world the way I did. Frankly, it changed me. Ultimately, I came to see Jesus's words: 'Love others as I have loved you.' I see the world differently now." (He would not vote for Trump in 2020.)

Most people had no intention of listening to people with differing opinions like my friend had, including some Democrats, one of whom told the *New York Times* that Trump voters were "a bunch of bigoted unthinking lizard brains." Once again, among the few writers on The Left who dared defy his own was Kristof, who told his readers that "tolerance is a liberal value; name-calling isn't."

"My hometown, Yamhill, Oregon, a farming community, is Trump country, and I have many friends who voted for Trump. I think they're profoundly wrong, but please don't dismiss them as hateful bigots.

"In Yamhill, plenty of well-meaning people were frustrated enough that they took a gamble on a silver-tongued provocateur. It wasn't because they were 'bigoted unthinkable lizard brains' but because they didn't know where to turn, and Trump spoke to their fears."[102]

I felt the same about many of the people I knew. Though their reasons for voting for Trump ranged beyond the economic sphere of the

Yamhill farmer, doing so didn't suddenly make them hateful, bigoted people, all cut from the same conservative cloth.

"When democracy fails," wrote Earl Shorris in *The Politics of Heaven*, "it is almost always because there is broad dissatisfaction with the government, which becomes unstable, like one of the jittery atoms of immense destructive power. A leader suddenly emerges to propose a single unifying idea, there is a coup d'état, and a new kind of state, perhaps totalitarian, rises in its place."[103]

What Hitler was to Germans in the 1930s, Trump had become to many Americans in 2016—that "unifying idea," at least for the Far Right. What he wasn't, and would never be, was a particularly *good* idea—at least from my perspective. Others disagreed. "We thank God every day that He gave us a leader like President Trump," said Jeffress, the Dallas First Baptist pastor.

Hearing such comments made me feel like an evangelical exile, feel pangs of guilt for not following the company line. Why couldn't I just put on a happy face and fly the far-right flag like most of the others in The Tribe?

LIKE CLOCKWORK, Marley's letters arrived each month, though he didn't gloat. Other letter-writers were not so civil. Letters with "stop whining, you lost" messages began arriving—and who could blame conservatives? The Left had hammered The Right in Eugene for decades. And Hillary Clinton, a seasoned political veteran, had been beaten by a guy with no political experience and more skeletons in his closet than an orthopedic surgeon.

Soon, conservatives began expressing frustration that *The Register-Guard* was still running so many letters critical of Trump, which, for the past eighteen months, had been our letter writers' No. 1 topic.

"How about if we see if they're right?" I said to my boss one morning in February 2017.

"What do you have in mind?"

"I've saved our letters. I'm half-curious myself to see if we—OK, if *I*—have some sort of implicit bias. I'll break down the number of pro- and anti-Trump letters that we got—and contrast that number to the 'pro' and 'anti' letters we ran."

"Go for it. But what if you find the readers are right—that we *do* run a higher proportion of anti-Trump letters than we get? Seems like we'd still need to report that regardless of what you find."

Clearly, this was risky, but he was right. "Totally agree."

The next day, after our section was put to bed, I dug in. I chipped away at it day after day until, after a few weeks, a month's worth was tabulated.

"The readers are right," I told my boss. "We're *not* being fair."

He narrowed his eyebrows. "Really?"

"Yeah, based on letters received, we're actually running a disproportionate number of *pro-Trump* letters."

He chuckled and shook his head.

"To be fair," I said, "we should be running more anti-Trump letters—and fewer pro-Trump letters—than we're currently running."

"Looking forward to your editorial on this."

Of the 496 letters we received in February 2017, we had run 70 percent of those with pro-Trump/anti-Democrat stances compared to 32 percent of those with pro-Democrat/anti-Trump stances. In other words, readers who sent us a pro-Trump/anti-Democrat letter had more than double the chance of being published as the anti-Trump/pro-Democrat folks had.

But that's not how conservatives saw it. Even though we had evidence to back up the results, conservatives pushed back, still convinced we were being biased. People, I'd long been reminded as a columnist, see what they want to see—and *don't* see what they *don't* want to see. It's like when you were a kid, waiting for your Mom to pick you up after basketball practice. You're standing in the cold. You're hungry. You desperately want to see your family car. And so when you see the lights of a car and its vague form, you think: *Good, that's her!* But it's not. And then you see the next car; *Oh, that has to be her.* Nope. And neither are the next six cars you're "sure" must be her.

Our biases skew our vision. The result? We don't seek the truth, per se, but a facsimile we *want to believe* is the truth. We see a squirrel, but our mind bends to tell us it's Jesus.

In the late 1970s, I was sports editor of a small daily newspaper that covered half a dozen high schools. Over the years, opposing coaches began getting increasingly vocal about their sense that one school—let's call it Riverdale High in honor of my favorite childhood comic book, Archie—was being "homered" by local referees. In other words, officials who lived in the same community might have been letting their bias influence their calls in favor of the hometown boys.

I decided to do some research—lots of research. I tallied all home-visitors' fouls called for the entire season in the conference. In almost every home game, Riverdale's foul totals were *dramatically down* and their opponent's *dramatically up*. Such a disparity was not the case for the league's other teams in their home games. The evidence seemed to confirm what other conference coaches suspected; local refs—intentionally or not—were doing some "home cookin'." Not surprisingly, the Riverdale coach—who knew the story was coming and had rationalized the discrepancy to me as just a statistical anomaly—went ballistic when he saw it. Riverdale fans were equally chagrined.

At the time I didn't glean some deep life lesson from this journalistic experience. But, looking back, I do now: allegiances can blind us to the truth. Emotions can cloud facts. Because what really matters to many people, in the end, isn't what's true, right, or just—what should be the bottom line for Christians, based on Scripture. It's that the home team must win.

"Many political scientists used to assume that people vote selfishly, choosing the candidate or policy that will benefit them most," wrote Jonathan Haidt in *The Righteous Mind*. "Not the case. People care about their *groups*, whether those be racial, regional, religious, or political. Our politics isn't selfish, but groupish."[104]

Haidt theorizes that when you agree with The Tribe, you get what's, in essence, a shot of dopamine. It makes you feel good to be affirmed; you're helping the home team win. "The partisan brain," he wrote, "has been reinforced so many times for performing mental contortions that free it from unwanted beliefs. Extreme partisanship may be literally addictive."[105]

We are products of our biases and presuppositions. Democrats think

44 percent of Republicans are sixty-five or older; the actual number is 21. Republicans think 38 percent of Democrats are lesbian, gay, or bisexual; the actual number is 11 percent.[106] We don't see the world as it is; we see it how we fear it is, or wished it was.

TRUMP HADN'T been in the Oval Office for more than a week when, on January 25, 2017, a draft of his decision to end the Deferred Action for Childhood Arrivals (DACA) program was leaked to the press.

In 2012, President Obama had established DACA, an American immigration policy that allowed some young people who entered the country as minors—and had either entered or remained in the country illegally—to receive a renewable two-year period of deferred action from deportation and to be eligible for work permits. Some 800,000 "Dreamers"—children of Latinos from Mexico—had been caught between a rock and a hard place. It hadn't been their choice to come illegally to the US; they'd been brought here by their parents. And, reasoned Obama, deserved some slack.

Trump disagreed. In September 2017 he announced his orders to end the program. "Congress," he tweeted, "get ready to do your job—DACA!" Donald Trump, clearly, was coming for Hispanic teenagers.

On Facebook, Obama called the action "cruel" and "self-defeating." "Let's be clear: the action taken today isn't required legally. It's a political decision, and a moral question. Whatever concerns or complaints Americans may have about immigration in general, we shouldn't threaten the future of this group of young people who are here through no fault of their own, who pose no threat, who are not taking away anything from the rest of us."

Obama, whose Christian faith had been scoffed at by evangelicals as not being the "real deal," chose grace. He chose others. Trump, who was introduced at the RNC as "a man who believes in the name of Jesus Christ," chose greed. He chose himself. The Tribe. Power.

Rich Stearns, former head of Christian-based World Vision, cut to the chase even more pointedly. "There is only one reason that the Dreamers don't have a path to citizenship," he tweeted. "A Republican party that uses them as political pawns." The GOP needed an early "win" to show its strength on immigration. And the DACA teens became the sacrificial lambs.

The politics of fear is strong. "People don't have to do heinous and evil things for us to see them as monsters," wrote Dan White Jr. in *Love Over Fear*. "We just have to feel a tad better than they are."[107]

Never mind that, at the time, your chances of being murdered by an undocumented immigrant were about one in 10.9 million per year, Trump would have us believe that such people were outside our window, ready to pounce.[108] After two years of Trump's "Build-the-wall!" fist pumps and his banning travel to the US from seven Muslim-majority countries, all immigrants were apparently threats, even teenagers.

IN 2017, WHEN Trump took office, nearly eighty million men, women, and children worldwide had been forcibly displaced from their homes, nearly half of them children. *Eighty million*—more people than California and Texas have combined. Since the refugee resettlement program had begun in 1980, the US had found places to live for more than 3 million, averaging nearly 100,000 per year, many of whom were Christians fleeing persecution. But Trump cut that number to 15,000 per year, the lowest in US history.[109]

That was the *need*. Here was the evangelical *response*: In 2018, more than any other religious demographic, white evangelicals had negative views of immigrants. Sixty-eight percent of white evangelical Protestants—many, presumably, whose ancestors immigrated to the US from somewhere else—did not think that the US had a responsibility to accept refugees. More than half of white evangelical Protestants thought a majority nonwhite US population would be "a negative development." Finally, white evangelicals believed that *Christians in America faced more discrimination than Muslims*.[110] [Italics mine.]

When I learned the latter, I thought of a Sikh client of mine, a born-in-India firefighter and paramedic whose book I was ghostwriting. Though Sikhs aren't Muslims, they are often mistaken for them, which my client found out as a little boy after he'd arrived in America just before 9/11. After the terrorist attack, he was beaten in a bathroom by two second-grade classmates at his Sacramento, California, elementary school;

had a tetherball rope wrapped around his neck, nearly strangling him to death; and a decade later, while playing high school basketball, would often hear the same chant from opposing fans every time he touched the ball: "Nine-eleven! Nine-eleven!" This in a country where some on the Far Right remind us that racism is a myth.

As a white evangelical, I had never faced discrimination like that, nor did I know any white person who had, which is why I scratched my head at the "we've-got-it-worse-than-the-Muslims" survey.

When I pondered the question, the only hint of discrimination I realized I'd faced, weirdly, was because I worked at a newspaper. It was the early 1990s and I was teaching a sixteen-student Reporting I class at the University of Oregon School of Journalism & Communication. At the start of one term, I had a student who seemed skeptical of me and my ability to teach. By that, I mean her disposition toward me was cold; she routinely questioned grades I gave her as being unfairly low; and, in her notes to me, she was demanding in an obnoxious sort of way. One day, I invited her to stay after class.

"Have I done something to offend you?" I asked.

No comment.

"Please, if you have something to say, just say it."

"OK, I will," she said. "For five weeks I've sat through this class, noting how you have all the *rest* of the students, like, totally cowed because you're a big-shot at the local paper. You go on-and-on, spewing this story and that from your experience as part of the *liberal media!*"

Ah, there was the proverbial "buried lede." I wasn't quite sure how to respond so I simply feigned that she was right.

"So," I said, "why haven't you been similarly 'cowed?'"

Her eyebrows raised like a typewriter carriage after you hit the shift-key.

"Because," she said, "*I* am a *Christian!*"

I wanted to tell her that we had something in common—or "Let's just keep that our little secret"—but didn't think either response was appropriate for a professor. But in her eyes, I'd been pigeonholed as The Enemy.

I'm aware that such stereotyping works both ways. That said,

Scripture tells us we can, as believers, expect persecution; it comes with the territory. "... Everyone who wants to live a godly life in Christ Jesus will be persecuted (2 Timothy 3:12)." But in Matthew 5:10, Jesus seems to say: Don't sweat it; wear it as a badge. "Blessed are those who are persecuted because of righteousness, for theirs is the kingdom of heaven."

Such verses contradict what Reed and the Christian Coalition had preached for decades, even if done so in code: *We need to be victims. We need "the others" to be seen as vicious.* In a February 2017 survey by the Public Religion Research Institute nearly twice as many white evangelicals (23.6 percent) believed "white Americans face "a lot" of discrimination as believed that black Americans face "a lot" of discrimination (14.9 percent).

Trump, Limbaugh, Fox News, and their ilk had done their job well in scaring evangelicals, in convincing us that our "God-given right" to claim what is ours—freedom, power, and entitlement—was being "undermined by the socialists."

Sure, I'd seen cases where evangelicals got a bad rap, but I'd never felt what apparently so many were feeling: that the world was discriminating against us. In many countries, yes, Christians were persecuted—I'd written a book about such believers, *i am n* (yep, lower case)—but in America I'd felt privileged to be able to worship at a church without government interference, even express my faith in newspaper columns without fear of retribution from some gate-keeping editor. That's not the case for 75 percent of the world's population, where many societies impose strict religious restrictions.[111]

What were evangelicals in the US so angry about? Jesus didn't translate his anger into leverage to protect himself but to protect something good or someone he loved. Stephen, when being stoned to death, said, "Lord Jesus, receive my spirit ... do not hold this against them (Acts 7:59-60)." And some evangelicals were enraged because refugees were seeking safety in our country?

Meanwhile, I wondered, when had we gone from being "I-was-a-stranger-and-you-welcomed-me" Christians to "build-the-wall" Christians? When did we adopt this "us-first" political agenda? Before the 1990s, evangelicals were too busy resettling newly arrived refugees to worry about political power.

In the late 1950s, Bertha and Harry Holt, Christians who lived on a Creswell, Oregon, farm a half hour from where I now live in Eugene, felt deep compassion for Korean orphans following the Korean War. Eager to adopt some of those children, they learned that US laws did not allow such practices; "you'll literally need to get an Act of Congress," they were told.

So they did just that. They fought and fought and fought. Got federal laws changed. And were the catalyst for a new law allowing such adoptions. The Holts adopted eight children themselves. And started an organization—now known as Holt International—that has helped hundreds of thousands of orphans around the world find homes.

Evangelicals were at the forefront of resettling Cuban refugees in the 1960s, and Southeast Asian refugees in the 1970s and '80s after the War in Vietnam.[112] Then, coincidentally just as the Moral Majority was playing matchmaker between Christians and the GOP, the us-first/others-last rhetoric intensified. Donald Trump didn't turn evangelicals into immigration fearmongers; he hopped on a horse that had already been well-ridden.

"Evangelical Republican support for Donald Trump is based more on immigration policy than his view on abortion," wrote Eastern Illinois University professor Ryan Burge in 2018. Trump's views on immigration, in fact, took a harder line than the GOP platform in general. Wrote Burge: "It's fair to say that white evangelical Republicans follow the doctrine of Trump more than the platform of the GOP."[113]

How could that be? Why wouldn't Jesus's followers be the *most* compassionate group when it came to welcoming in people in need?

"The answer is simply that this group of voters [white evangelicals] are Republicans first, white people second, and evangelicals third," wrote David French, senior editor of *The Dispatch*, staff writer for the *National Review*, and an evangelical Christian. "It's not true to think of white evangelicals as an 'uneasy' type of Republican—one that's not sold on the GOP economic policy but votes with them because of gay marriage and abortion. The reality is this: the overwhelming majority of white evangelicals are Republicans, through and through."[114]

In other words, evidence suggested that the answer to Nouwen's "To whom do I belong—to God or to the world?" question was, at least for an increasing number of evangelicals, *the world*.[115]

In Matthew 25, Jesus offers a parable to his disciples suggesting that by ministering to the sick, the needy, and the foreigners, they would be serving Him, because "I was a stranger and you welcomed me." He was suggesting that *how we regard others is, in essence, how we regard Him.* Could He have placed a higher value on how we treated others? No.

"When Jesus healed the daughter of the Canaanite woman (Matthew 15:28), he made his position clear," Texas pastor Max Lucado tweeted in 2020. "He was more concerned about bringing everyone in than shutting certain people out."

But, without hesitation, most prominent evangelical leaders—and the majority of evangelicals in general—supported Trump's executive order to ban travelers from seven Muslim-majority countries. A rare glimmer of hope had come in February 2016 when a group of evangelical leaders—including Lucado, Tim Keller, Kathy Keller, and hundreds of signees—bought a full-page ad in the *Washington Post* to protest Trump's ban. Ann Voskamp, author of one of my favorite books, *One Thousand Gifts,* came to Washington, D.C., from Canada to protest Trump's DACA decision. And others voiced their concern. But the president and his evangelical inner circle weren't budging.

As for immigrants as threats, in 2015, in Texas, natives were more likely than illegal immigrants to commit sexual assault and more than twice as likely to commit murder than illegal immigrants.[116] In 2013, whites accounted for 71 percent of all sexual assaults documented, *above* their total percentage of 63 percent of the US population, while Latinos accounted for 9 percent, *below* their total percentage of 17 percent, according to the Bureau of Justice Statistics' (BJS) National Crime Victimization Survey.[117] And in the forty years from 1975 and 2015, nationals of the seven Muslim-rich countries banned by Trump—Iran, Iraq, Libya, Somalia, Sudan, Syria, and Yemen—hadn't killed a single person in a terrorist attack, according to the libertarian Cato Institute.[118]

Which prompted this question for me: Whose words and examples were we as evangelicals following—Christ's or the Far Right's?

8.
Lilies of the Field

I had come to believe—naively, some apparently thought—that God wouldn't abandon us, even if Hillary had won.

Have no fear of robbers or murderers. They are external dangers, petty dangers. We should fear ourselves. Prejudices are the real robbers; vices the real murderers. The great dangers are within us ... worry about what threatens our souls.

—The bishop in Victor Hugo's *Les Misérables*

I blinked and the year 2017 was nearly half over. We celebrated my mother's 90th birthday with a luncheon, complete with spontaneous tributes and a slide show of her life. The turnout—more than 100 showed up—spoke volumes about her many friends, one of whom I asked how she'd met Mom. "We were standing in line at a show," she said. "By the time we paid for our tickets she'd invited me for dinner."

In late April and early May, Sally and I visited the Czech Republic and the nearby Auschwitz death camp in Poland, both fascinating for decidedly different reasons: the former because we stayed with a schoolmaster and his family and got a ground-level view of Czech life amid our guest-teaching at a high school. The latter because I'd written a few World War II books whose themes had ties to the death camp. By late afternoon, I was numb, queasy, and haunted by a question that kept coming back to me: *How could the German government have done this and how could German citizens have been complicit in letting it happen?*

Back home, I managed 150 miles on the PCT until a fire on the Oregon-California border prevented us from finishing our last two days. And I celebrated my one-year anniversary of being back at *The Register-Guard*

On the national scene, Charlottesville exploded in the summer. In August 2017, two years after the white supremacist killing of nine African Americans at a church Bible study in Charleston, South Carolina, an avowed anti-black group held a "Unite the Right" rally in Charlottesville, Virginia. Things quickly went south. Nineteen people were injured. One person died when a self-identified white supremacist rammed his car into a crowd of counter-protesters.

Afterward, Trump "condemned hatred, bigotry, and violence on many sides." In defending those remarks, which some critics thought implied neo-Nazis and white nationalists were no worse than the counter-protesters, Trump said there were "very fine people on both sides." Supporters argued that he'd clearly denounced white nationalists; critics interpreted both remarks as sympathetic to white supremacists. "Very fine people on both sides," they argued, was like describing people sitting across from each other at a dinner party; some of these "very fine people" in Charlottesville were carrying Swastika flags, chanting anti-Jewish rhetoric, shouting "Heil, Trump!" and driving their cars into people. (If it's any indication of how Trump's comments were interpreted, avowed white supremacist David Duke thanked the President for his "honesty & courage to tell the truth.")[119]

Even those on The Right, including Florida's Rubio, tweeted about Trump's unwillingness to condemn white supremacists. Vice President Mike Pence, Sen. John McCain, R-Ariz., and Sen. Orrin Hatch, R-Utah, all decried the white supremacists. And though Trump ultimately said all the right things in a subsequent video, he did so like a man being coerced by his staff, which, we later learned, was the case. He said he thought having to walk back his statements made him look "weak." But it wasn't about him. It was about others. About justice for all.[120]

According to Bob Woodward in *Fear,* Charlottesville was where Trump's staff gave up hope on having any influence on the man. "This was no longer a presidency," said Staff Secretary Rob Porter. "This is no longer a White House. This is a man being who he is."[121]

IN NOVEMBER, my boss suggested I write an editorial in conjunction with the one-year anniversary of Trump's triumph. I did so, the article, headlined "Evangelicals' dilemma," focused on evangelicals' continual defense of Trump—at the expense, I contended, of their faith. Read the editorial:

> When evangelical Christians cast their lot with Donald Trump a year ago to the tune of 81 percent, many did so not because they were particularly enamored with the man. They did so because they saw him as a means to an end: a more conservative Supreme Court, a voice for religious liberty, an alternative to Hillary Clinton. And, frankly, because they missed the power they enjoyed during the Bush years.
>
> Still, it was an all-in leap. Like being a passenger in a car with a tipsy driver, they understood Trump could be dangerous, but he was offering a ride and he promised to get them where they wanted to go.
>
> A year later, only a small percentage have said, "Stop the car. I want out." Trump's approval rating among white evangelicals has dropped, but only to 62 percent in August from 73 percent in January. And most evangelical leaders continue to defend him and others of his ilk.
>
> Liberty University President Jerry Falwell Jr. defended Trump after the Charlottesville, Va., violence: "He does not have a racist bone in his body."
>
> Franklin Graham, who, during the campaign, was quick to reiterate his support for Trump after the latter's lewd comments about

having his way with women, voiced support last week for Roy Moore, whose Senate run in Alabama has been spiked with stories that while in his 30s, he pursued young women, one of whom was 14 at the time. (A shopping mall was concerned enough about Moore's behavior that it banned him from the premises.)

Roy Moore is only forcing more hard questions for evangelicals: How much are they willing to compromise the tenets of their faith, truth, honesty and "care for the least of these" to fly the proper political flag? The answer seems to be a lot.

After reports of Moore's pursuit of teenage girls, a poll showed 40 percent of evangelical Christians in Alabama were now *more likely* to vote for him. As if the thinking was: *He may have assaulted young women, but at least he's not a Democrat.*

Some evangelical Christians get it. "Evangelical Christians ought to be the most dogged opponents of sexual predation and violence in the universe," tweeted Russell Moore, president of the Southern Baptist Convention's Ethics and Religious Liberty Commission—and no relation to Roy Moore or, for that matter, Beth Moore. "Christian, if you cannot say definitively, no matter what, that adults creeping on teenage girls is wrong, do not tell me you stand against moral relativism."

But evangelicals who consistently give Trump and others a pass no matter how they behave beg a question: Just what do they, as believers, stand for? Love for others, which the Bible suggests should be their calling card? Or political power, even if it means standing for the very people Jesus would rebuke?

Wrote the Apostle Paul in Philippians 2:5-7: "Your attitude should be the same as that of Christ Jesus, who, being in very nature God, did not consider equality with God something to be grasped, but made himself nothing, taking the very nature of a servant."

Said Mahatma Gandhi: "I like your Christ, I do not like your Christians. Your Christians are so unlike your Christ."

If conservative Christians want their faith to remain at all relevant, it's not going to be because they're inextricably fixed to the team in power. It's going to be because they show the same concern for victims that Jesus did. Because they're as quick to defend the disenfranchised who are alive as they are the unborn. Because they're courageous enough to ask themselves a hard question:

Just who are they all in for? Trump? Moore? The GOP? Or the Jesus they ostensibly follow?

I wasn't surprised to soon hear from my old friend Marley, whose letter read, in part:

> Dear Brother in Christ, Bob Welch,
>
> Did you happen to be the person who wrote the latest editorial on "Evangelicals' dilemma"?
>
> I feel this newspaper, through its editorial columns, has been singling out evangelicals for criticism in this four-year election cycle. If it wasn't coming from you, I would say the editorial board is biased. Yet I feel it is coming from you.
>
> Satan and unbelievers in our community may rejoice to see a fellow Christian rail against his brothers and sisters in Christ publicly, setting a precedent for them to follow. My understanding is that Christians ought to go to their fellow Christians, usually via the pulpit or one on one.
>
> I don't "consistently give Trump and others a pass no matter how they behave." I deplore all that Trump does that is wrong … .
>
> Best to you,
>
> Marley

I didn't initially respond—and not because I was plotting my next editorial with Satan. But after Marley wrote a letter regarding racism—and spent much of it talking about himself as a victim of "reverse racism"—I couldn't resist. My response—my tone—clearly suggested I was tiring of the evangelical defenses for Trump:

> Marley:
>
> I appreciate the thought, time, and passion you put into your responses. And I would assume if we sat down and talked—and I'd be happy to buy you coffee sometime if you'd like to do that—we would agree on much.
>
> I totally agree—two sad options. Clinton and Trump. The reason I've continued to hold evangelicals' feet to the fire is because of this: it is one thing to vote for someone. That's done. I get it. Like nearly all conservative Christians, you weighed the options and cast your lot with what you considered to be the least of evils. What galls me,

however, is the continual excuse-making for Trump, for the GOP, for all things conservative, in the year since the election.

Doesn't matter what the issue is. The answer is always: *We're right, you're not. We're winners, you're not. It's all about us.* It's almost never about a victim. Never about the poor. Never about the disenfranchised. Never about humbling yourself. Never about the stuff that Jesus continually preached as being important. Instead, it's almost always about—how else can I put it?—winning, which Jesus never was about.

Look at the world through a black man's eyes? No, no, no. Instead, your letter is about how blacks exploited *you*. (When was the last time you missed out on a job because you were white?)

Write a letter saying you voted for Trump but are disappointed in him because you've been in locker rooms for half a century and never once heard someone talk about grabbing a woman's xxxxxxxx? No, no, no.

Question the integrity of an Alabama senatorial candidate who, evidence suggests, is just about everything Jesus says a leader should *not* be? No, no, no. Instead, the email from a Christian I got today says: "Just goes to show that beauty is in the eye of the beholder. In my opinion, Jesus would tell the so-called sexual harassment 'victims' that they should forgive and forget. Many Americans have."

Where is the courage to say: *God is bigger than America, than elections, than parties?*

Where is the faith to say: *God will not abandon us even if my candidate doesn't win?*

Where is the humility to put yourself in the shoes of those who have been discriminated against or assaulted?

Are Christians sometimes discriminated against? You bet. Liberals can do that. I just wrote a book about persecution of Christians around the world. But there's nothing scriptural that suggests our life on earth is to be spent trying to be given a fair shake. And here's the difference between the persecuted Christians around the world and American Christians: the ones around the world, sometimes after having their testicles cut off, praise God and forgive their assailants. But here in America we gnash our teeth as if Jesus gave a hoot whether someone says, "Merry Christmas" to us or "Happy Holidays."

Think bigger, Christians!!!!!! Don't major in the minors. Don't obsess about not being treated fairly.

Jesus did not do that, and nobody was discriminated against worse than he was. Instead, he devoted his life to justice for others. Today, Christians really worry about a few things: themselves. And money. Forget all that lilies of the field crap. *I want mine. Now. And I fear, more than anything, me not getting what I deserve!* Whenever a tax issue comes up, who [writes] the up-in-arms letters about "how dare you take MY money"—uh, I thought it all belonged to God—"for the community's benefit?" Christians.

And that's why so many Christians voted for Donald Trump. He is going to be our great, almighty protector.

Hate and fear are an odd, and unbiblical, combination on which to base any choice we make. But those are the two things that won Trump the election. Sorry, in a time when a few Christians are still trying to build bridges to non-believers, still trying to be salt and light, still trying to live out the gospel of Jesus Christ instead of the gospel of prosperity and Trump, et al, I'm not going to live my life in fear of some Democrat.

I've never once said conservatives should become liberals. Should vote for Hillary. Should leave the GOP. I've simply said: If you're going to be a Christian, then be a Christian—and not a conservative who flies the Jesus flag, a la Donald Trump. Decide who your household is going to serve: Christ or conservatism. Because I got news for you, Marley: they ain't interchangeable.

Thanks for letting me vent. All my best. And, as I said, coffee is on me.

Bob

Reading the email four years later, I realize I sounded like an over-amped Chevy Chase in *National Lampoon's Christmas Vacation* when he realizes his expected huge Christmas bonus was a jelly-of-the-month-club certificate. In response, he goes bonkers, ultimately cutting down a tree in his front yard to replace the one inside that had caught fire in the electrical surge that did in the cat. Clearly, I was agitated. And my editorials, though fairly argued, were more barbed than they needed to be; my "drinking the Trump Kool-Aid" line, in particular, was out-of-line hyperbole that ignored how reluctantly some had stuck with Trump.

Why was I so angry? Was it pride? Did I have to *win*? Did I have to make Marley and other evangelicals feel suitably guilty for having voted for Trump?

After introspection, I answered no to all three. I think it went far deeper than that. I think Trump unleashed four decades of repressed feelings I had had about my complicity in allowing conservatism to cloud my God-breathed mission as a Christian: to love other people, even my enemies. In church, I might have heard that message on Sunday mornings and thought: *All right, let's do this.*

But when I left those doors, I played it safe. With exceptions, I hung out with my own kind. I still allowed the subtle "liberals-are-the-enemy" thinking to cloud whatever progress I was making in the open-minded category.

In fourteen years of column writing, I had written pieces that chided Christians for not always being very Christ-like in the public square. For thinking that you can slap a Jesus-is-the-Reason-for-the-Season sign in your yard at Christmas and call it good. For being hypocritical. But beyond those columns, I don't know that I was particularly courageous in practicing what I preached. Mainly, I kept quiet. I embraced the status quo. I maintained my *comfort* level.

But when Trump won the Republican nomination the same month that I was given the privilege of writing editorials, it created a perfect storm of sorts. For the first time, I found myself forced to take a hard look at myself as a Christian; what I discovered was both frightening and freeing. Frightening because the deeper I plumbed my soul, the more I realized the Christian faith I'd been following had been diluted by a pronounced conservative political spin—and I hadn't done much to resist it. Freeing because even if I'd realized I'd be swimming against the status-quo current by admitting my opposition to Trump and the Christian Far Right, I was at least swimming—instead of just blithely going with the flow as I had been.

Because in my job as a journalist I spent so much time around nonbelievers, I think I was extra-sensitive when an evangelical leader made news for some hypocritical statement or action. It shamed the faith I followed.

In my first newspaper job, a new reporter all but introduced himself with an "Are-you-saved?" line, then refused to cover city council meetings because they were on his Bible study nights. His work ethic was terrible. He played the victim card; the paper was violating his freedom of worship, he claimed. He didn't last long and left a sad legacy—as opposed to a Christian I knew at *The R-G* who quietly lived out his faith. He was among the hardest workers in the newsroom—and left a great legacy.

At *The R-G,* I valued relationships with my colleagues and felt warmly accepted by all but a few. I fit in because I was a team player, worked hard, looked for the best in others, and tried to make the atmosphere fun, the topper being a miniature golf tournament I and a colleague cooked up to raise money for a colleague who'd nearly died from Guillain-Barre syndrome. (For a hole located in our sports department, as I recall, participants had to putt their ball beneath an outstretched jockstrap.)

"Welch, before I met you, I used to hate evangelicals," said a left-of-left colleague on my last day at *The Journal-American* in Bellevue Washington, in 1989. "Now I hate them just a little bit less." (Hey, I'll take that compliment!)

Finally, I had come to realize, some of my anger had to do with the fundamentals of faith, embodied in the "lilies of the field" phrase I had mentioned in my latest reply to Marley. Faith is what should separate us from others; we *believe*, we *trust*, we *hope* in things unseen. Not the stuff of man but the stuff of God. We are encouraged to believe that God will take care of us, regardless of what might come our way: death, illness, storms, Democrats, Republicans, Hillary—*anything*.

The truth is, I was frustrated that many of my fellow evangelicals appeared to be doing the opposite: not only seemingly *not* resting in the promises of God, but, like James Dobson, acting as if a Trump loss would mean the end of western civilization as we know it. That's not faith in God, that's fear of man.

I'd decided I'd rather take my chances with the lilies of the field. The phrase is from Luke 12:27-28, a verse I credit for helping save me from the most depressing time of my life: my first two years of college.

"Consider how the lilies of the field grow," the King James Version says. "They do not labor or spin. Yet I tell you, not even Solomon in all his splendor was dressed like one of these. If that is how God clothes the grass of the field, which is here today, and tomorrow is thrown into the fire, how much more will he clothe you—ye of little faith!"[122]

PART OF MY troubles at college in the early 1970s involved loneliness. I lived alone in a dorm. Sally was back home. And I was a fledgling Christian with no support group—not that I made much of an effort to find fellowship—in an environment that was decidedly anti-Christian.

As a sophomore, I lived alone on a dorm floor comprised almost entirely of the UO swim team. One night, I heard a lot of hooting and hollering in the dorm room next to me; I later found out why when the swim-team captain knocked on my door with the Instamatic photos. He and half a dozen other guys had been taking turns with the team's female "groupie." I shut my door.

Beyond such darkness, 1973-74 was one of the rainiest winters in Oregon's well-saturated history. I was depressed, suffering from an ulcer, uncertain of my future, and living a yo-yo life of being sky-high on weekends while home with Sally in Corvallis, forty miles away, and snake-belly low on weekdays back at school. Dark times. But each morning on my way to class, as I popped my umbrella, I'd see a Bible verse that some guy had stuck to the window of his first-floor room so passers-by could see it—the "lilies of the field" verse. And each time I saw it, the words encouraged me that: (a) there was at least one other believer on campus—strangely, that was incredibly encouraging—and (b) I wasn't alone; God was going to take care of me. I could get through this.

He did. And I did. I got a part-time job in the sports department of my dream newspaper, *The Register-Guard*, was named sports editor of the student newspaper, *The Oregon Daily Emerald*, met a fellow journalism student who remains one of my closest friends, grew in my faith, and married Sally before my senior year.

Now, as Trump began his second year in office, I had, over the decades, seen God's faithfulness work so many times in my life—jobs, money, relationships, family—that when the "but-Hillary-will-win!" panic hit, I wasn't toiling and spinning. I wasn't trying to orchestrate whatever outcome I wanted. I'm no super saint, but my faith in Christ assured me that I needn't fret about the future.

I was simply trusting that, as the poet Robert Browning reminds us in a paraphrasing of Scripture, "God's in his heaven—All's right with the world!"

My Hope for the Future

That we might find the courage to live beyond fear

SINCE THE Moral Majority began in 1979, evangelicals have been encouraged to be afraid, very afraid. When you fear The Enemy, you're more likely to pledge your loyalty to those who have promised to keep you safe: the politicians, the televangelists, the hard-right media, the advertisers, the purveyors of conspiracy theories, and, in some cases, the pastors who exploit your fear.

Think about it: We write checks to our protectors. We listen to their radio broadcasts and podcasts, which impresses their advertisers, which makes the companies more money. We vote for the candidates the leaders tell us to vote for. We click on their social-media bait. We propagate the message of fear they've implanted in us. And our fear fuels their rise to power, prestige, and larger paychecks.

The problem? The fear-fanning folks win but those whose world view is skewed by lies and distortion lose.

We need to stop being fearful Christians and be courageous Christians.

During the Trump years, a stockbroker friend in Houston told me he had clients who were incredulous that he and his wife weren't "armed."

"They're like, 'You've got to get guns!'" he said. To which

I wanted to say: Is that a Jesus thing? Is there some Scriptural precedent for followers of Christ to weaponize?

"We are," said historian Jon Meacham, "living in the most vivid manifestation of fear in our country's history."

To explain why Trump was the answer for evangelicals, Ralph Reed offered a straw-man argument to rattle the faithful: "... if the voice and role of faith were relegated to the sidelines by hostile federal courts and the enforcement power of the federal government, *what then could the faithful do?* [Italics mine.] Trump had tapped into their concerns."

What then could the faithful do? As if to ominously say: *You're doomed without Trump. God isn't enough.*

Fear gives those who fan its flames a sense of grandeur, power, and control. Heightens The Tribe's sense of purpose. And, frankly, is effective; politically, Richard Nixon blazed the trail in 1968 with a dog-whistle campaign based on white people's fear of black unrest. Others, on both sides of the aisle, have done it since. Why?

"Fear flat out works," wrote White Jr. in *Love Over Fear*.

And here's an insidious truth: deep down, many of us *like* fear. "Fear offers something in return," wrote White. "A sense of control and safety, placing our wants, our needs, our anxieties at the center of importance .... Fear gives us a strange kind of focus."

"Fear is a powerful thing," said a pastor friend of mine, not at the church I attend. "Fear-led religious people put Jesus on the cross. Both parties use it, but the Republican Party—despite its non-fearful, strong, tough persona—is especially given to fear: Fear of socialism, fear of China, fear of lockdowns, fear that 'they' will take away my religious freedom, fear they will take away my guns, fear of terrorism, fear of Antifa, fear of BLM, fear of rigged elections."

As Christians, we are to fear only one thing: God—and,

even then, the biblical word "fear" refers to reverence and awe, not outright terror.

Fearful people can become all about themselves, their tribe, and lose whatever compassion they had for others.

"There is no fear in love," says 1 John 4:18. "But perfect love drives out fear, because fear has to do with punishment. The one who fears is not made perfect in love."

Love and fear can't coexist. Fear is the opposite of God. Fear hardens hearts; love softens hearts.

When we live fearful lives, our default is to attack or avoid anyone whose perspective on life is different from our own. And yet Scripture calls us to love others, period, which means those who agree with us and those who don't. You can't love someone without engaging them, without venturing out of your Christian cocoon and hearing someone else's story.

"If you love those who love you, what reward will you get?" says Matthew 5:46. "Are not even the tax collectors doing that?"

"I am convinced," said Martin Luther King Jr., "that men hate each other because they fear each other. They fear each other because they don't know each other and they don't know each other because they don't communicate with each other, and they don't communicate with each other because they are separated from each other."

One of the first books I was given as a fledgling Christian was from my brother-in-law, a pastor: *Your God is Too Small* by J.B. Phillips. Its most compelling feature? The title. Over the years, I've thought of that title countless times when I was up against something that seemed insurmountable. But what I was seeing now was how some Christian "leaders," in the guise of making America great again, were stuffing God in a box—making Him small. Putting Him in His place.

We need the wisdom to discern what's happening, the faith to flee from people who would deceive us, and the courage to step outside the false safety of The Tribe. Faith is all about courage—the courage to stand for a principle when you know it will cost you something.

It's what President George H. Bush showed in 1995 when, knowing it would cost him support among Republicans, he resigned his lifetime National Rifle Association membership after its leader, Wayne LaPierre, said a federal assault weapons ban would give "jack-booted government thugs more power to take away our constitutional rights, break in our doors, seize our guns, destroy our property, and even injure or kill us." *Really?* It's what Washington State football Coach Nick Rolovich showed in refusing to get vaccinated in 2021, knowing it would cost him his job. I didn't agree with his decision, but that doesn't mean he wasn't courageous. He stuck to his convictions even though he knew he'd pay a huge price to do so.

"I truly think anyone who wishes to say anything of real consequence or conviction is going to have to practice some pretty radical acceptance regarding backlash," tweeted Beth Moore in 2020. "It's going to take strong stomachs to voice strong convictions."

Indeed, it's time to be bold. Time to risk. Time to get beyond the comforts of far-right conservatism, knowing we aren't alone in this struggle. "The Lord sustains me," writes the Psalmist. "I will not fear the tens of thousands drawn up against me on every side (Psalm 3:5-6)."

Bad things happen when fear runs our lives. Good things happen when Christ-based courage runs our lives. God is glorified. The Kingdom *comes*.

9.

'Fire the SOB'

After Trump's reaction to Kaepernick, I find perspective in an Olympian I interviewed who raised a black-gloved fist in Mexico City.

There is the Christianity of this land, and the Christianity of Christ. To be the friend of one, it is of necessity to be the enemy of the other.

—Frederick Douglass

Colin Kaepernick and Donald Trump had at least three things in common: money, pride, and outspokenness. Beyond that, the two could not have been more different. Kaepernick, twenty-eight, was smart (straight 4.0 GPAs through high school and college), talented (in his first season as a starter in the NFL, the quarterback led the San

Francisco 49ers to the Super Bowl), and—whether you agreed with him or not—courageous. The son of a white mother and black father, he had, beginning in 2016, started to kneel before games during the playing of the national anthem to protest racial injustice and police brutality against blacks.

Trump didn't like it. Never mind that three-quarters of NFL players were black but less than a quarter of the coaches—and none of the CEOs or presidents—were black.[123] Or, when a victim was unarmed and posed a "minimal or less" threat, the police killed blacks at a *per capita rate* nearly triple that of whites, according to a Northeastern-Harvard study.[124] Or that, whether it was Rosa Parks refusing to be ordered out of her "white-only" seat on a bus or three black college students daring to eat at a Woolworth lunch counter, justice often begins by someone protesting injustice—with non-violence. Trump had had enough. And at a GOP fundraiser in September 2017, he let it be known.

"Wouldn't you love to see one of these NFL owners, when somebody disrespects our flag, say: 'Get that son of a bitch off the field right now. Out! He's fired. He's fired!'"[125]

Some Trump backers loved it, the folks who insist police violence against African Americans could end with two words at a routine stop: "Yes, sir!" This was exactly the kind of bull-by-the-horns style that had attracted them to Trump in the first place.

Others bristled, myself included. Trump's reaction to Kaepernick's taking a knee—and the reaction of those who agreed with him—was classic "this-makes-me-uncomfortable-so-it-must-be-wrong" thinking. We see what we *want* to see (the American flag being dissed), not what we *need* to see (an inequality so profound in Kaepernick's eyes that he was willing to sacrifice his career to make his point; he was essentially banned from the league and would never play again).

A few years earlier, I might not have understood so well. But when researching a book about an Olympic high jumper, Dick Fosbury (*The Wizard of Foz*), I did an interview with US sprinter Tommie Smith that recalibrated my perspective.[126] In the 1968 summer Olympics in Mexico City, Smith and John Carlos, while on the victory stand, had raised black-gloved fists in the air in support of human rights. Avery Brundage, head of the International Olympic Committee—and, not incidentally, a guy who routinely called US's black athletes "boys" and belonged to a country club that didn't allow Jewish people—demanded Smith and Carlos be banned from the Games. Back home, they were sent death threats. Had difficulty getting jobs. Were, like Kaepernick, basically ostracized for taking a non-violent stand against racial discrimination.

"But, Bob, how else was the world going to know what was happening?" Smith told me in our phone interview in 2017. "That this was real? Look, when I was running for San Jose State, I'd win a handful of races on Saturday and people would cheer for me and pat me on the back. But when I'd try to rent an apartment the next day, I'd be told none were available. But I'd ask my white friend to call and the landlord would be like: 'Sure, come on by, we have plenty of units available.'"

When I considered that experience through his eyes, not mine, I better understood why he raised his fist. When I imagined two decades of such experiences, I better understood the courage it took for him to raise that fist.

After the Olympic incident, Brent Musburger, then writing for the *Chicago American,* called Smith and Carlos "black-skinned stormtroopers," a reference to Hitler's henchmen. *Los Angeles Times* columnist Jim Murray mocked the pair by feigning to write a column while "wearing my black gloves"—as you might expect from a white man who'd never had a problem renting an apartment. *Time* magazine played off the Olympics' "Faster, Higher, Stronger" motto with "Angrier, Nastier, Uglier."

Countered Carlos: "Where was the outrage when blacks were being billy-clubbed?"

That was *it*: as white people who haven't experienced the disadvantages people of color have, we don't see, in basketball lingo, the original foul, we only see the retaliation. To see the original foul—the actual reason for the anger—is to have to take some ownership, to feel uncomfortable. So, in our minds, we quickly reconfigure the narrative so it fits our pride and politics: *My son fought in Iraq. He's a hero. How dare Kaepernick diss our flag like that. He's being disrespectful.*

As I pondered the kneeling, I asked myself: Couldn't two things be true? I'd written a handful of books on war and interviewed hundreds of vets. I speak regularly at Memorial Day services in Eugene and Springfield. I once put on a banquet in Washington, D.C., to honor World War II nurses. I love this country and am quick to honor those who sacrifice to protect our freedom. But, I wondered, couldn't the son have been courageous for his sacrifices in Iraq to keep the US free—and to keep nonviolent protests like this one possible? At the same time, couldn't Kaepernick be courageous for calling attention to the kind of injustice too many of us ignore?

Political parties abhor "both/and" thinking; they prefer "either/or." It keeps the good guy/bad guy narrative alive, even when the truth sometimes bleeds into—and sometimes eludes—each camp. I have no illusion that black people are all good and white people are all bad. We're all created in the image of God and all have, in various ways, gone astray.

Couldn't most police officers be ethical, caring, courageous people—I've met, interviewed, and done ride-alongs with plenty—but some exhibit racist tendencies that lead to the unfair treatment, sometimes even the deaths, of people of color?

Finally, I wondered: which elicited the most anguish among white evangelicals—watching a black man be shot by police after a routine traffic stop or Kaepernick kneeling during the national anthem? If what triggered our deepest emotions about the Kaepernick case was the flag and the anthem, I reasoned, we were missing the deeper story. The people story. The God story.

We've been called, first and foremost, to love our neighbors as ourselves; to hurt when they hurt; to encourage them when they need encouragement. Doesn't that begin with listening to them—with empathy? With wondering why a guy like Kaepernick who seemingly "had it all" would, like Tommie Smith, give it all up by protesting in such a manner? Finally, as Christians, was it possible—just *possible*—that our filter for Kaepernick had more to do with the tribe we represented and the politics we supported than with the Jesus we ostensibly followed?

Nowhere in Scripture does it say the bottom line for our opinions should be our political persuasions, our choice of presidents, or our country's national symbols or songs. That's the world's way, but for fifty years I'd been taught from the pulpit that we were supposed to *transcend* the world's way—not consider ourselves better than others but think *differently*. Think godly thoughts, not worldly thoughts. And consider that we might need to look at others from a different perspective—and adjust our opinions accordingly.

"Do not conform to the pattern of this world, but be transformed by the renewing of your mind," says Romans 12:2. "Then you will be able to test and approve what God's will is—his good, pleasing and perfect will."

In 2004, a group of people from Eugene's miniscule African American community—less than 2 percent of the population—went to the city council and suggested that one of Eugene's main parkways be renamed in honor of Martin Luther King, Jr. It played out, unfortunately, like too many of these kinds of situations play out: a cluster of white citizens dug in to oppose the idea for reasons that suddenly became fall-on-their-sword significant. ("But 'Centennial' was named for Oregon's first 100 years!") In the end, the street name was, indeed, changed, but only after a long, ugly battle. What could have been a wonderful way for the city to affirm the African American community became, instead, a vicious fight that did just the opposite.

Afterward, I was so frustrated by what I'd seen that I enrolled in a ten-week multicultural class at our local community college. I learned tons. I faced, and owned, biases that I never knew I had. I began seeing the world through the eyes of people whose experiences were far different from my own. And I wrote a six-part series to enlighten readers.

BIAS IS PAINLESS if you're on the side in power, painful if you're not. In 1985, I was riding in the passenger seat of a convertible being driven by a young African American outside Mendenhall, Mississippi. A law student at the University of Pennsylvania—and a Christian—he was in Mendenhall as a volunteer helping the ministry with legal matters. I was there representing my Kirkland, Washington, church, gathering information to help our congregation better understand the Mendenhall Ministries we supported.

"So," I said, notebook in hand, "I know there's racial tension in Mendenhall. How are you treated by the white people in town?"

"Just fine," he said, "until they find out I'm a law student. Then everything changes."

"How so?"

"As long as they sense they're better than I am, they're OK. But when they find out I'm smart—I'm a law student— suddenly I'm a threat. I'm uppity. I'm too big for my britches. I don't know *my place*."

Isabel Wilkerson's book, *Caste: The Origins of our Discontent*, is the best I've read about understanding the roots of racial bias and how insidious it is. She writes:

> By adulthood, researchers have found, most Americans have been exposed to a culture with enough negative messages about African Americans and other marginalized groups that as much as 80 percent of white Americans hold unconscious bias against black Americans, bias so automatic that it kicks in before a person can process it, according to Harvard sociologist David R. Williams. The messaging is so pervasive in American society that a third of black Americans hold anti-black bias against themselves.
>
> "All racial ethnic minority groups are stereotyped more negatively than whites," Williams said. "Blacks are viewed the worst, then Latinos, who are viewed twice as negatively as Asians. There is a hierarchy of rank."[127]

Like the Pharisee who huffs of his righteousness rather than humble himself, we are quick to defend ourselves regarding racial bias. We ascribe it to Proud Boys/KKK-types as if to distance ourselves from any possibility that we might need to see more clearly. Continues Wilkerson:

> What kind of person is likely to carry this kind of unconscious bias? "This is a wonderful person," Williams said, "who has sympathy for bad things that have happened in the past. But that person is still an American and has been fed the larger stereotypes of blacks that are deeply imbedded in their subconscious. They have all these negative images of African Americans so that when they meet an African American, although self-consciously they are not prejudiced, the implicit biases nonetheless operate to shape their behavior."[128]

And, so, when Wilkerson, who is black, flies first class on an airplane she says she often experiences a rudeness that the white person next to her does not. A pattern develops, a pattern of people telling her, in essence: *We both know you don't belong here.*

"Oh," says the skeptic, "everyone's tired and cranky on planes these days. She probably misinterprets that."

And despite her being a teacher at Princeton and winner of the Pulitzer Prize, did she misinterpret the time she was trying to catch an airport shuttle and the Drug Enforcement Agency began peppering her with questions? And the time when, as a *New York Times* reporter, she was waiting in a restaurant to interview a man, who showed up, took one look at her and promptly ordered a glass of water?

IN FOURTEEN YEARS of column writing, I quickly learned that race-related topics touched a hot-spot with white readers like no other.

"I've lived here a long time and Eugene is not a racist place!" a male caller said to me after I wrote about a black man who'd been pulled over by police numerous times, he said, for no reason.

"May I ask your race?" I asked the caller.

"I'm white."

"Can I ask where you live?"

"Spyglass Hill."

"Can I ask what kind of car you drive?"

"A Mercedes."

"OK, you're a white guy driving a Mercedes in one of Eugene's most exclusive neighborhoods. I wrote about a black man driving a beater in one of Eugene's least exclusive neighborhoods. Do you understand why your experience might be different than his—and that just because *you* haven't experienced discrimination doesn't mean *he* hasn't?"

"Makes no difference."

Click.

In other words: *Even if I wasn't in the black man's car and didn't experience the traffic stops from his perspective, it's obvious the man could not have been a victim of racial profiling. My experience as a white person outweighs his as a black person. I know better what he's experiencing than he does.*

Consider a trivial example of lack of perspective, one that happens often when I'm doing radio interviews for books, sometimes as early as 4:30 a.m. because I'm on the West Coast and the station is on the East Coast: even though the hosts know I'm in Oregon, they often nevertheless assume that if it's 7:30 a.m. where they are, it must be 7:30 a.m. where I am. Nope. That, of course, isn't some egregious sin, it's just a failing to see that an inconvenience for me is not an inconvenience for them. My being white in a predominantly white world conditions me to do the same thing—to think that everybody else's experiences are like my experiences. *Comfortable.* But the experiences *are* different; we assume people of color are in the same time zone as white people—but they're not.

Kaepernick bothered Trump, and millions of others, because he refused to look the other way. And that made it uncomfortable for those who did. As Christians, we can defend ourselves with "I-don't-see-color" and "I-work-with-a-black-guy" lines forever, but those who study religion and people offer a sobering reality that we can no longer ignore.

"The models reveal that, in the United States today, the more racist attitudes a person holds, the more likely he or she is to identify as a white Christian," wrote one of the country's foremost experts on race and religion, Robert T. Jones. He's founder and CEO of the Public Religion Research Institute and the author of *White Too Long: The Legacy of White Supremacy in American Christianity*.[129]

As an evangelical, I don't want to own that. It makes me feel guilty, ashamed. And, no, I don't believe if you're an evangelical Christian, you're automatically a racist. But when I hear this kind of data I have two choices: I can humble myself and, with the empathy of Christ, open my eyes to the oppression of others. I can listen to people of color whose experiences are different from mine. Or I can arm myself with defenses to protect my pride.

I can listen to the Word—"for all have sinned and fall short of the glory of God" (Romans 3:23)—and adjust my behavior or I can cozy up to the see-no-evil pact of The Tribe.

2018

10.

'One of Us'

**I'm reminded that the
power of The Tribe can be so subtle
that we might not even notice it shaping us.**

It's hard to make your adversaries real people unless you recognize yourself in them—in which case, if you don't watch out, they cease to be adversaries.
—Flannery O'Connor

In January 2018, the news hit me like a sneaker wave on the Oregon Coast: *The Register-Guard*—dating back to 1867 and owned by the Baker family since 1927—had been sold. The buyer was Gatehouse Media, which, in the last decade, had been buying struggling newspapers left and right.

Gatehouse's approach was regimented and ruthless: Gut the staff and reduce the number of pages each day. Outsource the design and copy editing—sometimes even the printing and editorial writing. Run tons of wire copy. And, meanwhile, pretty much ignore readers, the existing staff, the community—all that makes a place unique. In short, forgo what was working to maximize profits for stockholders.

One day we were a popular local restaurant—except to the Far Right, which had dubbed us *The Red Guard*—serving fine Northwest cuisine. The next day we were a journalistic McDonald's.

My future at the paper, I realized, was in jeopardy. But I'd long told myself never to put my trust in my workplace; God was bigger than any newspaper.

IN THE FIRST two weeks of 2018, Trump tweeted that his "nuclear button" was larger and more powerful than that of North Korea leader Kim Jong-un; ordered an investigation of FBI Director James Comey, whose loyalty he questioned; had his lawyer send Henry Holt and Company a "cease and desist letter" demanding they not publish Michael Wolff's book about Trump, *Fire and Fury*; tweeted that he (Trump) was a "very stable genius"; stayed mum on a *Wall Street Journal* report that, in October 2016, Trump's lawyer, Michael Cohen, arranged a payment of $130,000 to porn-star Stormy Daniels in exchange for her silence regarding a 2006 affair that Trump denied having anyway; and, in a meeting with Senators Lindsey Graham, R-SC, and Dick Durbin, D-Ill., referred to African countries and Haiti as "shithole countries," expressing preference for immigrants from Norway. [130]

In other words, just a typical two weeks in the life of a US president.

Tweeted Voskamp, regarding Trump's immigration comment: "Whenever we demonize & dehumanize people—that is the first step toward justifying anything. And now is the time to season words with anti-racist, Gospel Truth."

When fall arrived, I signed a contract with a former University of Oregon associate athletic director, Jimmy Bartko, to write a book about his being sexually abused by a priest as a child. I also decided to leave *The Register-Guard*—this time for good. The slim hopes that Gatehouse would just "let us be" wilted like late-summer blackberries.

I liked the security—and, frankly, needed the money—of a job, but my conscience wasn't going to let me stay at a paper where profit, not people and quality local journalism, was the priority. Life was short—and God was still taking care of the lilies of the field. I left the paper for good on September 4, 2018, thankful for the 25 years I'd had at *The R-G*, sad for the way it ended.

This will sound weird, but one of the things I was going to miss most was working with the huge network of letter writers, especially Marley. We'd had our differences, but I was going to miss that guy.

AS THE YEAR 2018 wound to an end, I found myself feeling lonely in ways I'd never experienced. I began sensing a loss of connectedness to something—not to Jesus but to the Christian world that had always framed my faith. I didn't feel myself estranged so much from individuals as from the once-comforting assumption that, as a church, we all saw the world, and God, in similar ways.

Now, I'd come to realize that wasn't the case.

I'd never felt the Church thought its mission was to create cookie-cutter people. To the contrary, I'd always marveled at how people's distinctive gifts fulfilled 1 Corinthians 12:12 and its talk of us as being "one body" with "many parts." But amid this diversity I'd also always imagined us then piling on to the same bus, going the same direction, for the same purpose. "Love people where they're at," was our church motto, "and help them follow Jesus."

I was now wondering if that was compatible with "Make America Great Again," a theme that conveniently twined church and state. Our church never officially encouraged such a melding of the two themes—we'd long since taken the American flag off our stage—but it was rampant in evangelicalism at large.

My problem wasn't that I didn't think we could love our country deeply and, at the same time, love God with all our heart, mind, and soul. My problem was that God and country have different leaders, goals, and methods; they are at cross-purposes with each other.

What had begun gnawing at me—what furthered my feeling of

disconnectedness—was a sense that "loving people where they're at," like God's grace, was supposed to have an "unconditional" sense to it. And Trump, the guy for whom eight in ten evangelicals voted, shamed that notion with regularity.

He was *all about conditions*, foremost among them that people be loyal not to God, not to the Constitution, not to historical realities, and not to facts, but to *him*. As believers, could we not see the hypocrisy of welcoming in people "wherever they're at" and supporting a president who only welcomed those who, in essence, bowed to him?

Women? No. The poor? No. Immigrants? No. People of color? No. People who didn't vote for him? No. People with disabilities? No. People who he'd hired but disagreed with him? No. POWs who were captured? No. People from Haiti? No. The list was endless.

The problem wasn't that friends of mine had seemingly become different people under Trump; not at all. But across the country, evangelical leaders whose faith ostensibly rested in the "Prince of Peace" kept excusing a man who thrived on sowing division. Hypocrisy was rampant within The Tribe. And few seemed daring enough to call out the elephant in the room.

AS I TRIED to find my equilibrium, Beth Moore became an encouragement. In October 2018 *Atlantic Monthly* did a major story on her, the first time she'd allowed a reporter to her home in Houston.[131] The focus was on Christian women in the age of Trump. Moore told writer Emma Green that she had written in a third-party candidate for president in 2016, that she was "horrified by church leaders' reflexive support of Trump," and that their giving him a pass on the 2017 *Access Hollywood* comments not only opened others to similar abuse but enabled Trump to win the presidency.

In a mid-2018 blog she referred to her shabby treatment from men. "I came face to face with one of the most demoralizing realizations of my adult life: Scripture was not the reason for the colossal disregard and disrespect of women among many of these men. It was only the excuse. Sin was the reason. Ungodliness."

When we don't hold leaders accountable, bad things happen to good people. At times, we need the courage to stand up and say: *This is wrong.* But, too often, we think: *I must be loyal to The Tribe. I can't say what must be said.*

When my older son was in college, he invited a friend home one weekend to watch the Oregon-Washington football game with us. The Huskies are one of the Ducks' two major rivals—Oregon State being the other—and this kid was from Seattle, home of UW. He wore his Husky sweatshirt, which he had every right to do. We joked about it. But sitting at a long table at lunch in the Ducks' Moshofsky Center, a UO fan—probably with a few beers under his belt—started needling the kid about the sweatshirt. At first, I thought he was kidding; just a grown man having some fun. But, no, I realized, he wasn't; he was a forty-something man picking a fight with a college kid because the kid favored "the other team." I didn't do anything heroic—I've never been in a fight in my life and didn't want this to be my first—but said something like, "Hey, he's with us. He's OK. Relax."

The lesson: *You can't always defend the home team.* At times, it is simply indefensible. It acts in wrong ways. Simply put, being a Christ follower means putting others above your defense of The Tribe. It's a lesson I learned the hard way.

IN THE LATE 1990s, when I was features editor of *The Register-Guard,* one of my reporters came to me with the idea of writing about students at a local Christian college. I was surprised. This idea seemed out of the wheelhouse for this edgy young reporter. I'd hired her, in part, because she was an amazing writer—in her resume, she had me at "I spent all night at a twenty-four-hour copy shop for a story"—and, in part, because she was my polar opposite: young, female, and well-pierced, a young Cyndi Lauper ("Girls Just Wanna Have Fun") to my Fred McMurray ("Chip, can you help Uncle Charlie with the garbage?") But she was enthusiastic about the idea, and I gladly told her to go for it.

When the story was finished, I was pleasantly surprised by how insightful and fair it was. The piece ran on a Sunday features cover. Monday morning, I got a call from an administrator at the college. He was livid.

"I should have known that's the kind of *junk* we'd get from the liberal media," he said. "Your reporter made us look like a bunch of uneducated idiots. You should be ashamed of yourself."

I took a breath, then remembered my interaction at church the previous morning with a professor from the college who, with his usual bright smile, had complimented me on the story.

"It's interesting you say that," I told the man on the phone, "because Edgar Cheasten, one of your profs, goes to the same church I do and told me he thought it was great."*

The phone line seemed to have gone dead.

"Wait," he finally said, "you go to the same church as Edgar?"

"I do."

Another pause. I wasn't sure what amazed him more, that I went to Edgar's church or that I went to church, period. I suspected the latter.

"I'm sorry, Bob," he said. "I didn't realize you were 'one of us.'"

ONE OF THE things I tried to do when researching this book was listen to as many points of view as possible; I did nearly fifty interviews over a year's time. Why? I wanted to challenge my assumptions, listen to different perspectives, and dare to learn something from people unlike me. My life in journalism had taught me that every time you listen to someone, you learn something you didn't know. And that helps you understand deeper truths.

But though I've aspired to operate like this, I've also realized that doing so grates against my sense of allegiance to The Tribe. My default format is comfort—and comfort means clinging to people who are like me. To broaden my world I have to *consciously accept discomfort*. Sometimes that means interacting with someone who sees the world differently than I do. Sometimes that means rethinking a position I have. Sometimes that means rethinking *myself*, period.

More than a decade ago, I was at the public library when I heard a little girl singing while standing next to her book-browsing mother. I mentally shook my head; this was a library. A formerly quiet library. She

---

* Not his real name.

was, I noted, dressed much like her Mom—Birkenstocks, peasant dress, tights. I immediately pigeonholed her, as if scanning her with a bar-code device whose digital readout said: "Earth Muffin," "Hippy in Training," "Lefty." As I moved toward her in search of a book, the singing continued.

I wanted to say: *Freedom is a beautiful thing, Mom, but this is a library. Perhaps this would be a great time to teach your daughter a lesson about respecting others and the value of being quiet.*

Closer.

But Mom didn't seem to notice, lost in her book search, too.

Closer still.

So close, in fact, that for the first time I heard the song the little girl was singing.

> Jesus loves me, this I know
> For the Bible tells me so
> Little ones, to him belong
> They are weak but He is strong

Oh, my gosh. I hadn't realized she was one of us.

FOUR LESSONS: First, we are instinctively driven by tribe, which doesn't always work for the glory of God. Second, we sometimes expect from others more than we expect from ourselves. Third, our assessments can be limited by a lack of information that could provide us better perspective. Finally, even when we know the full story, we still might be thinking "too small."

My obvious hypocrisy was that I'd been offended when a college administrator had pigeon-holed me as not being part of The Tribe—and treated me shabbily because of it. However, I had no compunction doing the same thing with the littler girl.

But here's the deeper truth: My root sin was not arrogance or small-mindedness. Instead, it was not seeing the little girl as Jesus would have seen her: worthy of love and respect regardless of what song she was singing, what she was wearing, or to what tribe she belonged. My hidden hypocrisy was defaulting first to tribe, not to Christ. When realizing she was playing one of my tribe's theme songs, I immediately accorded her value—but not until then. In other words: she needed to prove herself worthy to me; my evaluation of her was *conditional.*

Melding Christianity with politics is dangerous—and, frankly, impossible—because they run on different operating systems; they're Macs and Windows. Politics is based on force and power, Jesus on love and grace. Politics is based on conditions; *if you'll vote for me, I'll do this for you. If you're loyal to me, I will give you a seat at the table.* Jesus's love, on the other hand, is unconditional; He died for all. Politics begins with the premise that our side needs to win something for *us*; Jesus gave his life for *others*. Politics is temporal; Christ is eternal. Politics is fear-driven; Christianity is love-driven.

Back in June 2016, Trump wasn't inviting evangelicals to the table because he cared about them. (Sen. Ben Sasse, R-Nebraska, said Trump "mocks evangelicals behind closed doors."[132] Of evangelicals, Trump said, "they're all hustlers," according to his former attorney, Michael Cohen.)[133] No, Trump was courting them because he *needed* them to win the presidency. They were a means to an end: power. *His* power.

Conversely, Jesus doesn't need anything from us; instead, he wants our hearts. He beckons us to "Come to me, all you who are weary and burdened, and I will give you rest (Matthew 11:28)."

IRONICALLY, AS the year wound to a close, I found myself only a few blocks from Donald Trump's digs in Washington, D.C. I'd helped a Vietnam combat nurse, Diane Carlson Evans, write a book, *Healing Wounds,* about how she'd spent ten years fighting for a statue at the Vietnam War Memorial to honor the 265,000 women who served during that war.[134] On Veteran's Day 2018, thousands gathered to commemorate the twenty-five-year anniversary of the memorial's dedication.

Earlier, I'd toured the Newseum, a seven-floor building on Pennsylvania Avenue that honored the contributions of journalism to the world. It moved me deeply, particularly the memorial for 1,800 journalists who died in pursuit of the news—news that helped preserve the world's freedom. I was also impressed with the gallery of Pulitzer Prize-winning photographs, among the more iconic being *Raising the Flag on Iwo Jima*; a firefighter cradling a mortally injured infant after the Oklahoma City bombing; and *Burst of Joy*—the picture of a family at California's Travis Air Force Base greeting their husband/father, who'd been a POW in Vietnam. In words, pictures, and graphics, journalists help us make sense of our world. And newspapers, in particular, help galvanize communities, giving us a "public square," as it were, to see what's happening (news), share our opinions (editorial), see who won and lost (sports), see who's alive (features), and see who no longer is (obits).

In the absence of understanding, we resort to tribe-spun stereotypes to define one another, sometimes based on info from less-than-credible sources. Which is why I always appreciated a memorable column written by my former features editor at *The R-G*, who later became managing editor. It came amid some vicious heat from the Far Right. In a piece headlined "Newspaper's employees are just like you," he bared his soul about losing his son to muscular dystrophy, and about how it pained him to hear readers call the paper "arrogant," "heartless," and "pandering." About how easy it was to stereotype entire groups of people.

> We're all just regular people here inside *The Register-Guard*, just like you. We count among our employees cancer survivors, marathon runners, single parents, foster parents, grandparents, Kidsports coaches, evangelical Christians, recovering alcoholics, mountain climbers, secular humanists, book authors, soup kitchen volunteers. We love our families and our dogs. We wrestle with bottomless uncertainty. We pay the same ungodly price for gasoline … .

In other words, we weren't just some monolithic, faceless enemy that some labeled just to justify their hate—anymore than people in a church, school, military unit, police department, or ethnic group were.

AS MY TOUR ended, I was surprised how emotional the experience had become for me; in part, I suppose, because I never really grieved for what was becoming the slow death of *The Register-Guard*. I saw chunks of the Berlin Wall, rubble from 9/11, and hundreds of headlines from history, including the 1860 "The Union is Dissolved." And I sat there, alone amid a whirl of people, feeling privileged to have had a tiny role in it.

That night, at a candlelight ceremony to honor the Vietnam Women's Memorial, I was moved once again. I knew what this decade-long effort had required: a combat nurse who'd overcome nagging PTSD, death threats from men who felt threatened by the idea of the memorial, and blatant sexism, the worst example being the male head of the Commission of Fine Arts who, in a hearing, worried that if women were given a memorial then the "Scout Dog Association" might want one, too.

Diane had persevered with the same resolve that, in Vietnam, had helped her and a single corpsman—in the dark, during a mortar attack—keep twenty-eight just-arrived wounded soldiers alive.

Whether in combat or in a decade-long fight for long-overdue recognition, she had exuded the epitome of leadership: taking responsibility for the benefit of others.

BACK HOME a few weeks later, just before Christmas 2018, our five grandchildren were coming for our traditional Welch Grandkids Christmas Overnighter & Pizza Feed. I did the math. If each of the five children—ages 12, 10, 7, 5 and 3—brought their age in dollar bills, that would equal $37. If Sally and I chipped in $63 for our common ages, we'd have an even $100 to give to the Domino's pizza-delivery person as a random act of Christmas kindness. I emailed our two sons and their wives; they were all in. Good lesson for the grandkids.

The night arrived. The children arrived, though some without the agreed-upon amounts of money. They brought *more*; they wanted to chip in some birthday money, too, I was told. As I waited for the pizza, I counted our tip: $123.

There was a knock at the door. The grandchildren came running. I invited the pizza-delivery guy in. Later, I would learn his name was Mukhtar Jaballa. He was born in the US but had grown up in Libya. He was Muslim.

"That'll be $19.66," he said, looking at the pizza receipt.

"Oh, good," I said. "I can give you a $20 bill and you'll have a nice tip."

He didn't know how to take my sarcasm. I reached for the money.

"Actually, this is our tip," I said, handing him the $123. I explained the whole dollar-per-year thing. "Merry Christmas!"

My Hope for the Future

That we might be people who welcome in, not wall off

ONE OF THE most inspiring people I was privileged to write about for *The Register-Guard* was a blue-blood Fortune 500 manager with a vacation home on Cape Cod. He gave up his have-it-all life on the East Coast to become manager of the Eugene Mission. He went from the "high life" to the homeless.

What particularly impressed me was what he did before he started: He dressed up like a homeless guy, showed up at the front door of the mission, and went through the system: eating, hanging out, sleeping. Nobody knew who he was so the treatment he got from the staff was authentic. How was the mission treating these down-and-outers? What could he learn from this experience? How could he be a better leader by seeing the process through his guests' eyes?

That kind of risk-taking—walking a mile in the shoes of someone far different from us—is what helps us empathize with the kind of people Jesus empathized with: the poor, the outcasts, the disenfranchised.

Why shouldn't Christians be foremost among those who help and defend such people? Who welcome in instead of wall off people?

At times, I realize, we are. Recently, a Hispanic neighbor showed up with her new baby—and a thank-you card to give to my wife. Another neighbor, a Christian, had suggested that she and Sally honor the new mom with food and gifts—and they had done so.

You want to change the world? Change it like this—one batch of cinnamon twists at a time. The benefit to the world of grassroots Christians simply acting Christianly will surpass anything any elected leader will ever provide us. People resist force but they can't resist love.

In one of my parking-lot interviews, a former newspaper colleague, a Democrat, told me of a manager at *The Register-Guard* who was staunchly evangelical—and pro-life. "Like others, I was suspicious of her until I started to get to know her—and I learned that she and her husband were taking in these young women—not just being 'anti-abortion,' but doing the work, even if nobody even knew."

What had impressed him was her and her husband's willingness to welcome in, rather than wall off, those in need.

"By God's design, people are not to be won over to his kingdom primarily by our clever arguments, scary religious tracts, impressive programs, or our sheer insistence that they are going to hell unless they share our theological opinion," wrote Pastor Greg Boyd, author of *The Myth of the Christian Nation*. "No, they are to be won over by the way in which we replicate Calvary to them. They are to *see* and *experience* the reality of the kingdom in us."

But when we buy into we-win-you-lose thinking, that's impossible. That's not evangelizing others with the "good news." That's bullying.

If we see only bad things in liberals and good things in conservatives, we are not seeing clearly. If we see only bad things in conservatives and good things in liberals, we are not seeing clearly. God is not a "take-sides" god. He loves Democrats, Republicans, liberals, socialists, communists, even the lamestream media.

In an ahead-of-its-time book, *Blinded by Might: Can the Religious Right Save America?* (1999), Cal Thomas and Ed Dobson probed the failure of the Moral Majority, whose life span was not much more than a decade. "We failed because we were unable to redirect a nation from the top down. Real change must come from the bottom up or, better yet, from the inside out."

Preaching a message and later doing a writers' workshop at the Oregon State Penitentiary gave me renewed respect for men who'd made huge mistakes but were no less redeemable than you or I. Because I saw them face to face, as fellow human beings. I listened to them. And they listened to me. As such, we tore down the walls of "us" and "them."

"Each time we play into the sick glee of winning an argument, we lose the space for the presence of Jesus Christ to work in our lives," wrote David E. Fitch in *The Church of Us vs. Them*.

Our lives are not to be about dominating others but caring enough about others to sacrifice for them. Former Oregon half-miler Steve Bence, a client whose book, *1972*, I helped write, tells of trying to advance in the 880-yard race of the Pac-8 Championships back in the 1970s; if he didn't finish in the top four, his season was over. But coming down homestretch he got pinned to the rails by other runners—and he wasn't in the top four.

"C'mon, Bence, *move*!" said Steve Svoboda, a runner from Oregon's arch-rival school, Oregon State.

"Can't! Boxed in!"

Svoboda, who *was* in the top four, instinctively sped up, opening a gap for his rival. But in the process, the OSU runner got cut off by another runner. He finished fifth in the heat, not advancing to the finals. Bence made it.

How could we change the world if we evangelicals embraced the welcome-in style of Svoboda, if we placed others above ourselves—even if it cost us something?

What if Christians saw others as God sees them—in His own image, and gloriously redeemable—instead of defaulting to "socialist/communist" labels as a way to dehumanize them?

What if we worried less about building walls than building bridges?

"To remove from the mind the label of 'enemy' is like removing the blinds from a window and letting the light in," wrote Patrick Woodhouse of a Dutch Jew who refused to hate her guards at the Auschwitz death camp. "If you will not hate them, then you may begin to see them."

2019

11.
Wise Men & Folly

**As the 2020 election approaches,
I double down on my doubts that
policies render character unimportant.**

O sweet spontaneous earth ... how often have religions taken these upon their scraggy knees squeezing and buffeting thee that thou mightest conceive gods.

—e.e. cummings

In February 2019, when I looked out at a group of writers at a workshop I was leading, there he was in the audience: Marley. He'd been to another workshop of mine years before, but I hardly recognized him now. It was fun seeing him in person. We chatted during breaks.

By now, the golf-loving Trump was starting the back nine, halfway through his four-year term. Gone was talk of why people voted for Trump in 2016, replaced by talk about whether they would do so again. There was every reason to think pro-Trumpers were going to order another round. When a group of no-Trump Republicans tried to change some minds in the heartlands prior to the 2020 election, for example, they reported the effort fruitless.

> When [a facilitator] played [Trump voters] videos that clearly showed Trump lying, they shrugged it off. In part, this was because they did not hold him to the same standard as other politicians. Instead … they saw him as a businessman and a celebrity, someone exempt from normal morality. "They say, 'Yes, he lies. But he's honest, he's authentic, he's real,'" [one of the facilitators] said. Even more powerful, though, is the pull of the group. "I'm a Republican, my parents are Republicans, all my friends are Republicans," [they'd say]. To vote differently wouldn't just be an intellectual decision for these voters. It would tear them away from their tribe.[135]

To go with the flow is comfortable; to question The Tribe—or dare to veer from its tenets—is not.

"When I speak out against racism, police brutality, gun violence, and discrimination against the LGBTQ community, many Christians sneer at the concept of justice and accuse me of being 'divisive' and 'too political,'" wrote a Texas evangelical, Elizabeth Baker, who didn't vote for Trump. "This was when we realized that everything we had been told was non-negotiable didn't matter when power was on the line. The [2016] election was like a floodlight on the underbelly of the evangelical church, and this is when the church started gaslighting me.[136]

"The church that warned me against moral relativism now calls me a heretic when I apply the very principles they taught me to apply to real situations, with real stakes for real people."[137]

A FEW MONTHS after the workshop, Marley sent me an article entitled "Yes, Christians Can Support Trump Without Risk to Their Witness."[138] Written by a Presbyterian, the premise was that flawed people can do good things. It was written by Chris Buskirk, an eloquent writer whose op-eds occasionally ran in the *New York Times.*

"Can an adulterer be a great surgeon?" he began. "If your child needed care and the best surgeon had cheated on his wife, maybe more than once, would you let him operate? What if you are a Christian and he is not? Does that matter? Should it?"

Over and over, Trump apologists kept pointing to the Bible to show that God uses people with moral failings to do good. I had no qualms with that; of course He does. I wouldn't be writing this book if I didn't believe that—because I, too, have moral failings. But I also seek God's forgiveness and beseech the Holy Spirit, with some regularity, to reboot me. I listen to the wisdom of mentors, friends, authors, pastors, podcasters, and others. I try to learn and grow into becoming a deeper follower of Christ. In short, I *repent.*

Yes, God used Paul, who once persecuted the church, to do great works. Same with David, who not only had sex with a woman who wasn't his wife, but had her husband killed. But these men *changed.* They once were blind, but now they *saw.*

Trump had no interest in listening to others, seeing his blind spots, and changing. That was the essence of his folly, the crux of who he was—a man who saw himself so unflawed that he was perfect "as is."

"I like to be good," he told an interviewer in 2016. "I don't like to have to ask for forgiveness. And I am good. I don't do a lot of things that are bad. I try to do nothing that is bad."[139] Given such flawed thinking, evangelicals who publicly defended Trump became enablers—acquiescing to his foolishness rather than holding him to even basic standards of decency.

For me, the fact that Trump had had affairs represented only minor stops on this bus trip to the abyss: in addition, he was a serial liar and a serial cheater. His "private failings" had become embarrassingly *public,* often because of his incessant, and juvenile, tweets.

I had come to realize that the repetitiveness of Trump's foolishness—some would call it evil, though I'd resisted going that far—had dulled at least some evangelicals to the seriousness of his wrongdoings.

"When we are overwhelmed with false, or potentially false, statements, our brains pretty quickly become so overworked that we stop trying to sift through everything," wrote Mario Konnikova in *Politico* magazine. "It's called cognitive load—our limited cognitive resources are overburdened. It doesn't matter how implausible the statements are; throw out enough of them, and people will inevitably absorb some. Eventually, without quite realizing it, our brains just give up trying to figure out what is true."[140]

And like walking with a pebble in our shoe, we forget what it was like to walk without one. Can you imagine Trump saying anything close to what Republican President Ronald Reagan once said: "In the party of Lincoln, there is no room for intolerance and, not even a small corner for anti-Semitism or bigotry of any kind. Many people are welcome in our house, but not the bigots."

While Trump could never "go there," never—without prompting from his staff—decry bigotry, he was quick to tweet that four congresswomen of color—their points of view not aligning with his—should "go back to where they came from."[141]

But by now it had become easier for many to simply eye-roll his latest comment with, "Oh, that's just Trump being Trump."

Interesting.

No pastor I know has justified intolerance or arrogance of parishioners with, "Oh, that's just a Christian being a Christian."

No parent I know would invite a babysitter back if he or she bullied, lied to, or mocked his or her children. But as the year deepened, it was clear that evangelicals had no qualms about re-upping with Trump. To even question him was, in the minds of his staunchest defenders, to be labeled a moralist gone mad.

"This is a common problem in American evangelicalism," Buskirk wrote. "Too often it forsakes true religion for a moralistic therapeutic deism. The prigs and scolds replace the Gospel with idealistic rhetoric and aggressive social and political agendas. That's why the spirituality of the church must be defended."

Wrong.

The "spirituality of the church" was the very thing some evangelicals were willing to sacrifice by allowing Trump and the Far Right a front-center pew. And the "prigs" and "scolds"—better defined as Christians who care about evangelical integrity—were the ones defending such spirituality.

IN READING Proverbs, I noticed a pattern: when the author wrote "don't be this, be *that*," Trump was invariably the *this*. In Proverbs 11 and 12 alone: "The way of a fool seems right to them, but the wise listen to advice (Proverbs 12:15)." "Fools show their annoyance at once, but the prudent overlook an insult (Proverbs 12:16)." "The Lord detests lying lips, but he delights in people who are trustworthy (Proverbs 12:22)."

Psychologist Henry Cloud contends there are three types of people in the world: wise, foolish, and evil. The way you tell who fits where is how each of us reacts when confronted with truth, feedback, and correction.

"When the truth presents itself, the wise person sees the light, takes it in, and makes adjustments," wrote Cloud, a Christian, in *Necessary Endings*. "When you give them feedback, they listen … and adjust their behavior accordingly … They own their performance, problems, and issues and take responsibility for them without excuse or blame."[142]

Fools are different. "The fool tries to adjust the truth so he does not have to adjust to it," Cloud wrote—long before Trump ran for president. "… He is never wrong; someone else is … " In a business setting, this person "constantly produces collateral damage for others, does harm to the cause, and everyone but [him] feels the effects …."[143]

And when confronted with feedback?

"They are defensive and immediately come back at you with a reason why it is not their fault … they 'shoot the messenger' ['Fake news!'] and make it somehow your fault … their emotional response has nothing to do with remorse … they have little or no awareness or concern for the pain or frustration that they are causing others or the mission … they see themselves as the victim, and they see the people who confront them as persecutors … their world is divided into the good guys and the bad guys. The good ones are the ones who agree with them and see them as good, and the bad ones are the ones who don't think that they are perfect."[144]

As America turned its eyes toward the 2020 election, most evangelicals weren't once again planning to entrust their country to, as Buskirk wrote, a man with a few "private failings" tucked safely in his past. They were planning to again entrust their country to a fool.

IN JUNE 2019, I flew to California's Bay Area to meet with Jimmy Bartko. He showed me where he'd grown up, in Pinole, north of Berkeley. He showed me the outside of the rectory in which he was abused. We met with an attorney who hoped to represent him in a class-action suit against the Archdiocese of Oakland.

Nearly a year into the project, Jimmy and I had become friends. I found him quietly courageous; I doubted I'd have the guts to tell such a difficult-to-share story—even if I knew doing so might help others avoid what I'd been through, which was Jimmy's motive. He estimated he'd been sexually assaulted by the same priest nearly three dozen times in elementary school. He was now fifty-four—and had kept his secret for more than four decades before going public with it in January 2016.

"I haven't really slept," he told me, "in more than forty years."

I believed him. From the time I first met him in Eugene in July 2018, Bartko had appeared tired, stressed, on edge. In recent years, he'd twice been hospitalized for kidney-related problems. Once he sent me a photo of two large cups of liquid that had been drained from his kidneys. He was not a healthy man—physically or emotionally, though, with therapy, was making progress.

A former University of Oregon associate athletic director who was the university's unofficial liaison to Nike co-founder and UO alum Phil Knight, Bartko had assumed the head AD job at Fresno State in January 2015. Nearly a year later, at a treatment center in Arizona, he'd first admitted to someone else—a counselor—that he'd been abused. In January 2016 he told his story to the *Fresno Bee*. Within a year, despite overwhelmingly positive performance reviews to that point, he'd been fired by the university. His wife later filed for divorce.

When I met Bartko he was a broken man, a man who felt as if a priest and a university had betrayed him, and a wife had passed up a chance to start over with a "new him." He was tired, he said, of others defining who he was; he wanted to write a book to tell his side of the story.

When I was scheduled to preach at our nondenominational church,

I thought of inviting Jimmy, then changed my mind. He'd been raised Catholic and, despite his abuse, had remained Catholic. Once, I'd asked him why he hadn't left the church.

"The church didn't abuse me," he said. "One priest abused me."

"Yeah, but the church covered for that man," I said. "And a church leader who covered for that man would someday become the Pope [Benedict XVI]. And you said yourself that not a single church leader has reached out to you to apologize."

"I've forgiven the Church," he said. "But that doesn't mean I've *forgotten*."

The night before I was to preach, something inside me said: *Invite him*. I texted him and went to bed. When I stood in front of the two hundred folks in our church the next morning, there he was, back row, sitting next to a former Oregon assistant football coach we both knew.

I spoke on how God gives second chances to those who run to Him, my talk based, in part, on Psalm 103: "The Lord is compassionate and gracious, slow to anger, abounding in love. He does not treat us as our sins deserve or repay us according to our iniquities. As far as the east is from the west, so far has he removed our transgressions from us."

"Loved it," said Jimmy afterward. "Thanks for the invite."

IN JULY 2019, Sally and I began writing a marriage-coaching guide for our church. And, in August, I spent a beautiful day on our back deck interviewing three people whose fathers—one a German soldier, one an American soldier—had fought against each other in the Battle of the Bulge, and late in life, become friends. The information was for a book I was writing for Regnery History called *Saving My Enemy*.

Late in life, Fritz Engelbert was suffering from terrible shame for having been a pawn of Hitler, and Don Malarkey feeling terrible guilt for having killed so many Germans. But, in 2004, they met over beers in a boutique hotel in Bastogne, Belgium, and essentially, forgave each other. Told each other "it wasn't your fault; you had no choice." And, as the snow fell outside, the pain ebbed in each. Not only did the two men ultimately die in peace, but Don's daughter, Marianne McNally, became the "little sister" Fritz's sons, Volker and Matthias, had never had. The two families had melded as one, hopping over "the pond" for frequent visits with each other.

The story inspired me. If two men once charged with killing each other could forgive each other, wasn't it possible that opponents in the American culture war might find some common ground?

IN AUGUST 2019, I headed back on the PCT, doing a 210-mile Lake Tahoe-to-Yosemite stretch that was among the most beautiful I'd seen on the trail. My brother-in-law and I would be up at 4:30 a.m., and on the trail for at least twelve hours, averaging just under eighteen miles per day. In the afternoons, when the legs started wobbling, the blisters started flaming, and the mind started fading, I'd sometimes resort to ear buds and audiobooks. James Comey's *A Higher Loyalty* was on the Tahoe-Yosemite listening menu.

Comey, a Republican at the time, had been appointed FBI director by President Obama but was kept on by Trump. That said, the two were wary of each other, Trump of Comey because the director didn't seem like a "team player," Comey of Trump because the President didn't seem to understand, in a democracy, the importance of keeping the FBI separate from the White House. And because Comey believed Trump had a propensity to lie.

"Much of life is ambiguous and subject to interpretation, but there are things that are objectively, verifiably either true or false," wrote Comey. "It was simply not true that the biggest crowd in history attended the inauguration, as [Trump] asserted, or even that Trump's crowd was bigger than Obama's. To say otherwise was not to offer an opinion, a view, a perspective. It was a lie."[145]

What mattered, Comey believed, wasn't the crowd size; that was irrelevant, inconsequential bragging rights. What mattered was the *truth*.

Three weeks after he became president, Trump invited Comey to a private dinner in the oval office—just the two of them. After small talk—and, again, this is only Comey's recollection—Trump started talking about the director's job. He suggested that he could "make a change at FBI" if he wanted to.[146]

Comey told Trump, "He could count on me to always tell the truth.

I didn't do sneaky things, I told him, and I don't leak. But, I said, I am not on anybody's side politically and could not be counted on in the traditional political sense, explaining that such a setup was in the president's best interest."

Comey sensed an uneasiness in the president, as if Trump didn't think that *would* be in his best interest.

A short time later, with a serious look on his face, he said, "I need loyalty. I expect loyalty."

> During the silence that followed, I didn't move, speak, or change my facial expression in any way. The president of the United States just demanded the FBI director's loyalty. This was surreal. To those inclined to defend Trump, they might consider how it would have looked if President Obama had called the FBI director to a one-on-one dinner during an investigation of senior officials in his administration, then discussed his job security, and then said he expected loyalty.[147]

Later, Trump circled back to the same topic, saying again, "I need loyalty."

"You will always get honesty from me," said Comey, who recalls Trump replying, "That's what I want, honest loyalty."

> In that moment, something else occurred to me: The 'leader of the free world,' the self-described great business tycoon, didn't understand leadership. Ethical leaders never ask for loyalty. Those leading through fear—like a Cosa Nostra boss—require personal loyalty. Ethical leaders care deeply about those they lead, and offer them honesty and decency, commitment, and their own sacrifice.[148]

On May 9, 2017, at a Diversifying Agent Recruiting event in Los Angeles, Comey was talking to FBI recruits when a giant-screen TV beyond the audience caught his attention. On the screen were two giant words: "Comey Resigns."[149]

He'd been fired—not that Trump or his staff had bothered to tell him. Afterward, in fact, Trump was enraged because he hadn't wanted the FBI to allow Comey to fly back to Washington, D.C., on the government's nickel—and Acting FBI Director Andrew McCabe had allowed him to do so.[150]

At the end of *A Higher Loyalty*, Comey referred to something that a lot of Trump supporters used to defend their support of him: policy over character. "Policies come and go," he wrote. "Supreme Court justices come and go. But the core of our nation is our commitment to a set of shared values that began with George Washington—to restraint and integrity and balance and transparency and truth. If that slides away from us, only a fool would be consoled by a tax cut or a different immigration policy."[151]

12.

'Opposite Day'

The shaming of Beth Moore makes me realize that, increasingly, some evangelicals are doing exactly what Jesus would *not*.

Christ is always being remade in the image of man, which means that his reality is always being deformed to fit human needs, or what humans perceive to be their needs.
—Christian Wiman

In October 2019, at a Truth Matters Conference for evangelical pastors in Sun Valley, California, the host pastor, John MacArthur, was part of a word-association panel when it happened. The idea was for panelists to blurt out whatever came to mind when the moderator gave them a subject.

"Beth Moore!" came the opening pitch.

A tittering of laughter swept through the evangelical audience.

"Go *home*!" said MacArthur, which, like the *ka-thump* of a cannon ball jump into a pool, triggered a geyser of laughter. "The church is caving into women preachers! There is no case that can be made biblically for a woman preacher. Period. Paragraph. End of discussion."[152]

Moore, sixty-two at the time, was the popular Bible teacher from Houston who, after the video of Trump's "grab—'em-by-the- …" comment two years earlier, had dared to stand up for women who've been sexually abused. She was scorned for it. And later revealed she did not vote for Trump.

MacArthur, eighty, had been pastor of Grace Community Church, a conservative megachurch, for fifty years. He'd written more than 150 books, started The Master's University in Santa Clarita—I was once invited to speak there and did—and was the third in a line of pastors in his family, his father having once been an icon at First Baptist in Eugene, where I lived. In other words, MacArthur was a stalwart on the national evangelical scene. And after initial misgivings, was now all-in for Trump.

A second man on the panel made it a tag-team match when he called Moore a "narcissist" because of her preaching style, an interesting perspective given that she basically does what men do: holds a Bible and speaks. Then MacArthur compared her to a "TV jewelry salesperson"—interesting, given that my wife and most women I know love Moore's down-to-earth, don't-take-yourself-too-seriously style; some jokingly call her "Beth Le Ham." For his closing act, MacArthur then criticized the #MeToo movement in general.

Ironically, his comments came just months after the *Houston Chronicle* released the findings of a massive investigation that found Southern Baptist Convention leaders had been covering up widespread sexual abuse for years; over a 20-year period, 380 churches had allowed 700 members to be sexually abused. And, ironically, the Moore bashing happened at a Truth Matters conference at Grace Community Church, a double irony that brought to mind wisdom from pastor/author Tim Keller: "Truth without grace is not really truth, and 'grace' without truth is not really grace."

"We were in the middle of the biggest sexual abuse scandal that has ever hit our denomination," Moore later told the Religion News Service, "and suddenly, the most important thing to talk about was whether or not a woman could stand at the pulpit and give a message."[153]

Tweeted Moore: "I did not surrender to a calling of man when I was 18 years old. I surrendered to a calling of God. It never occurred to me for a second to not fulfill it. I will follow Jesus—and Jesus alone—all the way home!"

When the YouTube video of the MacArthur event and word of Moore not bowing to Trump were posted, some evangelicals were livid—with Moore. "You have such terrible theology and [are] so dangerous to anyone who follows you," tweeted one woman.

Then came the "Go home!" t-shirts—you can't make this stuff up—that some evangelicals began wearing. And for those who'd called for Moore to remain barren, lest she taint the world beyond her two grown daughters, she tweeted: "To those who have gone so far as to curse my womb, I had a hysterectomy 11 years ago. Just saving you some time."

Earlier, when Moore had stood up for sex-abuse victims in the wake of Trump's "locker room" talk, a cluster of pro-Trumpers—including some big names, like Dallas First Baptist's Jeffress—demanded she recant. She would not. Though some people came to her rescue, the blizzard of written and spoken abuse was blinding. Breitbart News claimed Moore was "standing in the gap for Hillary Clinton," borrowing a turn of phrase from the Book of Ezekiel. (Moore was not a Clinton supporter.)

Some evangelical pastors defended Moore. Lucado asked, "Are we, white, male, middle-aged leaders of the church, listening? Are we heeding the message of our sisters in Christ?"[154] Other Moore supporters piled on. But, ultimately, Moore—the target of the verbal abuse—took the high road, tweeting: "Hey, y'all. Let's cool it on the slander toward JMac et al. Doesn't honor God. Let's move on."

In the wake of this, as I tried to unpack it, I realized this didn't happen directly because of Trump, but was clearly part of the bully culture he encouraged. This is what Hard-Right hate incited—not only scorn for The Enemy, but for Our Own. And this is what Trump had modeled from the beginning: those who aren't loyal to The Tribe, like Comey, must be ousted.

Think about it: A pastor who ostensibly believes in a Bible that says "If I have not love I am a clanging cymbal (1 Corinthians 13:1)" publicly ridicules a woman whose "offenses" were that she: (a) defended sexual abuse victims; (b) wouldn't support Trump for president; and (c) taught Bible lessons to millions of women. It was evangelical cannibalism at its worst.

In the last three years, these were the kind of things that had me shaking my head. They represented more than just evangelicals getting riled up over someone making an off-the-cuff remark that they later regretted and apologized for. No, they were premeditated, hateful, hurtful remarks that, were I a non-believer, would *make me want to stay that way forever*. Which is ironic, because the very term "evangelical" means "good news"—as in the *love*, the *grace*, the *truth* stuff—that's supposed to attract people to, not repel them from, the Lord.

To a large degree, people act on emotions. But the emotion stirring many evangelicals wasn't *concern for others*—remember Seamand's view that "the good news of the Gospel of grace has not penetrated the *level of our emotions?*"[155]—but *protection of ourselves*, which apparently had.

Trump's bully demeanor emboldened some evangelicals to do likewise. Of a protester who'd been ejected from one of his rallies, he said, "I'd like to punch him in the face." In a similar incident, "If you see somebody getting ready to throw a tomato, knock the crap out of them, would you? Seriously, okay. Just knock the hell—I promise you I will pay for the legal fees."[156] He treated women like play toys.

"I honestly don't know what makes me more sick," said evangelical podcast host Julie Roys (The Roys Report). "Listening to Trump brag about groping women or listening to my fellow evangelicals defend him."[157]

How else can you say it? Trump gave permission for evangelicals to be mean. Never mind that, as Christians, we had no business taking our cues from the likes of him. And never mind that Jesus didn't "do mean." Weirdly, some evangelicals had taken that permission and run with it— as if Trump had become, in the eyes of at least some, the very "pastor in chief" that his early defenders said we weren't expecting him to be.

"God, Guns, Trump" sweatshirts sold briskly. In Texas, pickups flying Trump flags tried to run a Biden bus off the road.

In response, Trump tweeted a photo of the scene with "I love Texas!"[158]

"An alarming number of evangelical males think that since Jesus threw the money changers out of the temple, they have license to turn Christianity into some sort of gnostic virility cult," tweeted Scott Coley, a philosophy professor at Mount St. Mary's University in Maryland.

Coley got part of it right—the virility cult part—but he was wrong in suggesting bully attire only came in men's sizes; Marjorie Taylor Greene of Georgia and Lauren Boebert of Colorado—Republican members of the House—would later revel in their taking guns to work at the Capitol. In Idaho, Lieutenant Governor Janice McGeachin would release a video of herself sitting in a pickup truck whose camper was draped with an American flag, a Bible in one hand, a pistol in the other.[159]

Brennan Manning's "ragamuffin gospel" was out, replaced by the gospel according to Rambo.

IN AN OLD *Seinfeld* TV episode, George Costanza realizes his life is going nowhere so decides to do everything just the opposite of what he would typically do. Opposite Day. Elementary schools picked it up. Kids wore their shoes on opposite feet and parted their hair left to right instead of right to left. They wore their shirts, pants, and hats backwards.

As I watched the MacArthur/Beth Moore video again, I realized an uncomfortable truth: *Some evangelicals are locked into a sort of infinite Opposite Day.* Instead of peace, war. Instead of love, hate. Instead of bridges, walls. Instead of grace, payback.

"Woe to those who call evil good and good evil, who put darkness for light and light for darkness, who put bitter for sweet and sweet for bitter," says Isaiah 5:20, 23. " … who acquit the guilty for a bribe, but deny justice to the innocent."

This wasn't about issues, this was about attitudes. Where, among this anti-Beth-Moore throng, was the compassion of Christ? Where was plain old civility? I wanted to say: *Count me out. Kick me out of the club.* Like Moore, I was going to cling to Jesus, but please, God, don't lump me in with this lot. I didn't mean it in the way the proud Pharisee huffs that "I am glad I am not like other men (Luke 18:11)" regarding the humble tax collector; hey, I was a sinner saved by grace. But I did shake my head, wondering if my concept of God and the concept of some evangelicals were even remotely the same.

NOT THAT I couldn't occasionally unleash my own self-righteousness. Years ago, I was helping coach a youth basketball team that was playing a Christian school in town. Even though the other team was leading us by thirty-five points, their two coaches were screaming at their players, arguing with the refs, embarrassing their school—at least from my vantage point. Part of my anger, of course, was because we were getting trounced—and my kid was on the losing team. But what bothered me more was that the two coaches were making a mockery of our common Christian faith.

Finally, when they whined after a fourth-quarter foul called on *us,* contending their players deserved two shots and not a one-and-one, I'd had it. As the game ended, I got in the face of one of the coaches.

"How can you even sleep at night?"

"What?"

"Really? Arguing a call with a thirty-five-point lead? You guys were like that the entire game. Look, I'm a Christian and—."

"Well, then take the log out of your own eye first, pal!"

Not my finest moment, I admit; not his. In fact, it reminded me of a cartoon I had on my wall at work of two therapists, nose to nose with each other, fists clenched. One says, "I could take you."

"Yeah?" says the other. "You and what other co-dependents?"

Although I could have handled it better, I wasn't apologizing for the anger that provoked me. Wasn't Jesus's anger aimed at those who were making a mockery of the faith, the money changers in the temple, the proud-as-a-peacock Pharisees, the "hypocrites," as he called them, who "pray standing in the synagogues and on the street corners to be seen by men (Matthew 6:5)?" As Christians, shouldn't we be angry when our brothers and sisters disgrace the Gospel we're called to love, share, and defend? And shouldn't we wonder about ourselves if we're *not*?

But here's what I'd begun noting: The anger of many evangelicals, unlike the anger of Jesus, wasn't aimed at the hypocrites. Instead, it was laser-beamed on The Left—or fellow evangelicals, such as Moore, who didn't blindly defend The Right. Or on the media. The focus of their anger was not spiritual, but political, in nature.

In November 2019, I was editing a manuscript written by an evangelical client and was stunned to find the depths of anger he felt toward liberals. *Yowza.* I appreciated his honesty, but I'd never felt the anger for liberals that seemed to fuel his fears. As I said earlier about evangelicals, some of the most ethical, trustworthy, honest, humble, fun, sensitive, giving, loving, upbeat, compassionate, and empathetic people I know were liberals: Colleagues at work, hikers I hiked with, swimmers I swam with, clients I collaborated with, writing students I taught, folks I met for coffee—I spent considerable time with such people and, just as with my evangelical friends, considered myself blessed to have them in my life.

Our annual Beachside Writers Workshop in Yachats, which drew fifty people from all sorts of backgrounds, had always been one of the highlights of my year; the Saturday night read-aloud session was the cherry on top. We laughed, we cried, and, occasionally, winced as we learned each other's stories.

My mother, a Democrat, was a lifelong encouragement to me. How could I forget the time, as a college freshman, when I was playing in the annual Turkey Bowl football game and saw her on the sidelines, wearing her 1942 Corvallis High rally uniform and leading cheers that hadn't been heard since the Roosevelt Administration? She saved virtually every column I ever wrote.

On the other hand, when I read Philip Yancey's 2021 memoir, *Where the Light Fell,* my heart ached for him. His mother, a Bible study leader, so desired he become a missionary that she considered him a failure because he did not. She never read one of his books, which have sold 15 million copies and been published in 40 countries.

Being a Christian isn't a tried-and-true indicator of who's generous and empathetic, and who's not. Did people on the Far Left look at the world differently than I did? Of course. But to judge people as inferior simply because their politics are different from ours is to miss their nuances as human beings.

This wasn't a *head* problem within evangelicalism, I realized, it was a *heart* problem. It was as if some hearts had hardened to the love-one-another values of God.

"Vision depends on character," wrote Chambers. "The pure in heart see God."[160] That's *it*: some evangelical hearts had been so clouded by the Far Right, whose get-tough ways are not Jesus's ways, that their vision had suffered because of it. They'd lost sight of what we're supposed to be as Christians.

Athletic teams, it's been said, mirror the demeanor of their coaches. If he or she is composed, committed, and compassionate—a person of deep character—the players tend to play like that, and treat their opponents, fans, and officials with respect. If he or she is angry, anxious, and argumentative—a person lacking character—the players tend to play like *that*, and treat others without respect.

By 2019, the behavior of some evangelicals suggested that they were playing for the wrong coach.

My Hope for the Future

That we might value character over comfort

IN 2021, A STUDY of 166 countries over a ten-year period showed a fascinating connection between government support of Christianity and the percentage of that country's population that actually embraces the faith: "As governmental support for Christianity increases, the number of Christians declines significantly ... ," wrote social researcher Nilay Saiya. "Christians attempting to curry the favor of the state become distracted from their missions as they become engrossed in the things of Caesar rather than in the things of God to maintain their privileged stations."

In short, the temptation of privilege and not the threat of persecution appears to be the greater impediment to Christians living out their faith—which is just the opposite of what some far-right leaders had been telling their American flocks: it's all about power, protection, and political gain. It's all about the government empowering the Church—the Christian Church.

"Seven of the ten countries with the fastest-growing Christian populations offer little or no official support for Christianity," wrote Saiya. "Paradoxically, Christianity does best when it has to fend for itself. In short, Christianity in Africa, as in Asia, is thriving not because it is supported by the state but because it is not supported."

As evangelicals we need to value character over comfort.

"Most of the things Jesus asked His friends to do were simple, but they weren't easy," tweeted Bob Goff, author of *Love Does* and founder of a human rights organization with the same name. "He told them to drop their plans because He had new ones for them, and it meant they had to give up being in charge. They had to let go of their need to be in control."

Harvard psychologist Robert Coles, after studying people and empathy, learned that comfortable people were apt to have a stunted sense of compassion. Ultimately, he came to believe that the most dangerous temptation of all was the temptation of "plenty." And nationalism is based on that very idea; when twined with Christianity, it promotes white evangelicals feeling good about themselves, often at the expense of others. It promotes our comfort, even if it means discomfort for refugees, people of color, or those who are neither Christian nor conservative.

The Tribe tells us that we are owed something, that someone is keeping it from us, and that we must fight to get it back. In other words, *life isn't fair—and it's their (The Enemy's) fault.* Which, frankly, clashes mightily with Scripture that basically says: yeah, life *isn't* fair—period.

"The first shall be last" clashes with "we must win."

"The humble shall be exalted" clashes with "we rule!"

"Love one another" clashes with "take care of me."

When, among evangelicals, did self-sacrifice get replaced by self-preservation?

"God is not interested in your *comfort*," our African American pastor in Kirkland, Washington, would boom from the pulpit, "he's interested in your *character*."

One of the most inspiring people I've had the privilege of writing about is Michael Fechner Sr., a Texas millionaire who sold his security-alarms business and began a ministry to the Dallas poor (*Lessons on the Way to Heaven*). He made a conscious decision to give up the so-called "good life" to live a "God life." At times, he was extremely uncomfortable; he'd be the only white person in a black church, for example. But the impact he had on the community for Christ was deep and wide.

As Christians, we need to decide our priorities: fulfilling the command to "love God with all your heart, mind, and soul, and love your neighbor as yourself" or lording our power and self-righteousness over "them."

We can't do both. We can't cling to a conservatism that's thirsty for power any more than we can cozy up to a liberalism that, at times, eschews necessary boundaries. We need God's love and God's laws, both of which transcend any political party. But we can only make the transition from the political trough to the spiritual treasures if we muster the courage to *be uncomfortable*.

The Republican party and the Democratic party each has an elephant in the room called Hypocrisy. The former's is a sense of me-first protectiveness that belies an others-first Christian faith that fuels the party. The latter's is a pro-abortion policy that clashes with Democrats' "everything's-connected-to-everything-else-and-needs-protection" broad-mindedness that informs the party's climate-change positions and snail-darter defenses. In both cases, comfort rules: it's easier to not go the extra mile for the needy and more convenient to abort a baby than to raise that baby or put it up for adoption.

"I am a safety-first creature," wrote C.S. Lewis. "Of all arguments against love, none makes so strong an appeal to my nature as 'Careful, this might lead to suffering.'"

Earlier in the book, I mentioned how evangelicals I visited at Christian TV and radio stations in the South and Midwest seemed to be going through the motions. A glaring exception was The Voice of the Martyrs nonprofit in Bartlesville, Oklahoma. The irony? These people's lives were spent in support of Christians being persecuted around the world for refusing to denounce their faith. Tortured. Maimed. Dismembered. Raped. Killed.

My job was to craft forty-eight stories from these martyrs' firsthand experiences—as described in magazine articles—into a book. I could hardly get through the project because I found reading of the torture so emotionally wracking. But the people at Voices were incredible: upbeat, inspiring, imaginative, and fun—and the providers of the best barbecue brisket I've ever eaten.

I was dumbfounded: "How can you guys be so upbeat given the tragic nature of your work?" I asked my point person, the director.

"Easy," she said. "We have a purpose. Our goal is to support those on the front lines, those whose faith is so strong that they withstand torture and terror and worse. Luke 21:12-15 tells us we can expect persecution. We're honored to serve these people. So, 'tragic' might not be the best word. 'Triumphant' would work better."

That's character over comfort. That's the gritty stuff of Christ we need to replace the "gimme" stuff of culture.

If, as Christians, we retreat to the cocoon of comfort instead of daring to engage with those who don't share our faith, we're not living for Christ, we're guarding ourselves from an enemy of our own—not God's—making.

13.

Flags & Crosses

**While exploring the depths of
Christian nationalism,
I experience an "aha moment."**

Christians become convinced that they are pursuing the purposes of God by pursuing the purposes of the empire.

—Lee Camp

The memory of the moment shames me but vulnerability leads to lessons and growth, so I'll gladly share my small-mindedness. When I first went to Haiti on a medical mission in the late 1980s, our team was attending a worship service when I was overcome by the passion with which the Haitians sang hymns in their native Creole.

And I thought: *Huh, they love God as much as we do.*

My default format was tinged with a subtle sense that Americans were the gold standard for the worship of God, the fixed spiritual planet around which all others must orbit. A week later, I was shamed by my myopia after learning that some of these people walked up to ten miles just for a chance to worship. Despite the resistance of geography, poverty, governmental neglect, and voodoo worship, they seemed to have a joy for Jesus that left me thinking: *As Americans, do we love God as much as they do?*

Through no effort of my own, I'd been born into a land of plenty. And yet, as I described in the Prologue, there had been times when I was angry at God for seemingly being silent when I flailed in choppy financial seas. I had forgotten the lessons of Haiti: that God transcends the richest and poorest countries, and was to be found, instead, in the hearts of the faithful, regardless of where they lived and how much money they had.

GOD AND COUNTRY comprise a difficult dance. As 2019 deepened, evangelicals and America had bled into one another like the reds, blues, and yellows of a child's water-color tray. In a few cases, it was difficult deciding where the cross ended and the flag began.

The result was what sociologists and historians were starting to refer to as "Christian nationalism." Not as if those who "qualified" were referring to themselves in such terms—if they'd even heard the phrase. All they knew was that they loved God and they loved their country. What was wrong with that?

Nothing, per se. The love of country only becomes problematic for believers when it starts wagging the tail of faith, when it demands privilege for "us" at the expense of "them," and when it blinds us to our historical failings as a country. Failings that, when ignored, reinforce a status quo that supports the "qualifiers" and silences the others.

David French, a vet who served in Afghanistan, is an evangelical and as good a critical conservative thinker as America has. Decidedly pro-life and pro-religious liberty, he had, at one point, sued more American universities than any other living lawyer to protect free speech and religious freedom on campus.

"What is Christian nationalism?" asked French. "It's a deep emotional attachment to a particular and exclusive culture, a skewed version of history, and a false sense of 'marked superiority' that must and will fade away."[161]

"I love this country," he says, "but I love it with my eyes wide open … The same nation that stormed Normandy's beaches to destroy a fascist empire simultaneously sustained a segregationist regime within its own borders. Our virtues do not negate our vices, and vices do not negate our virtues."[162]

An increasing number of evangelicals love America less broad-mindedly—and with an alarming sense that Christians deserve premier status while others should fly coach, if at all. Never mind that the First Amendment to the Constitution says "Congress shall make no law respecting an establishment of religion, or prohibiting the free exercise thereof," Trump's former national security adviser, Michael Flynn, has said, "If we are going to have one nation under God, which we must, we have to have one religion. One nation under God, and one religion under God."[163]

A 2017 Baylor University study showed that more than two-thirds of white evangelicals believe that the US Constitution and Declaration of Independence were "divinely inspired." And a 2020 ReligionData study showed that 53 percent of evangelicals believe being Christian is "very important" to being "truly American."[164]

The Muslim circuit court judge who I met while the two of us attended a Citizens Police Academy program—and whom I later asked out for a cheeseburger—might question that. And who could blame him? From all I'd heard, he was one of our community's finest judges—and the fact that he took a dozen nights out of his own time to attend the CPA showed his commitment to his community. Are we to believe that his faith—because it's not *our* faith?—would preclude him from being a good American? Would we be better off with a white, American-born president who, say, demeaned women, Gold Star mothers, war heroes, opponents' physical features, and the like?

Well, yes, Christian nationalism would argue, we would be better off. Because the prerequisites for belonging are not about what you do or say or how committed you are to the American ideal but whether you belong to The Tribe. It's not about character, it's about credentials.

Wrote Samuel L. Perry and Andrew L. Whitehead in their 2020 book, *Taking America Back for God*: "Christian nationalism is implicitly and sometimes explicitly committed to a specific social order in which the old hierarchies—native-born over foreigners, men over women, Christians over Jews and Muslims, whites over non-whites—are re-asserted and strengthened. Put simply, it is a view that you cannot be a *real* American if you are a Muslim or a Jew, an immigrant, a non-white Christian or even a political liberal."[165][166]

Taking data from the Baylor study, Perry and Whitehead began connecting the dots regarding those who were "accommodators" (supporters) of Christian nationalism (about 32 percent of Americans) and "ambassadors" (*strong* supporters, about 20 percent of Americans,) and what they believed about America. The results were fascinating and frightening:

First, "those Americans who adhere most strongly to Christian nationalist ideals have *political* interests primarily in mind. Religious interests rank second, if they rank at all."[167]

"Despite evangelicals' frequent claims that the Bible is the source of their social and political commitments, evangelicalism must be seen as a cultural and political movement rather than as a community defined chiefly by theology," wrote Du Mez in *Jesus and John Wayne*.[168]

Second, in determining why people voted for Trump in 2016, Christian nationalism was a more significant factor than affiliation with evangelicalism, believing in a literal Bible, or frequency of "religious practice." "In other words," wrote Whitehead and Perry, "Christian nationalism *explained almost all of the 'religious vote' for Trump*."[169] Not abortion. Not a conservative Supreme Court. Instead, an identity that preserves a particular status quo that involves the cross and the flag.

Christian nationalism is about "group think," not individual consciences. When we identify as a member of one group, it influences how we think about the world. "You like members of that group more than others," wrote Christopher Federico, a political psychologist at the University of Minnesota's Center for the Study of Political Psychology. "You want things to reflect favorably upon your group. You're biased toward believing things that will reflect positively on your group."[170]

Nationwide, roughly half of evangelicals embrace Christian nationalism to some degree, according to Whitehead and Perry, who identify ten ways of "spotting Christian nationalism in the wild," among them a professing believer who:

(a) Sees non-Christians as enemies to be defeated rather than served;

(b) Refers, when talking about Christianity, to a culture (values, morals, worldviews, behaviors) instead of a person (Jesus);

(c) Harbors contempt for laying down one's rights and, instead, displays a zeal to "win";

(d) Defines America's "faithfulness" in terms of religious and sexual purity instead of justice and fairness;

(e) Believes, despite no biblical evidence, that America is central to God's plan.

"Put simply, Christian nationalism does not encourage high moral standards or value self-sacrifice, peace, mercy, love, justice, and so on," wrote Perry and Whitehead. "Nor does it necessarily encourage conforming one's political opinions to those Jesus might have . . . .

"As it turns out, being an evangelical does not lead one to enthusiastically support border walls with Mexico; *favoring Christian nationalism does*. Being an evangelical does not seem to sour Americans' attitudes toward stronger gun control legislation; *endorsing Christian national does*." And, above all: "Being an evangelical was not an important predictor of which Americans voted for Donald Trump in 2016; *supporting Christian nationalism was*."[171] [Italics mine.]

FOR ME, this was an epiphany in solving the evangelical/Hard Right contradiction: if Whitehead and Perry's data analysis was correct, here's what I had missed: the "God-and-country" subset of evangelicalism. I'd known evangelicals weren't monolithic, but the demographic differences—race, age, location, etc.—ignored what might be the one thing that differentiates us more than all the rest, this emotional merging of flag and cross.

In a weird way, this news not only bothered me, but comforted me.

Whitehead and Perry's intensive dot-connecting went a long way in answering a question I proposed in my Prologue: "How could people who in so many ways saw the world as I did, assess Trump so differently?"

"Two people could both be from the same region of the country, worship in the same denomination, identify with the same political party, but still significantly diverge in their likelihood of voting for Trump depending on their orientation toward Christian nationalism," wrote the two authors.[172]

What may have separated me from at some of my evangelical friends, I now surmised, wasn't our faith but our willingness—or, in my case, *unwillingness*—to allow, or encourage, nationalism to bleed into that faith. My friends were loving, caring people; where we diverged, I believe, was in terms of how we regarded our stature as Christians in America. Many of my friends, even if they'd never heard the term, would, I suspect, qualify as at least "accommodators," casual endorsers of Christian nationalism. But I didn't begin to pass the five-way test that I alluded to earlier. I simply haven't felt the same fear so many evangelicals seem to have.

Yes, I'd seen some anything-goes sex-ed material being taught to sixth-graders, material that I found wildly inappropriate. But I'd also watched the country elect a president who'd paid off porn stars, talked about grabbing women by their genitalia, and creepily suggested that if "Ivanka weren't my daughter I'd be dating her."

To me, the danger to our country emanated not from the Left or the Right but from agenda-driven people in both parties without respect for others. Meanwhile, I'd never seen any scriptural call for making one's country *the* priority; to me, Christian nationalism smacked of The Tribe's values getting misconstrued for Christ's values—and fear, not faith, leading the way.

To return to my motorcycle-sidecar metaphor from the Prologue, I had, before Trump, assumed that wherever the motorcycle of faith ventured, the sidecar of hard-right politics had to come along. But Whitehead and Perry were suggesting something quite different: that, now, the Christian Far Right *is* the motorcycle; it's our faith, as evangelicals, that's only along for the ride.

Bingo! It's as if the scales had fallen off my eyes regarding why I might look at things so differently than other evangelicals.

I consider myself patriotic. I recently helped Tony Brooks, a young Army Ranger, write a book, *Leave No Man Behind,* about his experience in Afghanistan. In 2005, he was part of a unit that had to recover the bodies of sixteen men who'd died when their helicopter was shot down while on a rescue mission. As Tony talked of his concern that these men get back to their families, I was deeply touched. On an obscure, faraway mountain, every one of those soldiers gave his life for me and for other Americans—for our freedom.

That said, love for one's country and love for one's God are two different things. But the more I researched, the more I realized that I'd been naive in thinking all evangelicals are of the same mind. That our faith necessarily informs our life decisions; that it always comes first.

"I don't look to the teachings of Jesus for what my political beliefs should be,"[173] then-Liberty College President Jerry Falwell Jr., told the *New York Times* in 2018.

When I discovered this quote, I had to re-read his comment twice to make sure I had it right. It brought to mind Mark 7:9: "And [Jesus] continued, 'You have a fine way of setting aside the commands of God in order to observe your own traditions."

You're the president of one of America's largest evangelical colleges and you check your Bible at the door when it comes to politics? If, as Scripture reminds us, "thy word is a lamp unto my feet" (Psalm 119:105, KJV), isn't the purpose of that light to guide us wherever we go—politics, culture, marriage, libraries in which we might get judgmental regarding a little girls who is singing? So why, then, would we not look *first* to the teachings of Jesus for our political beliefs? Isn't that what the Holy Spirit is supposed to do through us: guide us to wise decisions, regardless of the context of those decisions?

Granted, the Bible isn't going to tell us how to vote on a particular tax measure or whether Candidate A or Candidate B would be better. But Scripture does tell us what God's priorities are for us (love for Him and others, per Matthew 22:37-40); what the "fruit of the Spirit" we are to uphold in ourselves and others ("love, joy, peace, forbearance, kindness, goodness, faithfulness, gentleness and self-control," per Galatians 5:22-23); and what our dispositions should be. ("Your attitude should be the same as that of Christ Jesus: Who being in very nature God, did not consider equality with God something to be grasped, but made himself nothing, taking the very nature of a servant ... ," per Philippians 2:5-6).

Try as I might, I couldn't reconcile how such wisdom translated to support for a Christian nationalism that makes sure that we, as believers, are the priorities. Please don't misread me. True patriotism is good, particularly when it inspires us not to just wave a flag but make sacrifices to help our country and communities. But there's nothing in Scripture to suggest God values Americans any more than He values, say, Haitians or Mexicans or Germans. And anything beyond a mere cherry-picking of the Constitution would suggest that our country was never intended to be some sort of members-only club.

Should we, as believers, want the US to espouse Christian values? Yes, in the sense that that means patriotism as working for justice, caring for the poor, sacrificing for others, and being Good Samaritans to our neighbors all over the world—the true stuff of Scripture. No, in the sense that our president's "Make America Great Again" campaign carries with it an exclusivity weighted toward a John Wayne America that favors "the chosen" rather than, as our Pledge of Allegiance says, "liberty and justice for all."

AFTER A YOUNG woman wounded in a 2013 workplace shooting in Virginia wrote *When Thoughts and Prayers Aren't Enough,* she was stunned at the reaction.

"I expected the backlash and the criticism," Taylor Schumman wrote about reaction to her 2021 book advocating that Christians work against gun violence. "What I did not expect were the attacks on my faith and my character from people who claim to follow Jesus ... I was somehow labeled unpatriotic and un-American for wanting to reduce gun violence. I was told that I hate my country, that I should be more grateful to be an American, that I was attacking a God-given right."[174]

I didn't get it. It made no sense to me, this indisputable pattern over the years: Politically, as Christians, we *don't stand* for much of the stuff

Jesus stood for and we *do stand* for much of the stuff He didn't.

Asked Stephen Mattson in *The Great Reckoning:* "Did Jesus spend any time and energy trying to improve, let alone dominate, the reigning government of his day? Did he worry at all about ensuring that his rights and the religious rights of followers were protected? Does any author in the New Testament remotely hint that engaging in this sort of activity has anything to do with the kingdom of God?"[175]

Christian nationalism, wrote Whitehead and Perry, "often influences Americans' opinions and behaviors in the exact opposite direction than traditional religious commitment does."[176] The two found that *the more people attend church, pray, or read the Scripture,* the more likely they are to express values that consider the common good. OK, that makes sense. But *the more they adhere to Christian nationalist views,* the less likely they are to, say, acknowledge discrimination in policing or welcome refugees.

Biblical values and Christian-nationalism values are simply not cut from the same cloth. They are only alike in the minds of those who have found ways to pound square political pegs into round scriptural holes—and rationalize, or don't recognize, the impossible fit. Simply put, hard-right politics and Jesus's ways are often at cross-purposes with each other.

And when you try fit them together, as we did on our cover illustration with the flag being part of the cross, you can see what happens: the image of the cross is obscured, not enhanced. The addition of the flag distorts the image of the cross, which was meant to stand on its own as a symbol of Christ's sacrificial death for us. And the flag looks out of place; it was meant to stand on its own as a fifty-state, thirteen-original-colonies symbol representing not just Christians but people of all religious faiths—and no faith at all—who are Americans.

THE QUESTIONS that Christian nationalism prompted for me were these: At our core, what drives us? What do we default to in forming an opinion? As Christians, I suppose most of us want to say "Christ"; that's our auto-response, our "I-know-the-answer's-Jesus" response, right? But what does the evidence say? What do those outside the church say—the ones who we're supposed to be engaging, sharing the gospel with, the ones to whom we're supposed to be offering salt and light?

What do the oppressed say about us? What do the surveys say about us—the objective analyses that are based on what we tell the pollsters about what we value and don't?

This: That we too often default to a Christian nationalism that's rooted not necessarily in the love of Christ but in the fear of us losing power and privilege. That's rooted deeply in affirmation of, above all, The Tribe, with preference afforded those who are white, conservative Christian, and male at the top of that list.

Let me show you what I mean: A thirty-something woman whose book I'm helping write learned that she was conceived through artificial insemination in 1987. Through DNA testing, she later discovered that her father was her mother's gynecologist, who, without her mother's knowledge or permission, had contributed his sperm to the effort. Three decades later, he was still practicing in the same small East Texas town, a pillar in his evangelical church.

In 2019, when my client went public with the story on ABC's "20/20," saying what the doctor had done to her mother was morally wrong, people in the doctor's church not only overwhelmingly defended the gynecologist but lambasted the young woman for speaking up. "He gave you *life*," was the going rationalization. "And, look, you're beautiful. What are you complaining about? It was clearly God's will that this happened."

Such a reaction was neat and comfortable. It affirmed the church. It affirmed the tribal status quo. It affirmed the conservative, Christian nationalist, white-male-as-hero narrative.

Question: Would the people in the church have rallied behind the doctor—and chastised the young woman—just as fervently had the gynecologist been, say, a liberal African American? If not, why not? Wouldn't he have given the young woman life? Wouldn't he have been part of the reason she was beautiful? Wouldn't this have clearly been God's will?

The rightness or wrongness of the doctor's decision had nothing to do with *who he was* and everything to with *what he did*. But when Christian nationalism, not Scripture, becomes our priority, right and wrong become the sacrificial lambs.

We give passes to the those who wear the right-colored uniform

(Trump, for example) and punish those who don't (my client). What someone says or does has become almost irrelevant; what matters is that those in The Tribe be defended and those, like my client, with the courage to question The Tribe, be castigated.

When we cling to The Tribe with at-all-costs fervor we make enemies of the world. "If Jesus doesn't transform the way you relate to your enemies, then it's not Jesus you're following," tweeted Dan White Jr., author of *Love Over Fear*.

Russell Moore insists that, "Christians should defend religious liberty, they should defend life. But they should not even begin to presume that their ongoing 'othering' in American society is a product of their virtues. Sometimes the world rejects Christians because it rejects Christ. Sometimes, however, the world rejects Christians because Christians are cruel. In that case, alienation isn't persecution. It represents righteous judgment for our own political sin."[177]

Some far-right evangelicals have assumed that the world they want, and the way they want to achieve it, is the world God would want. They haven't hijacked a theology and pretended it was theirs; they've built a theology and pretended it was God's.

"The problem isn't that the average white evangelical is a rabid Christian nationalist," tweeted Coley. "The problem is that the average white evangelical is not uncomfortable with Christian nationalism."

IN SEPTEMBER 2019, National Security Advisor John Bolton resigned—at Trump's demand. What Bolton had found in his fifteen-month stint was unsettling, at least for those who had hoped Trump's supporting cast could guide a man who was proving to be, said Bolton, "un-guide-able." " ... He second-guessed people's motives, saw conspiracies behind rocks, and remained stunningly uninformed in how to run the White House, let alone the huge federal government," wrote Bolton, an old-school Republican, in *The Room Where It Happened*.[178]

By mid-autumn, the House of Representatives was looking into impeaching Trump for abuse of power and obstruction of Congress. At issue was a phone call from Trump to Ukraine President Volodymyr Zelensky. In the conversation, the US president had allegedly asked the

Ukraine leader to dig up dirt on political rival Joe Biden, a likely Trump opponent in the 2020 election, and his son Hunter, who had worked for a Ukranian energy company when his father had been vice president under Obama. Meanwhile, Trump had blocked—but would later release—payment of a congressionally mandated $400 million in military aid to Ukraine. At the time, the House's judiciary committee said Trump had "betrayed the nation by abusing high office to enlist a foreign power in corrupting democratic relations."[179]

I MISSED MOST of these details because my attention had been focused on convincing my 92-year-old mother to move to Eugene, then, in November 2019, helping her do so. Knowing that she loved her fourth-floor apartment over the Willamette River in Corvallis, I found a place in Eugene, Willamette Oaks, with a fourth-floor apartment overlooking the same river. Despite living her entire life in Corvallis, she gladly accepted the invitation.

She loved her new digs. Picking her up on Thanksgiving morning, I marveled at being a mere ten-minute drive from her. Soon the house was packed with people: our two sons, daughters-in-law, and five grandchildren. Suddenly, there was a knock on the door. Our special guests had arrived: Mukhtar, our Domino's pizza guy, and his wife Hayfa. Mom, sitting next to them at our table of fourteen, was infatuated with both.

"You are," she said to Hayfa, "so beautiful."

Sitting down for our turkey dinner, I looked at my Mom, the rest of my family, our new friends, and exhaled. It had been a wild month. Alas, as November 2019 became December—as the House of Representatives followed through with its expected impeachment of Trump on December 19—something happened across the Pacific Ocean that would make the short-term past seem placid by comparison.

A resident of Wuhan, China, fell sick with a never-seen-before virus.

2020

14.

Death & Deception

**As the 2020 election draws near,
COVID-19 arrives, a friend departs,
and I struggle with both.**

Truth is the enemy of power. Power is the enemy of truth.
—Unknown

The virus didn't stay in China. On January 21, 2020, the Center for Disease Control and Prevention (CDC) confirmed that a resident in Snohomish County, Washington, returning from China had tested positive for what was being called the "coronavirus." He was in the same hospital in Kirkland where I'd interviewed a family for a story on hospice care back in the 1980s when I worked for the nearby *Journal-American* in Bellevue.

President Trump wasted no time assuring the American people. "We have it totally under control," he told CNBC. "It's one person coming in from China. It's going to be just fine."

With 20/20 hindsight, of course, we know the coronavirus got terribly out of control and it wasn't "just fine." But at the start of such an insidious virus and with so little information, you could understand why Trump might have underplayed the seriousness of it; after all, in late January, Dr. Anthony Fauci, director of the CDC, said, "right now ... this is not a major threat." He also said the virus was "an evolving situation" and that "every day, we have to look at it very carefully."

The difference between Trump and Fauci was this: as the situation evolved, as new information became available, Trump—even if he believed it was a serious threat, which he seemed to—stuck to his "nothing-to-sweat" narrative and Fauci let the truth alter his thinking. What separated the two was that Trump, with an election to win and a tribe to appease, politicized the virus and Fauci did not.

COVID-caused business closures would lead to a sagging economy, which might cost Trump votes. COVID-caused cancellations of his rallies might cost him votes. Appearing weak, and not blaming China, might cost him votes. Ironically, he'd had no problem working his base into a fear-pocked frenzy about nonexistent threats—Antifa, the cancellation of Christmas, and the like—but now that he had an *actual* threat, he downplayed its danger and spun the narrative to the advantage of himself and to the detriment of others. People were dying.

On January 28, 2020, national security advisor Robert O'Brien told Trump, "This will be the biggest national security threat you face in your presidency ..."[180] Matthew Pottinger, the deputy national security adviser, concurred. He told the president that the situation in China was dire, meaning the world faced a health emergency on par with the flu pandemic of 1918, which killed an estimated 50 million people worldwide. In late January, *The Washington Post* reported that China had canceled its Lunar New Year in Wuhan and Beijing, which would be like the US "axing Christmas and the Super Bowl simultaneously."[181]

Initially, Trump respected the seriousness of the virus. At the time, he was allowing *The Washington Post's* Bob Woodward to interview him on an ongoing basis for his book *Rage*. The virus, he told the Pulitzer-Prize-winning journalist (Watergate), was "deadly stuff."[182] That said, Trump chose to downplay it to the public. He held six indoor rallies in the next few weeks, none with mask and social-distancing requirements.[183]

On February 26, he said the COVID case total "within a couple of days is going to be down to close to zero." Instead, within three months the virus had killed 100,000 Americans, nearly double our casualty rate in the nineteen-year Vietnam War.

South Korea, which discovered its first "positive" the day before the US but took the virus more seriously, had fewer than 1 percent the number of deaths the US had. With just 4 percent of the world's population, the US soon had 25 percent of the COVID cases.[184]

"We've done a *great* job on COVID response," Trump tweeted at the time, "making all Governors look good, some fantastic (and that's OK), but the Lamestream Media doesn't want to go with that narrative, and the Do Nothing Dems talking point is to say only bad about 'Trump.' I made everybody look good, but me!"

By then, as expected, Trump had been acquitted by the Senate on both impeachment counts, few Republicans willing to risk veering from the company line. More surprising was that the bedrock Christian magazine founded by Billy Graham, *Christianity Today*, had, six weeks earlier, called for Trump's removal from office.

Granting that "the Democrats have had it out for him from day one," the facts were "unambiguous: The president of the United States attempted to use his political power to coerce a foreign leader to harass and discredit one of the president's political opponents. That is not only a violation of the Constitution; more importantly, it is profoundly immoral." The editorial called Trump "morally lost."[185]

In my estimation, the most powerful paragraph in the magazine's editorial was this one:

> The President's failure to tell the truth—even when cornered—rips at the fabric of the nation. This is not a private affair. For above all, social intercourse is built on a presumption of trust: trust that the milk your grocer sells you is wholesome and pure; trust that the money you

> put in your bank can be taken out of the bank; trust that your babysitter, firefighters, clergy, and ambulance drivers will all do their best. And while politicians are notorious for breaking campaign promises, while in office they have a fundamental obligation to uphold our trust in them and to live by the law ... Unsavory dealings and immoral acts by the President and those close to him have rendered this administration morally unable to lead.[186]

Significantly, the magazine's reference was not to Trump's lies regarding Ukraine in 2019—but to President Bill Clinton's lies regarding his affair with a White House intern more than two decades before; the magazine was pointing to an undeniable double standard among evangelicals. In repeating what the magazine had written in favor of Clinton's impeachment in 1998, the same standards, *CT* wrote, must apply to Trump, whose removal "is not a matter of partisan loyalties but loyalty to the Creator of the Ten Commandments."

> To the many evangelicals who continue to support Mr. Trump in spite of his blackened moral record, we might say this: Remember who you are and whom you serve. Consider how your justification of Mr. Trump influences your witness to your Lord and Savior. Consider what an unbelieving world will say if you continue to brush off Mr. Trump's immoral words and behavior in the cause of political expediency. If we don't reverse course now, will anyone take anything we say about justice and righteousness with any seriousness for decades to come? Can we say with a straight face that abortion is a great evil that cannot be tolerated and, with the same straight face, say that the bent and broken character of our nation's leader doesn't really matter in the end?[187]

I was surprised—and inspired—by the magazine's stance, which, among evangelicals, represented an island of courage in a sea of cowardice regarding Trump's me-first leadership. But his followers defended him with vigor. A 2020 Pew Research Center survey would show that, by a nearly 2-to-1 margin, white evangelicals were more likely than other Americans to say the terms "morally upstanding" and "honest" described Trump at least "fairly well."[188]

AFTER SPENDING eighteen months helping Bartko write *Boy in the Mirror: An Athletic Director's Struggle to Survive Sexual Abuse as a Child,* the book was out. I gave a copy to Mom, who wrote Bartko a word of encouragement. "You are to be commended for finally coming forth with your abuse," she wrote, "and you are to be admired for your courage to do so. Hopefully this will encourage others who find themselves in similar circumstances to also take a similar course."

By now, news of the virus had become the nightly lead on the major networks, though Fox was naturally downplaying it.

"Just stay calm," tweeted Trump on March 10, 2020. "It will go away."

The next day, before flying to California for a press conference at which Jimmy was to announce his lawsuit against the Archdiocese of Oakland, I tweeted: "It was a privilege to tell Bartko's story. So much more courage than those who betrayed him."

From the moment I saw him in Oakland, Jimmy seemed more tightly wound than usual.

"You OK?" I asked in the hotel lobby.

"Just tired. Want this to be over."

"Hey, you're gonna do great."

Because we knew the clock was always ticking—the book needed to be out in time for the press conference—we'd done nothing together but work on the project.

"When we get back to Eugene, let's head for Tokatee [Golf Club]," I said.

"Great idea."

Before going to sleep, I called Sally to say goodnight, then was scrolling through my Twitter feed when I saw it: The World Health Organization, after noting there were now 118,000 COVID cases in 114 countries and 4,291 people had lost their lives, had decided to officially call it what it was.

A pandemic.

THE NEXT MORNING, as the videographer set up for a live feed in a hotel meeting room, I stacked dozens of our books for the media. The public relations folks had already propped a huge foam-core poster of the book cover on an easel to the side of the podium. I met Jim's sister, Kim, with whom he had an unusually close relationship, then, all set, again scrolled through my Twitter feed.

Like a drift boat ramming a rock, my thoughts came to a thudding halt. There were tons of retweets of WHO declaring the coronavirus a pandemic. I scrolled further. The Pac-12 men's basketball tournament had been canceled—in mid-tourney. Everywhere: ominous news about what scientists were calling "COVID-19." It was only five minutes from showtime and I counted only two dozen people, many California friends of Jimmy, a few of them victims of the same priest, I later learned.

"Where are the media?" I whispered to a guy next to me.

"It's the virus. Reporters are either out covering it or staying home because of it."

Bartko's attorney announced the lawsuit and the book, then turned things over to Jimmy. His voice was weak, his body slumped, his delivery pained. At times, he wiped away tears. But he shared his story. I was touched when he chose to read a portion of the book that I'd helped him write, talking about abuse victims who'd been …

> … swept away in a tsunami of addictions, broken relationships, and failure to hold a job. Still others, unable to reconcile with the hurts of the past, have killed themselves.
>
> For those who remain, the irony is that what ultimately frees us is our willingness to stand up and bear witness to what happened to us—perhaps to family and trusted friends, to the police, to a therapist, and maybe—as I'm doing here—to the public at large. We finally share what our betrayers hoped we would take to our graves, because our silence allows them to continue to prey on those afraid to speak up.
>
> One by one, as if bombing victims in a war not of our making, we wander out of the smoke and rubble, daring to tell our stories.
>
> This is mine.[189]

Afterward, I joined Jimmy, his family, and friends for lunch at the hotel. The mood was more subdued than I would have expected. Partly, I figured, because Jimmy wasn't feeling great and partly because this virus news was subtly unsettling. What, exactly, it meant, nobody knew; but in the last twenty-four hours, it was as if the world had tilted.

Our flight home to Eugene was leaving early evening. At 2:45 p.m. I texted Jimmy: "Awesome job today. Doesn't matter who showed up and how many will see it via internet later. All that matters is that you carried through on your convictions in a big way. You looked the monster straight in the eye—and spit in his face. Proud to call you my friend."

We met at the airport for dinner with a woman from a Eugene public relations firm who'd helped organize the press conference. We made small talk, then boarded the plane, though Jimmy and I weren't sitting together. Heck, nobody was sitting together; because of the sudden COVID panic, only a few dozen people were even on our flight, the return-trip a stark contrast to the previous day's full flight.

In Portland, where I still had to catch a half-hour flight to Eugene, Jimmy waved goodbye. "Staying with my sister," he said.

"Take care," I said. "Good job, man."

"Thanks."

He smiled faintly and soon blended into a small stream of on-the-go travelers, swept away—as it turned out—forever.

FOUR DAYS LATER, on a Monday, I met a *Register-Guard* reporter in the newspaper's parking lot—employees were already working remotely because of COVID—for an interview about the book. Beyond this worrisome virus, life was good. *Boy in the Mirror* was going to get front-page billing in the paper. And my brother-in-law and I had booked our flight to LA for April 24 to do the first of two PCT stretches to finish our 2,650-mile, decade-long quest to complete the trail.

While in my pickup outside an OfficeDepot, my phone buzzed. It was a friend common to me and Jimmy.

"What's up, Brad?" I said.

"Bob, it's Jimmy. He's—."

"What?"

"I'm here at the hospital. Jimmy's dead."

15.

COVID Nation

I wrestle with white privilege, black rage, an ailing mother, and, like us all, a pandemic.

Men never do evil so completely and cheerfully as when they do it from religious conviction.

— Pascal

Bartko's death at fifty-four knocked me sideways. When word spread, lots of people asked me if he'd died of COVID. Others, frankly, wondered if he'd taken his own life. Neither was true. After four decades of working long hours, getting little sleep, and sometimes medicating with wine and prescription drugs to get through the nights, his body had simply shut down while he was working out at a fitness club. Officially, he died of complications while in surgery to repair his kidney. But when John Canzano, a Portland sports radio-show host and *Oregonian* columnist, asked me—on air—what I thought killed him, I didn't hesitate.

"I think a priest murdered him more than forty years ago and it was just a slow gestation period."

My mother was crushed at the news. She'd read a late draft of the manuscript before it had gone into print. "What's wrong with people?" she said, referring to the priest. "They're sick. They're *evil*." When hearing he had died, she asked for his parents' address.

"I need to tell them they raised a good son."

SINCE THE moment I'd read the word "pandemic" on my iPhone six days before, the world had grown stranger and stranger. On the night Bartko died, I had been scheduled to have dinner with Mom and a friend who also had a mother at Willamette Oaks—my buddy and I representing two-thirds of The Three Amigos coffee group that had been meeting for more than a decade. But the staff had closed the restaurant; all residents would need to eat in their rooms until the virus passed, we were told.

Three days later, the Pacific Crest Trail Association recommended that hikers stay off the trail because of COVID. My brother-in-law, a doctor, suggested we bag it for 2020. I reluctantly agreed.

On March 20, a reporter asked Trump, regarding COVID: "What do you say to Americans who are watching you right now who are scared?" It was a fair question for a nation looking for assurance, hope, and direction—the same way America was looking for such things after the attack on Pearl Harbor in 1941. At the time, President Franklin Roosevelt told listeners "the only thing we have to fear is fear itself." And, in 2001, after the terrorist attacks on America, President Bush said, "Terrorist attacks can shake the foundations of our biggest buildings, but they cannot touch the foundation of America. These acts shatter steel, but they cannot dent the steel of American resolve."

Trump wasn't Roosevelt or Bush. "I say that you're a terrible reporter, that's what I say," he responded. "I think it's a very nasty question, and

I think it's a very bad signal that you're putting out to the American people."[190]

THE OLDER you were, the CDC reported, the more vulnerable you were to dying from COVID. Mom and the hundred-plus other residents at her retirement community were placed in lockdown. No visitors. No leaving, even to do her laundry just across the hall. No social interaction whatsoever. Though a total "people person," she didn't complain. Still, Sally and I could tell that, after just a few weeks, she was growing lonely. We called. We emailed. Our two sons and their families even managed a Facetime interaction with her on her iPhone, a device she normally used only to cheat on her *New York Times* crossword puzzles.

Meanwhile, the saving grace for Mom was that she had a deck and could sit on it, wrapped in a quilt Sally had made for her, and watch the geese fly down the river. Each week, we'd deliver whatever supplemental food she needed and return her laundry after washing it.

When I started calling Mom from below her fourth-floor apartment, she'd come out on her deck, wave, and we'd chat. I decided that for the next few weeks—maybe even *months* if this COVID stuff hung around—I'd try to do this every day. Just a month after celebrating her ninety-third birthday with Sally and a granddaughter at her favorite restaurant, Sabai, Mom was fading. She got slower and slower getting out onto the deck.

The day I was supposed to have left for LA and a PCT trailhead was the day Mom wound up in the hospital: April 24, 2020. A Friday. She was there five days, suffering from atrial fibrillation, not COVID. We then brought her home to our house—in essence, to die.

"I'd say she has a couple of weeks," the hospice nurse whispered to us afterward. "Maybe a little more."

We put a hospital bed in our living room, at whose foot we placed the Ruth Bader Ginsburg action-figure we'd gotten Mom for Christmas. On May 5, we learned that Ginsburg had been hospitalized for treatment of a gallbladder issue, the latest in a series of health scares for the eighty-seven-year-old Supreme Court Justice. It prompted something we'd never heard from Mom, an Episcopalian-turned-Presbyterian who kept her faith quiet.

"Can ... we ... pray ... for her?" she said, her voice weak.

We did.

In Mom's final days, we never talked about this being "the end" but I'm convinced she knew it was. She'd cheated death twice—a car accident and a tour-boat capsizing in which four people had drowned. She had outlived two husbands, my father Warren and her second husband, Bob, both good men. But this was different. This was farewell to not only a mother but a friend. Since my father's passing in 1996, sailing at Fern Ridge Lake west of Eugene had drawn Mom and I closer together than ever.

"I just love the sound of water on the side of the boat," she'd say nearly every outing. "We're blessed." Each summer's sailboat highlight was our "jungle cruise," a four-generation, sails-down, centerboard-up journey through winding Coyote Creek. She loved seeing her great-grandchildren swimming and, in blow-up rafts, having laugh-spiced water-gun fights.

Now, her breathing was getting more labored. One morning, I couldn't find Sally. I walked into the living room. There she was, tucked around Mom on the bed as if a mother bird protecting a baby, as if to say: *you're not dying alone*. I lost it. Just broke down and wept. And only later thought how painful it must have been, amid COVID, for loved ones—and doctors and nurses taking care of those loved ones—to experience a death with no in-person goodbye.

A few nights later, I was sure this was "the end" and felt compelled to say stuff to Mom that I might never again have a chance to say.

"Remember how, after Bob died we'd be sailing and you'd see a lone goose fly over and say, 'Maybe that's Bob, sending his love?'"

She nodded slightly.

"Mom, I'm going to miss you most when I'm sailing. You were my first mate. No, wait, I was *your* first mate."

Her *ET*-esque response caught me off guard. "I'll be with you," she rasped. "I'll be there."

My tears came harder.

A calligrapher, she had a handful of favorite sayings she liked to pen, among them one that said, "Time is so precious that it is dealt out to us only in the smallest possible fractions—one moment at a time."

And then came the last of those moments. Twelve days after we'd moved her in with us, just after midnight on May 12, 2020, I was asleep on the couch next to Mom when Sally suddenly appeared from the bedroom. Her instincts were amazing about such things.

"Bobby," she whispered. "She's gone."

It seemed odd to not have a service to celebrate Mom's life, but COVID precluded that; we planned one for October when this mess would be over; and, meanwhile, per Mom's request, we scattered most of her ashes into the Pacific Ocean off the rocks at Yachats, where her father had bought a beach cabin in 1936. She had played on this beach since she was nine, last going barefoot on it just two years ago as I videoed her. As we scattered the ashes, it was Sally who noted the lone gull hovering overhead—with not another in sight.

ON JUNE 1, 2020, Trump posed for a photo in front of Washington, D.C.'s St. John's Episcopal Church, defiantly holding up a Bible to make a "law and order" stand to protestors following the police killing of an African American man, George Floyd.

Floyd, forty-six, had died the previous week in Minneapolis, his life snuffed out by a white police officer, Derek Chauvin, after he was apprehended for trying to pass a counterfeit $20 bill in a quicky-mart. Four police officers responded to the call. Chauvin held the un-armed, handcuffed man on the pavement with a knee to Floyd's neck for nine minutes and twenty-nine seconds. The Hennepin County Medical Examiner's Office ruled it a homicide.

As the father of sons not much younger than Floyd, I tried to imagine what that would feel like for a parent: learning that your son, for trying to pass off a fake $20 bill at a convenience store, had been slowly killed by law enforcement—while officers fended off those trying to save his life.

Floyd's death at the hands of white cops was the latest in what had become—because of cell phones and police dash cams—almost common on the evening news and social media: black men being killed by white police officers. Floyd's death, however, set off arguably the largest wave of protests since the height of the Vietnam War in the late '60s.

Rioting is visual, ongoing, and spiced with police-vs.-protestors conflict; naturally, it is go-to fare for TV news, cable news, and social media. What triggered the anger is more easily ignored. Many seemed far less interested in learning about the roots of black rage—how, for example, in a nation where many think white privilege is a myth, the median net worth of a black family ($17,150) is roughly one tenth the net worth of a white family ($171,000).[191]

Some evangelicals saw a bigger picture than simply people looting and burning tires. "There is nothing—absolutely nothing—'conservative' about denying the reality of the consequences of centuries of intentional, racist harm," wrote David French.[192]

Former President George W. Bush said, "Laura and I are anguished by the brutal suffocation of George Floyd and disturbed by the injustice and fear that will suffocate our country."[193]

But many on the far right scurried to rationalize Floyd's death; he was on drugs, Fox News kept insisting, a desperate attempt to maintain the "not-our-fault" narrative of The Tribe when racism reared its ugly head. (Yes, he was, though that seemed a weak excuse for killing a man.)

When I learned that a post-Floyd survey by the Barna Group showed self-identifying white Christians were nearly twice as likely to say race is "not at all" a problem in the US than they were just the previous year, I was incredulous.[194]

WHEN I WAS in fourth grade, my ahead-of-his-time teacher at Garfield Elementary School in Corvallis, Mr. Brown, read the class *Black Like Me*. It was a true story about a white man from Texas, John Howard Griffin, who'd had a dermatologist darken his skin so he could experience, and write about, life as a black person in the South. Inside, he was the same person but, outside, he was suddenly seen by many white people as someone undeserving of even basic respect.

It left a huge impression on me; as a white kid in an almost exclusively white school, I learned not all people were treated equally—and some people could be cruel to others just because of their skin color.

Then came a far different experience involving race. When I was a high school sophomore I got mugged by three African American teenagers at Portland's Memorial Coliseum. My school, Corvallis High, was playing in the state Class AAA basketball tournament opener against Jefferson High, a predominantly black high school in Portland. Within five minutes of twalking into the arena, three guys cornered me and asked if they could borrow a dollar. They didn't wait for an answer. Instead, one ripped my back pocket off my jeans, another grabbed my wallet; I had about $50 in it. Another shoved me, and they ran. I was shaken by the incident, but don't recall it having any residual effects on me.

Two years later, Jefferson High and Corvallis High participated in a student exchange; a group of their kids spent a week at our school, a group of our kids spent a week at their school. My job, as an editor/reporter on the school paper, the *High-O-Scope,* was to interview our students and capture the experiences they'd had. It was a two-page spread—like nothing we'd ever done before—and included some great photographs by a friend of mine who'd been part of the exchange.

When classmates and teachers praised me for the effort, it felt good. When Jefferson High's administration wrote that the article was, in essence, racist, it felt bad. *Me, writing a racist article?* My advisor defended me. The principal defended me. My newspaper colleagues defended me. *Don't worry about it. Your reporting was objective.* "They're" just overreacting.

Decades later, when writing about race, I pulled out a musty scrapbook and found that article. In the intervening years, I'd become friends with the across-the-hall African American twins in my freshman dorm at the University of Oregon, guys who literally gave me the clothes off their backs so I'd look stacked-heel cool when taking Sally to her senior prom back home. I'd taken Black Literature and Black History classes at UO, my professor later becoming a friend whom I toasted at his eightieth birthday party. For stories I was writing, I'd interviewed dozens of people of color. And I'd taken a ten-week multicultural class at the local community college. Such experiences hadn't somehow inoculated me against biases—I will always struggle with such because my whiteness comes with advantages I seldom notice—but had helped me broaden my perspective on race.

As I read the yellowed article, however, I was stunned. *Oh. My. Gosh.*

If I'd been the folks at Jefferson, I'd have been angry, too. What jumped out at me wasn't anything overt, it was the subtle suggestion, throughout the article, that Jefferson wasn't only different, but wasn't as good as *us* because it was different than *us*. Again, I never said we were better—and, frankly, I never remember thinking we were better—but the result was an article that suggested we were. That the standard was *us* and Jefferson was *them*.

The mirror we hold up to see who we are is only as truthful as our perspective is broad; in the Bible, Paul says we see "through a glass darkly." When it comes to race, we see the world through self-colored glasses designed to protect that which we value most: ourselves.

What the eighteen-year-old version of myself revealed in that article didn't strike me as racist fallout from my having been mugged by black guys. Instead, it was a lack of human empathy, understanding, and perspective. I wasn't trying to appreciate life through the eyes of someone different from me. I was trying to uphold—on a completely subconscious level—my values as a white person by dismissing those unlike me. Just as I'd seen the Haitians in church through a blemished American lens, so had I seen the Jefferson kids through a blemished "self lens."

In George Lakoff's *Moral Politics,* he wrote:

> To conceptualize moral action as fully empathetic action is more than just abiding by the Golden Rule, to do unto others as you would have them do unto you. The Golden Rule does not take into account that *others may have different values than you do.* [Italics mine.] Taking morality as empathy requires basing your actions on *their* values, not yours. [Italics mine.] This requires a stronger Golden Rule: Do unto others as *they would have you do unto them.*[195]

As I was awakening to such lessons in 2020, I had a friend who was a small-college football coach. In 2016, after Kaepernick had begun taking a knee during the national anthem, an African American player on my friend's team wanted to do the same—not only to support Kaepernick but to call attention to racism in general and to police brutality in particular. My friend had never faced this issue as a coach and his default format had always been to stand for the national anthem to honor our country. But instead of simply saying no, the coach sat down and listened to the young man.

"He's a beautiful kid, Welchy," my friend told me, "and he has a father who is a disabled vet. He didn't want to do this to disgrace veterans, but he felt there were higher reasons. It wasn't about disrespecting anyone. It was about calling for respect for all."

The coach allowed it—and has continued to allow it as other players joined in. Whether the coach was sympathetic to the young man's values wasn't the point; the point was that, as in affirming Lakoff's perspective, the coach based his actions on his player's values, not his own.

That's empathy. And that, in the summer of 2020, was what some evangelicals couldn't seem to embrace regarding black lives. I understood why people were angry; during the protests, some people were torching buildings and looting stores. But like my friend the coach, were we as willing to listen to the frustration of black people that led to such violence—willing to honor their values, insights, histories, and perspectives rather than subtly keep imposing our own?

"For years, one of my coworkers treated me coldly," a Latino writer I mentor told me. "Finally, I asked her why. She told me how her family was robbed by Latinos when she was young. So, she'd assumed that 'we' all must be like that."

As with Juan's coworker, the comfortable act is to lasso people into convenient stereotypes—*robbers, looters, slackers*—instead of trying to see and understand who they really are as individuals. In Trump's case, to hold up a Bible to dramatize the toughness of The Tribe instead of perhaps visiting Floyd's grieving family. To deny that we, as white Christians, have any responsibility for the suffering of people of color who were created in the image of God just as we were.

When the Holy Spirit is alive in our lives, we don't default to *us*, we default to *them*—those in need, those who hurt, those who face injustice. That's how we get fed—by living beyond ourselves. "Blessed are those who hunger and thirst for justice/righteousness, for they shall be satisfied," says Matthew 5:6.

Ten months after George Floyd's death, nearly two-thirds of blacks considered his death a murder, but less than a third of whites did so.[196]

The discrepancy between whites doubting discrimination against blacks in general would seem to offer us only two conclusions. Either:

(a) What the majority of black people consider discrimination is actually *not*; they're misreading their own experiences;

(b) What the majority of white people *don't* consider discrimination against blacks actually *is*; as white people, we're misreading the experiences of others.

By summer 2020, I had come to believe the answer was (b). Yes, I'd seen cases where people of color had blamed race for something they should have owned themselves; believing race bias exists doesn't mean thinking all white people are bad and all people of color are good. But I'd also become convinced that such "own-it-yourself" cases were the exceptions, not the rules.

Let's say you and I are walking down the street on a winter day and I'm feeling particularly warm and cozy.

"I'm cold," you say.

"No, you're not," I say.

Who knows better whether someone is cold: you or the person shivering?

Experience, I'd come to learn, is *not* the best teacher. *Other people's experience* is the best teacher. That's what history is: other people's experiences. And history, too often, is written by the winners, whose position of power skews their perspectives.

Are there people of color who deny racism? Of course. But that doesn't mean we should discount those who suggest otherwise. The point isn't to slap the US with a one-size-fits-all label of "racist." As Christians, the point is to listen to those who grieve.

WAS IT POSSIBLE, I wondered, that our nation was being protected by heroic men and women in law enforcement, most of whom were honorable and trustworthy and fair, but some of whom treated people of color chillingly differently than they treated others? Was it also possible that some outsiders were quick to blame police for violence against people of color—violence that, unfortunately, was necessary to protect the greater good? (I've known of journalists with deep integrity, and some who fabricated entire stories; pastors who I'd want with me in a foxhole, and others who shame the faith.)

Thanks to the Eugene Police Department's Citizens Police Academy, I'd seen a seldom-reported side of police-suspect confrontations. Over more than a dozen sessions, which Sally attended with me, a handful of officers had taken us through every facet of their jobs. It was fascinating. The part that impacted me most deeply was the "final test"—putting on police gear, being given a blank-filled gun, and getting thrown into situations in an abandoned building at the training facility.

In a darkened hallway, with a man running toward me with something in his hand, I had to decide whether to shoot.

Chaos. I still remember much of what I learned in that experience, and it has helped me appreciate the nuances of such police-suspect confrontations.

"Every fight we come to there's at least one gun there—our own," an officer told our group. "And there's a chance we can lose that gun." In fact, odds are greater that an officer will be shot by his own gun than by someone else's.

For cops, every game is a "road game." "We go into the lion's den," the officer said. "And the law of nature says police officers don't win these. We have rules. They don't. That gives them an advantage."

This kind of intensive education over three months' time opened my eyes to perspectives I'd never considered; the experience deepened my already strong appreciation for law enforcement. In the absence of first-hand knowledge of someone else's experience, we tend to default to stereotypes that reinforce our pre-conceived notions—that make us feel *comfortable*—instead of considering more nuanced alternatives that nag our conscience.

IN LATE JUNE 2020, soon after Floyd's death, I learned of evangelical churches that were addressing the race issue by targeting the Black Lives Matter organization itself. I'd read up on BLM; it was unabashedly bold, edgy, and angry, not a great fit for conservative evangelicals.

But I found it interesting that of the many ways a pastor could have approached the race issue—an innocent man had been murdered right before our eyes—they chose the one that protected The Tribe. The one that required no introspection or obligation on our parts. The one that strained the gnat and swallowed the camel.

Could we as evangelicals be missing a deeper truth here? Could it be that focusing on the BLM organization per se—instead of the broader theme of racial bias—conveniently diverted us from considering the "least of these" victims? Instead of running *to* those in need, like Jesus did, why did so many evangelicals run *from* whatever bogeyman we had built in our minds—or *had built for us* by our president or hard-right media or, in some cases, pastors? Could we have learned nothing from the Civil Rights movement—yes, the one whose leaders, like MLK, were also routinely dismissed as Marxists and Communists in order to keep the status quo comfortably unchanged or unchallenged?

In my parking-lot chats—I had begun interviewing people but hadn't fully committed to the book—no topic I brought up made evangelicals bristle more than race. The most common line was: "I don't see color" or "I'm not prejudice" or "I treat everyone the same." The unspoken line was: *I don't wanna go there.*

The attitude wasn't unique to Eugene. Strangely, the more racism begged to be talked about, the less evangelicals wanted to talk about it. In 2016, reported *Christianity Today,* 90 percent of pastors agreed their congregation would "welcome a sermon on racial reconciliation"; four years later—coincidentally, after four years of Trump—that had dropped to 74 percent.

In 2021, a survey showed that 66 percent of white evangelicals agreed that "one of the most effective ways to improve race relations in the US is to *stop talking about race.*" [Italics mine.] It was like telling an embattled married couple: "If you want your relationship to get better, don't discuss your differences."

I couldn't disagree more—and not just because Sally and I were coming down homestretch on a marriage guide for the church that said just the opposite, that communication in relationships was essential. Head-in-the-sand thinking echoes a point I've been trying to make throughout this book: one of the reasons some evangelicals aren't more loving is that we've failed to accept—or accept but won't act on—the idea that love must sometimes force us out of our comfort zones.

Trump suggested that courage was tough-guy stuff, bully stuff. Wrong. Courage is humbling yourself to learn deeper truths for God's glory. Courage is daring to not instinctively defend yourself, but being willing to listen to the stories of others. Courage is standing for something that will cost you something.

"Racial bias is largely unconscious," wrote Robin Diangelo in *White Fragility,* "and herein lies the deepest challenge—the defensiveness that ensues upon any suggestion of racial bias. This defensiveness is classic white fragility because it protects our racial bias while simultaneously affirming our identities as open-minded. Yes, it's uncomfortable to be confronted with an aspect of ourselves that we don't like, but we can't change what we refuse to see."[197]

Daniel Hill, the white pastor of a multiethnic church in Chicago, agrees with Diangelo. In *White Awake,* he argues what prevents white Christians from "going there" is a subtle self-righteousness that compartmentalizes racism as the individual acts of "bad" people.

"The telltale sign of self-righteousness in everyday identity is drawing a circle around the in-group and pointing a judgmental finger at those in the out-group," he wrote. "This usually manifests as trying to prove that you belong to the group that 'gets' it—or as many in my congregation joke, as being the 'cool white person that's on the side of justice.' This inevitably leads to judgment, and at times even scorn, toward those who have other vices and behaviors."[198]

IN FEBRUARY 2020, Ahmaud Arbery, twenty-four, was gunned down by three men in a pickup truck while running down a road in Georgia. The video of it—yes, one of the three charged in the shooting videoed the man being shot to death—had gone viral.

What led to his death? He was a runner; neighbors often saw him jogging down the streets of Satilla Shores. He'd sometimes stop to shoot hoops with little kids, but on this day he did something different: a security camera showed he'd walked into a door-less house under construction, looked around, taken nothing, and left. Then jogged away.[199]

Wise? No. Legal? No. But I imagined a white couple walking their poodle and being curious about a floor plan of a house under construction; perhaps the layout looked like something they might want to replicate with the remodel they were planning. Sally and I had done it ourselves a few times, once at an exclusive resort in Central Oregon; nobody would mind, right? And, hey, it wasn't like there was even a door on the front.

Would that white couple—would Sally and I—have wound up being hunted down like rabbits by three guys in a moving pickup, one of whom filmed "the hunt?" Though unarmed, would we have died from shotgun blasts from close range? Would one of the three eventually charged in the murder, according to the video, have said "f---ing whities" as we bled out on the pavement?

Not likely. But in a 2021 NationScape survey, which of the eight demographic groups polled was least likely to agree with the statement, "The two men were motivated by racism and should be prosecuted for murder?" White evangelicals.

It was a fairly open-shut case; among other things, there was video evidence that showed Arbery took nothing from the house. Later, in the trial, one of the defendants said the victim never verbally or physically threatened any of the three. He had no weapon. So why would evangelicals seemingly be inclined to show leniency to the three white men charged in the murder—at the expense of the young black man they had gunned down?

AS THE SUMMER deepened, I learned of an evangelical pastor in Eugene who was speaking boldly about racism. While hiking, I listened to a handful of his sermons and was stunned at how courageous he was in addressing the issue.

I didn't know the guy and it was uncomfortable, but I invited him to a parking-lot meeting. When we sat down together on that August 2020 morning, he told me the church had lost nearly a quarter of its congregation since he'd preached two series on race.

"How'd you come to feel so strongly about the race issue in the first place?"

"A few years ago, an African American woman in the congregation came to me in frustration. 'Do you have any idea,' she said, 'how people in this church treat me? The things they say to me? The looks they give me?'"

She told him. It wasn't pretty.

"I'd had no idea," he said to me. "I was stunned. Ashamed."

He committed himself to listening and learning from people of color. Reading. Writing. Studying. Praying—often for forgiveness. The result, to begin with, was two sermon series on racial injustice—and a training session for the church elders on racial justice.

"What have you learned?" I asked.

"That as white people have some corporate responsibility to own this," he said. "And that people are prickly. The term 'white privilege' is incendiary; nobody likes it."

I asked the pastor if he had a better phrase for "white privilege."

"I think 'white advantage' is better. The best I ever heard it explained was the metaphor of two guys—one white, one black—sitting on two swim platforms, a couple hundred yards apart, each equal distance from the coastline. Both good swimmers, they decide to race to shore. After a few minutes, the white guy is far ahead. He can't figure out why the black guy is struggling, why he can't keep up. 'Come on, man,' he yells. 'What's the problem?' What the white guy can't see is that the black guy is swimming in a riptide, and he is not. The white guy thinks the black guy is doggin' it; after all, there's no rip tide working against *him*."

After all, when his son got his driver's license, he'd never had to tell him how to respond when being pulled over by the police. Never had to worry about his African American-sounding name leading to his application being funneled into the "no" pile as studies have shown. Never had to worry, like Tommie Smith, about being unable to rent an apartment because of his skin color.

When my father returned from World War II, he was able to get a loan through the GI Bill and buy a nice little house whose value, thanks to inflation, climbed, allowing my folks to buy a bigger house and, finally, a split-level house where I spent my teen years. True, my parents worked hard, but they also had twenty-five years of inflation momentum; when it was time for me to go to college in the early '70s, the money was available.

Not only were black veterans *legally* discriminated against in World War II—banned from fighting alongside white soldiers—but *illegally* discriminated against after the war; in what came to be known as "red lining," banks wouldn't make loans for mortgages in certain neighborhoods or to certain people. Thus, African Americans often found it impossible to buy a home because of exclusive deed covenants and flat-out racism.[200] No house, no chance to ride inflation. So, the hopes of an African American kid my age having the money to attend college were less promising.

I'd benefitted from a white advantage, an advantage that helped explain, at least in part, today's 10:1 ratio in white net worth compared to black net worth.

Do I need to wallow in guilt over that? No. But as a person of faith, I do need to add something to the list of stuff that I believe in even though I can't see it: riptides.

16.

The Decision

I had played it safe most of my life, but a writer-friend's shunning—and the courage of a friend now gone—push me off the branch.

You are not only responsible for what you say, but also for what you do not say.

—Martin Luther

The tweet from an African American father tore me up. "To hear my fifteen-year-old son say he won't take driver's training, because he's afraid police will shoot him took my joy this morning," he wrote. "I'm done with this. I don't know what to say."

I imagined what that must have felt like for those two—stolen joy—and I thought: Who among us evangelicals will speak for this man and his son? Who among us will set aside our fear of "white guilt" long enough to let their pain be our pain?

Contrasting his despair to the joy I had of watching my two sons get their licenses—and the three of us not having to worry about any of us being shot by the police if we were pulled over—grieved me. I thought of the father's words: *I don't know what to say.* For years, I'd been sensing *I know what to say.* But I hadn't had the courage to say it. Now, my conscience whispered, *write the book. Stand up. Say it.*

By now, the summer of 2020, I'd been seriously mulling a book but was reluctant to fully commit. The pastor of our church had been preaching "relaxed concern" and a book questioning the evangelical faith would represent deep concern; would make me, at least in some people's eyes, a disruptor, a traitor to The Tribe.

Trump's presence had sent political sensitivity to an all-time high; a writer friend of mine, a Presbyterian, had dedicated her September 2020 newsletter to social justice, basing her message on Micah 6:8; "What does the Lord require? To seek justice, act mercifully, and walk humbly with our God." She referred to George Floyd's death and acknowledged "systemic racism." She wrote about praying for a nephew she loved who was in law enforcement, though sensed the need to "stand with brown and black families who from the depths of tragic and violent histories, fear simply taking a run or wearing a hoodie," for fear of being killed.

While she received dozens of positive emails and "shares" from evangelical Christians for articulating views that they'd felt but couldn't express, sixty newsletter subscribers dropped her instantly. What's more, a member of her prayer team resigned; she didn't want her name associated with any effort that supported "the Marxist Black Lives Matter" movement. One person rebuked her in a two-page letter.

"She said I was trying to wipe out history," said my friend, a heart-of-gold writer who'd teamed up with me to teach numerous workshops. "Honestly, it felt like a shunning."

Here's what stung me so deeply about the response my friend got: her detractors *knew* her novels upheld Christian values and the dignity of women. *Knew* her heart. *Knew* her faith. *Knew* her life. If I were going to choose a handful of people who lived with integrity as the "hands and feet of God," she'd be on my short list. And yet because she dared to speak up for African Americans, dared to do the very thing I think Jesus would do, she was suddenly bad news. I began wondering if evangelical churches today would welcome Jesus Himself were He to show up; He might be considered too radical. Too *woke.*

While the Holy Spirit seemed to be guiding my friend's words and actions, those who turned on her seemed to be guided by something else—or some*one* else.

"I felt like, absolutely, Trump had given permission for his followers to be this way," she told me. "All these old grievances found a channel in Trump. It's OK to be aggressive, OK to be demeaning to immigrants and women because, well, the president of the United States feels that way."

Why were some evangelicals unable, or unwilling, to see that the values of Trump and the values of Jesus were, in many cases, polar opposites?

"I don't feel ashamed for having written it," my friend told me. "Artists have been making statements for generations. That's what we *do.*"

That's what I'd *done* most of my life, too, though I'd always kept my sailboat in the deep waters of caution and seldom skirted the shoal-pocked shallows that demanded more courage.

On a September 2020 sailing trip to Cultus Lake—I was scattering the last of Mom's ashes in a place we'd enjoyed a handful of magical vacations—I pondered the book idea. It was a surreal setting, mine among the few boats on a high-mountain lake shrouded in a pale-orange sky, the smoky residue of some of Oregon's worst forest fires in history.

Even if I wrote it, what evangelicals were going to read a book that suggested far-right politics had clouded our Christian conscience? And the book could imperil my relationships with many of my closest friends, good people who'd voted for Trump:

Pastors who taught me leadership, modeled integrity, helped me navigate life: *Trump.*

People who, year after year, brought hope to the hopeless in Third World countries by organizing, and serving on, medical missions: *Trump.*

People who were there to comfort me when I lost my father: *Trump.*

People who rushed to the rescue on a rainy night to drain our flooded basement: *Trump.*

People who live in California but, once COVID abates, plan to drive 2,000 miles roundtrip to attend my mother's memorial service: *Trump.*

People who popped their head in my office every morning when they arrived at *The Register-Guard* and not only asked how I was doing but listen to—and cared about—my response: *Trump.*

And others, including a guy who, in my troubled college years, was the only real friend I made—and remains my closest book-writing confidante: *Trump.*

Given the potential resistance, I realized this effort could be *masochistic*. Already, some evangelical friends had questioned my going forward with this; did I really want to risk this? But I couldn't imagine living with myself knowing that I'd refused to say what needed saying—just to maintain my personal comfort. Where was the courage in that? I would be bowing to the very thing I was arguing *against*—that going with the flow was wiser than reaching for, in Comey's words, "a higher loyalty."

Why does a preacher preach when it would be easier *not* to preach? To effect change. To awaken people. To say: *We are too much like this and God wants us more like that*. In other words, at what point did "relaxed concern" become negligence?

"There is only one way to avoid criticism: do nothing, say nothing, and be nothing," wrote Aristotle. Later, the Apostle Paul raised the idea of who, as Christians, we're living for.

"Am I now trying to win the approval of human beings, or of God? … If I were still trying to please people, I would not be a servant of Christ (Galatians 1:10)."

My calling, Scripture reminded me, wasn't to be popular or even successful in the eyes of the world; my calling was to "be faithful," says Revelation 2:10, "until death."

I thought of a quote from Pastor Rick Warren of Saddleback Church: "If you live for the approval of others, you will die by their rejection."

I thought of Jimmy Bartko, who'd had the guts to tell his story about abuse even though, as he told me, he knew the price might be high.

Finally, I thought of insight from author Annie Dillard that I used to offer at my Beachside Writers Workshops: "Write as if you were dying. At the same time, assume you write for an audience consisting solely of terminal patients. That is, after all, the case. What would you begin writing if you knew you would die soon? What could you say to a dying person that would not enrage by its triviality?"

This. Not as an attack on those who'd supported Trump, but as encouragement for those who, like me, had been quietly complicit in letting politics blur their clarity of Christ.

Midway through that sailing trip, I made the decision: I would write the book.

I came home, set my alarm for 5 a.m., and began research and writing each day. At times, the project evoked a sense of freedom in my being able to be more real about my faith; at other times, it felt as if I were passing a 100,000-word kidney stone.

THE FALL unfolded with much less grandeur than usual. Because of COVID, the football season that usually drew our family together in leafy, three-generation walks to Autzen Stadium for Oregon games on Saturdays was on indefinite hold. We stayed apart, hunkered down, and faithfully wore our masks when venturing out for groceries.

On October 27, 2020, Trump tweeted: "All the fake news media wants to talk about is COVID, COVID, COVID … ."

Wrote his niece, Mary L. Trump: "Donald's initial response to COVID-19 underscores his need to minimize negativity at all costs. Fear—the equivalent of weakness in our family—is as unacceptable to him now as it was when he was three years old."[201]

"Fear is necessary in war," Don Malarkey, one of World War II's Band of Brothers, had once told me for the memoir I helped him write, *Easy Company Soldier.* "It's what helps keep you safe."

Before now, I'd found Trump's dismissal of the virus merely worrisome; now, however, I looked at it differently. Three days before his "COVID, COVID, COVID" lament, after I'd felt some flu-like symptoms while helping our younger son and his family move into a new house, Sally had encouraged us to go in for COVID tests.

She tested negative. I did not.

My Hope for the Future

That we might rededicate ourselves to the Truth

A SIKH CLIENT of mine told me how, within his faith, the strongest incentive for making a big-life decision is The Tribe. But The Tribe, he says, is sometimes flawed in its own values; for example, "women," he said, "are considered second-class citizens." So, he doesn't always acquiesce to The Tribe.

I spent 40 years in the newspaper business, which taught me to listen to both sides of a story, to document the points I make, and to differentiate between fact and fiction—good things all. But that doesn't mean I acquiesce to the newspaper tribe for my truth.

Someone else might have a military background, which taught them discipline, teamwork, and pride of performance— good things all. But that doesn't necessarily mean he or she should automatically default to the military for their truth.

My measuring stick for truth needs to be God's Word. Not my background. Not my workplace. Not my circle of friends. Not what a political organization tells me is true. Not what my peer group tells me is true. Not what I *wish* were true. And, in some cases, not even what my pastor or elder board, whose visions can become skewed, might tell me is true. But what God's Word leads me to believe is true.

As evangelicals, it's time we rededicated ourselves to

something that God values highly: the truth.

Before we can even get to the point of having a discussion with someone about ideas, we must find common ground on the concept of truth. Either we respect it or we don't; it is an equal-opportunity concept that, in its absence, is like playing an athletic contest without officials.

"When we can't agree on truth, we can't have a functioning democracy," said economist and author Thomas Freidman.

And that means broadening the scope of where we get our information. If at the food-court of ideas, we're eating at the same restaurant each time, we're building a narrow worldview that will keep us safe but not sound. "Illusion," said Voltaire, "is the first of all pleasures."

To broaden our informational scopes doesn't mean forgoing our scriptural foundation; it simply means letting reason and discernment help us separate truth from fiction. Because The Tribe's interests often aren't Christ's interests.

"The greatest threat to our nation and to our Christian faith is not from liberals—it's not from conservatives—it is from the trashing of truth by extreme media outlets that spew information in exchange for ratings," tweeted Stearns, the former World Vision director. "There is still good fact-based journalism out there."

The truth mattered to Jesus—and it ought to matter to us. "If you hold to my teaching, you are really my disciples," He said in John 8:31-32. "Then you will know the truth, and the truth will set you free." Conversely, *not* knowing the truth—falling for lies and deceit—will keep us in bondage.

As evangelicals, we need to resist go-with-the-political-flow thinking, the stuff that traps us in echo chambers of personal affirmation, and dare to question others—and ourselves. We need to replace tribal thinking with Bible thinking; it's our responsibility, says John 7:24, to "not judge by appearances, but judge with right judgment."

If we don't realize how manipulative social media can be—see Netflix's *The Social Dilemma* (2020)—we are bound to fall for lie after lie.

If we spend forty-five minutes a week listening to a sermon and four hours a day listening to Fox News and other far-right bias, how nutritious is our informational diet apt to be?

"White evangelicals would do well to turn off cable news and listen to their sisters and brothers in the increasingly diverse pews of evangelical churches," said Ed Stetzer, executive director of the Billy Graham Center at Wheaton College.

Do we believe statements because they're true or because The Tribe wants us to believe they're true? Because they're documented by trustworthy people with no agenda—or because they support what we already believe?

After COVID hit, Francis Collins, then director of the National Institutes of Health, urged people to look at the facts, at the evidence, not the politics. At an event with Southern Baptist leaders, Collins, a Christian, implored people to not let "fear and anxiety" trigger bad decisions. He pointed to Philippians 4 for guidance: "Brothers and sisters, whatever is true, whatever is noble, whatever is right, whatever is pure, whatever is lovely, whatever is admirable—if anything is excellent or praiseworthy—think about such things."

"That would apply really well right here," he said. "So, 'whatever is true.'"

Even if it hurts, which the truth sometimes does. In my journalism career, I've written a handful of newspaper columns that I chose to rewrite, and have republished. Why? Because, provided new information and new insight by readers, I realized what I originally thought was true was not. Or what I originally thought was a fair stance was a flawed stance, in some cases caused by my own biases.

Each time I "redid" a column wounded my pride; to do so was to advertise to 50,000 readers that I had failed. But my pride had to bow to something more important: truth and fairness. And what I learned was that readers, at what seemed like a fairly deep level, honored my willingness to admit my mistakes.

Why would we begin to trust someone who never admits a mistake? A lie? A distortion of the truth? President Donald Trump lied or distorted the truth more than 30,000 times in his four years as president, according to *The Washington Post's* fact checker. [2]

In Texas, a new millennial friend whose book I helped write left his Baptist megachurch because, as he says, "our pastor—a guy who'd been my spiritual advisor—got sucked in by Trump. He bought this lie and that lie. The congregation is all Fox News-driven and it's all about how Republicans and Trump are the last great hope of the world; 'we gotta control that runaway socialism and distance ourselves from the evil Democrats.' They're 100 percent missing the point; they're closing the door to any Democrat who's lost and needs Jesus. Finally, we left."

Why? For the same reason my Sikh friend sometimes veers from the tenets of his faith—because faith groups consist of people, and people are flawed. Journalists are flawed. Politicians are flawed. Pastors are flawed. All of us are flawed, including The Tribe.

17.

Choosing Sides

As people decide their priorities about dealing with COVID, I lament a time when I had a "me-or-others" choice—and guess who I chose?

Silence and tacit consensus always, without fail, protect privilege. That is why the privileged are characteristically silencers.

—Walter Bruggemann, *Interrupting Silence*

By September 21, 2020, with COVID deaths in the US having reached 200,000, Trump's claim that it affects "virtually nobody" was apparently being believed by plenty of evangelicals, including financial guru Dave Ramsey. Ramsey, an evangelical who teaches Bible-based financial principles, drew fire for keeping his Nashville company open even after employees tested positive for the virus; for not requiring masks; for ignoring recommendations to avoid large gatherings; and for hosting a business conference in July after a Marriott Hotel canceled it because of safety concerns.[202]

"This is America—a voluntary thing, you choose what you want to do," Ramsey told the *Nashville Tennessean*. "But we're not going to have someone pay $10,000 for a ticket to have some $8-an-hour twerp at Marriott giving them a hard time about wearing a mask."

Later, he told Fox News that he didn't believe in COVID-related stimulus checks "because if $600 or $1,400 changes your life, you were pretty much screwed already. You've got other issues going on. You have a career problem, you have a debt problem, you have a relationship problem, you have a mental health problem . . . ."[203]

It was a little like Jesus saying to the five thousand: "You're hungry? Get a friggin' life, pal. This is on *you*." I found Ramsey's cockiness the kind of stuff Trump seemed to have emboldened in evangelicals, the same kind of unwarranted toughness my writer-friend had noted: a sense of oppression, particularly odd for Ramsey, whose house, in 2021, would go on the market for $15.45 million.[204]

As Christians, why wouldn't we be just the opposite? Why wouldn't we be the group *most concerned* about those around us falling ill or dying? Jesus's Golden Rule—"So in everything, do to others what you would have them do to you (Matthew 7:12)"— suggests that if we didn't want someone to transmit a virus to us, then we should try to avoid transmitting a virus to them. Asserting my rights was all about *me*, but wearing a mask was all about *them*.

That said, an early evangelical defense for COVID skepticism was to point out that the virus mainly affected only those with pre-existing conditions and older people. Scientifically, that was accurate. But, scripturally, it was shortsighted.

In November, a woman our age whom Sally had gone to Haiti with on a medical mission—and whose son I'd written about in a 1998 book—died of COVID. The knee-jerk "did-she-have-a pre-existing-condition?" question that some asked seemed disingenuous, as if a "yes" answer would somehow minimize her death. As if the death then somehow didn't count—wouldn't work against Trump's COVID-is-overblown spin.

A woman was dead, a woman who wouldn't have died had the virus not been real. A man lost his wife, children lost their mother. To us, the political ramifications were totally insignificant. But by now, it seemed, some were allowing the values of The Tribe to dilute the values of the heart.

Didn't "pro-life" mean caring about life, period, at any point in a person's existence, beginning with conception and lasting to death? Didn't "pro-life" mean standing up for the vulnerable, period? Didn't the shepherd in the Parable of the Lost Sheep leave the ninety-nine to save the one? To God, every life mattered—black, blue, white, brown, even old lives and those with pre-existing conditions.

LIKE TRUMP, Ramsey was apparently among those who believed COVID was being overblown by The Left to work against Trump. Like the President, he had a chip on his shoulder.

When Ramsey's company hosted a Christmas party for nearly one thousand people, caterers were asked to *not* wear masks—"so as not to scare those in attendance," a note from Ramsey's company to the catering company said.[205] It was as if suggesting that a Christian might intellectually agree with John 15:13—"Greater love has no one than this: to lay down one's life for one's friends"—*just don't ask me to go to the trouble of wearing a mask around you during a pandemic.*

When Religion News Service requested an interview with Ramsey about his views on COVID protocol, the financial and media company responded to the reporter with this:

> Thanks for reaching out. We want to confirm for you that you are right, we are horrible evil people. We exist to simply bring harm to our team, take advantage of our customers, and spread COVID. And YOU figured it all out, wow. Who would have guessed that an unemployed guy, oh I am sorry, a "freelance reporter" would be the one to show us how horrible we are so we can change and to let the world know of our evil intent, secrets, and complete disregard for decency, but YOU did it, you with all your top notch investigative skills have

been able to weave together a series of half-truths to expose our evil ways. You are truly amazing.[206]

When I read the response, I was struck by how Trump-like it sounded in its small-mindedness: Shoot the messenger. Act smug. Play the victim. And, of course, raise a smokescreen that obscures your unwillingness to show true leadership and take responsibility for the benefit of others.

I don't say this to disparage Ramsey, who has admittedly helped countless Christians get out of debt and manage their money better and who, privately, might be a model believer. I mention this because too many high-profile evangelicals, at least in their public comments, have lost their ways, people in leadership positions whose words and actions influence millions of evangelicals. They've flown off the scriptural rails, they arrogantly refuse to be held accountable, and the Kingdom is shamed because of it. With great power comes great responsibility, and it's wrong for Christians with far-reaching platforms to callously ignore that responsibility with "let-them-eat-cake" smugness. That's not Jesus; that's the pride and haughtiness He preached *against*. That's The Tribe.

After COVID hit, Tennessee Pastor Greg Locke tweeted, "We have a First Amendment right to worship. If that's impeded upon, we will invoke our 2nd Amendment right and meet you at the door. We will not be bullied."[207] In other words: "Let us gather to worship the Prince of Peace—*or we will kill you!*" Was anyone wondering how this kind of grandstanding looked to our "mission field," the non-believers wondering if God was even real?

"If Christians don't take the first step to humble ourselves and become less testy, less defensive, less easily offended, and less vindictive when we experience milder forms of opposition and criticism than the global norm, who will?" tweeted Pastor Scott Sauls, author of *A Gentle Answer*.

The attitudes of Ramsey and Locke were microcosms of a Trump-inspired attitude on the rise: *We can be as nasty as we want to be. Why? Because we're Christians and this is OUR country.*

Such thinking represents fingernails to the blackboard of Scripture. "Do nothing out of selfish ambition or vain conceit," says Philippians 2:3. "Rather, in humility value others above yourselves."

Too often, instead, we choose ourselves over others.

IN 2004, I learned that a grade-school classmate of mine had committed suicide at age forty-six. Immediately, I thought of the playground incident. It was sometime in the early 1960s. I didn't understand it at the time, but, looking back, I think he was a lonely kid. He lived with his grandmother because his parents had died when he was small. I think he saw me and most of his classmates as being in the inner circle. And saw himself as constantly outside looking in.

Why else would he have come up to me on the playground that day and made me the offer? A dollar to play two-square with him at recess.

After he made the proposition, my default format wasn't grace, it was greed. I said yes. I was the better player, but I didn't humiliate him; I remembered, after all, who had buttered my bread. That night after dinner I raced my Schwinn to the Cornet 5&10 store and was standing in line to buy a bag of plastic army men when I saw my mother.

"How do you plan on paying for those?" she asked. "You don't have any money."

I told her how I'd gotten the dollar. She had me return the army men. She told me to give the money back—and invite the boy to play two-square with me.

"He was only looking for a friend," she said. "Please, why don't you *be* one?"

I played two-square with the kid, even if it was a guilt-induced game for me. We never became buddies. He grew up, married, had a son, and worked much of his life in an auto parts store. The obituary said he enjoyed going "four-wheel driving." It didn't say how he died, but I knew. The sheriff's office confirmed to me what I'd already been told by friends: He killed himself. He drove out into the woods and swallowed a lot of pills. He left a note.

I don't know why he took his life. But I will always wonder if he was as lonely as a grown man as he seemed to be as a young boy. And I will always wonder if his life might have turned out differently had people like me befriended him for the right reasons, not the wrong.

People who succeed are quick to thank those who helped them in their pasts. By that same measure, don't we need to own some incremental part we may have played in the lives of those who have faltered? Words and actions matter; Bartko's story reminded me of that. One person's *evil* influenced Jimmy for the rest of his too-short life; it's not a reach to say it ultimately killed him. I'm not suggesting I'm responsible for my classmate's death, but neither do I think I can blindly slough off any responsibility. We affect each other—for better or worse. And I failed that kid big-time.

In our two-square and four-square games, we sometimes called for "do-overs"—say, if a ball landed on the line and we didn't agree whether it was "in" or "out." That's what I longed for after reading his obit: a do-over—a chance to go back in time and tell the kid to forget the buck. *You serve.* Alas, life rarely affords such chances. Instead, it can only beckon us to learn from our mistakes—the times we were asked to choose sides. And we wrongly chose ourselves.

I DON'T like remembering that story; it's *uncomfortable* because it reminds me that I've not always been the person I should be. It would be easier for me to ignore it or alter it with a little revisionist history so I would not come off as the Bad Guy. But the truth is the truth.

You can't fix what you don't own; you can't let the Holy Spirit work through you if you don't face your flaws. Remembering our transgressions doesn't mean wallowing in guilt; God forgives those who confess their sins. And we need to forgive ourselves. But we also need to do better. And so it was that, after I learned of my classmate's death, I promised to honor the man's memory the only way I knew how: by vowing to never again treat anyone as shabbily as I'd treated him.

COVID FORCED a lot of us to decide who to choose and who to trust. Many evangelicals made it clear they weren't trusting science. In spring 2020, only 54 percent of white evangelicals said they "definitely" or "probably" would take a vaccine.[208] A year later, when COVID numbers were dropping markedly because of the vaccine, that number would bump up only a single percentage point.[209] But 90 percent of atheists wanted the vaccine, polls showed, a rate nearly double that of evangelicals. It created another one of those "what's-wrong-with-this-picture?" moments for me regarding evangelicals and our priorities: why would we—people whose priorities should be caring for others—be so hesitant to do so when atheists—people with no sense of spiritual responsibility whatsoever—seemed to be acting with empathy for others? Why would people think that a vaccine that had *helped* millions would kill them but a virus that had *killed* millions would not?

"If you are a Christian or anybody not yet vaccinated, hit the reset button on whatever information is causing you to be doubtful or fearful, and look at the evidence," said Collins, then director of the National Institutes of Health—and, again, a Christian himself. "The evidence is overwhelming that the vaccine is safe and effective and can save your life."[210]

In Los Angeles, multiple members of John MacArthur's church—a church resisting state COVID restrictions—told The Roys Report that they feared retribution from church leaders for discussing a COVID outbreak.[211] In Louisiana, where state laws at the time restricted gatherings to fifty people or fewer, Pastor Mark Anthony Spell defied the order, and held six services that each drew more than 500 people. He said he did not believe his congregation was at risk of getting COVID.

"It's not a concern," Spell told CBS affiliate WAFB. "The virus, we believe, is politically motivated. We hold our religious rights dear, and we are going to assemble no matter what someone says."[212]

Faith over fear is commendable; negligence masked as faith is dangerous. COVID—on its way to killing more than 5 million people worldwide, including nearly 900,000 Americans of all religious and political affiliations—was apolitical. It only cared about how much we made our bodies available to its microscopic tentacles—not who we voted for or how much faith we had.

I knew firsthand; I'd had what felt like a head cold for nearly seven months and still wasn't tasting or smelling anything. But among those who tested positive, I was among the lucky ones; I had no breathing problems, had no lingering fever, and never wound up in the hospital.

Meanwhile, I assumed the same large-church pastors who resisted wearing masks thought nothing of having armed security teams guarding their flocks each Sunday—and certainly saw to it that the elements for communion were safely presented, right? Was that acting cowardly or simply being smart? Was that a lack of faith or following the biblical command to love one another?

What was different about COVID than, say, a church security system was that Trump had politicized the virus, making it a decision that delineated the Good Guys from the Bad Guys. And The Tribe quickly picked up on his signal.

Instead of seeing COVID for what it was—a non-discriminatory virus happy to infect anyone—many evangelicals let Trump, not the truth, guide their decisions. The bottom line didn't seem to be keeping others safe but staying consistent with the Far Right, some of whose followers wanted to arm teachers to protect students from school shooters but didn't want teachers to wear masks to protect those same students from a deadly virus.

How, I wondered, had it come to this? How had our God-breathed priorities as Christians become so skewed?

18.

Consider the Source

The response to COVID from many evangelicals has me recalling advice from a former professor of mine about who to trust.

The worst thing about being lied to is knowing you are not worth the truth.

—Jean-Paul Sartre

While initially believing that COVID was a serious threat, Trump decided it was in his best interest to not convey that to Americans at large. Beyond some evangelicals, The Left *was* taking COVID seriously—and to agree with The Enemy, he felt, made him look weak.

Trump's father, his niece had pointed out, had always taught Donald to "be tough at all costs" and that "in life, there can be only one winner and everybody else is a loser." In February 2020, Trump admitted to *Washington Post* reporter Bob Woodward that he knew the coronavirus was "more deadly than even your strenuous flu" but that he "wanted to always play it down." ("The president never downplayed the virus," White House Press Secretary Kayleigh McEnany, an evangelical Christian, told the media September 9, 2020:)[213]

Said Trump to the public on February 26, 2020: "This is a flu. It's a little like a regular flu that we have flu shots for."(In spring 2020, the number of deaths from COVID was running twenty times the number of deaths from the last two flu seasons—at their peaks.)[214]

That lie, like nearly all Trump's lies, didn't seem to bother most of the flock; like the political equivalent of the bride's mother standing for the wedding processional and everyone else following suit, what Trump did The Tribe did. Trump's chief apologist, Reed, had accurately called the man "the Pied Piper," and many evangelicals' blind obedience to him affirmed the aptness of that description.

Of all the available evidence suggesting conservatives blindly followed Trump, this, to me, was the most frightening: In March 2020, when it came to information on COVID, Republicans were much more likely to trust Trump (38 percent) than federal public health agencies (27 percent), according to an NBC News/Commonwealth Fund Health Care Poll.[215]

Let's unpack this. Republicans were more likely to trust *their lives*—that's the bottom line for a deadly virus, right?—to a serial liar who clearly had a dog in this fight; if COVID caused the economy to tank, the outcome might hurt Trump's presidential chances in 2020.

More likely to trust Trump than scientists who'd spent their entire adult lives becoming experts on infectious diseases—and had no dog in the fight whatsoever. As such, their priorities would seem to be the lives of Americans, their expertise would be obvious, and their opinions would not be sullied. Instead, Republicans trusted a guy who once posited—in a live press conference—that injecting the body with a disinfectant, like bleach, might thwart COVID.[216]

The sad result of mistrust? By October 2021, people in counties where

Trump won at least 60% of the 2020 vote were dying from COVID at a rate three times higher than in counties where Biden won a similar percentage, according to a *New York Times* analysis of the data.[217]

LONG AGO, a sage journalism mentor—and a fellow Christian—offered me three words of advice that saved me numerous times when, as a reporter, it came to trusting sources or taking criticism from readers: *consider the source.* People with integrity who value others and the truth will say what needs saying even if they have everything to lose and nothing to gain. People short on integrity who don't value others and the truth will say whatever is necessary for them to benefit, *especially* if it costs The Enemy. Trust the former, don't trust the latter.

Once, while I was lap-swimming to get in shape for the PCT, the guy in the next lane asked if he could offer me advice on my technique.

"You bet," I said without hesitation. Why? First, he was trustworthy; he was a well-respected doctor. Second, he had no reason to skew the truth to his political advantage; clearly, he just wanted to help me out. Finally, he'd won a bronze medal in the backstroke in the 1968 Olympics. I took his advice—kick with my feet at surface level and reach farther with my left arm. Within a week, I was getting twenty percent more distance in my hour-long swims.

WHEN TRUMP chose to defy CDC regulations and hold rallies with do-your-own-thing mask "rules," his campaign spokeswoman Courtney Parella said, "Americans have the right to gather under the First Amendment to hear from the President of the United States." That totally missed the point: The issue wasn't, "Do we have the right to gather?" The issue was, "Do we care enough about the citizens we serve to want to keep them from getting sick or dying?"

A Stanford University team analyzed eighteen Trump rallies held between June 20, 2020, and September 22, 2020, all marked by a general neglect for compliance with CDC protocol.

"All told, Trump's gatherings led to more than 30,000 confirmed new COVID-19 infections and at least 700 deaths directly attributed to the virus," the study reported. "Some of those who died were not even in attendance, meaning they were infected by someone who brought the bug home with them."[218]

One way to test whether a movement is truly "of God" is to ask the question: who, in the end, benefits? Is it the "least of these," those who Jesus prioritized, or the powers that be who Jesus often chastised for their self-interest? Granted, Trump was presiding over a nation, not a church, but, remember, from the get-go Trump had been packaged to evangelicals in spiritual gift-wrapping. On the night he was nominated, he was introduced as one "who believes in the name of Jesus Christ." Reed called the Trump/evangelical link a "holy conspiracy." Trump beat the God-and-country drum loudly. But who benefitted most? Beyond voters who wanted a more conservative Supreme Court, only Trump, bringing to mind Romney's 2016 remarks that he was "playing members of the American public for suckers. He gets a free ride to the White House, and all we get is a lousy hat."[219] Or, in this case, COVID.

When The Tribe anchored itself to Trump instead of the Truth, priorities got flipped, facts no longer mattered, and conspiracy theories rushed in to fill the void. Over coffee, an evangelical Christian man told me he and his wife live in "alternate universes." "She's angry because I got vaccinated," he said. "She spends her days glued to Far-Right conspiracy-theory podcasts."

Seventy-seven percent of white evangelical Republicans said the claim that an unelected group of government officials, known as the "Deep State," was working against the interests of the Trump administration is "mostly" or "completely" accurate.[220] White evangelical Protestants—27 percent—were more likely than any other religious group to say it was "mostly" or "completely" accurate to say that Trump "has been secretly fighting a group of child sex traffickers that include prominent Democrats and Hollywood elites."[221]

In South Dakota, Governor Kristi L. Noem, an evangelical, would boast that, regarding COVID, hers was "the only state in America that never ordered a single business or church to close." And in a sad twist of sow-and-reap reality, she would, by April 2021, be governor of a state that would have the second-most coronavirus cases per 100,000 population—and the country's eighth-highest per capita COVID death rate.[222]

Given Trump's almost hypnotic connection with his followers, he could have changed history, saved thousands of lives, and likely won a second term by simply encouraging people to wear masks—and done so himself. Evangelicals would have been far more likely to comply—because many were responding not to Scripture, health experts, or even practicality, but—surveys clearly showed—to *him*.

BY JULY 2020, nearly a thousand Americans a day were dying from COVID, but even death couldn't dissuade some conspiracy theorists from continually going down the rabbit hole. COVID was spread via the 5G wireless communication network and smart phones. The vaccine would implant microscopic chips in people so the government could track them. Hospitals were calling non-COVID deaths COVID deaths to get more money from the government, which led to inflated death rates. All false.

Stearns, the former head of Christian-based World Vision, put it well in a tweet: "Dear Christian, you can peddle in conspiracy theories, or you can believe in absolute, objective, transcendent truth. But you cannot do both. They are completely incompatible. Choose wisely."

Why, I asked myself, were evangelicals—who serve a God who says "I am the way and *the truth* and the life"—so susceptible to bowing to unproven theories? As Paul said in 1 Thessalonians 5:21: "Test everything that is said. Hold on to what is good."

First, I'd realized at least some—again, *some*—had lost their spiritual moorings. Trump and The Tribe called the shots; to some, God was a distant general manager, seldom, if ever, consulted—as Falwell attested with his admission that he didn't look to the Bible in making his political choices. For some, the subconscious go-to question didn't seem to be, "What does the Lord *lead m*e to think?" but, "What does The Tribe *require* me to think?"

Second, Christian nationalism had clouded the consciences of many evangelicals. Remember Ramsey's quote? "This is America—a voluntary thing, you choose what you want to do." On its face, the comment sounded noble, patriotic, even courageous. But it was none of the three. It imbued no sense of community. No sense of responsibility for the greater good. No sense of others. Only an overriding sense of "me" and "us." Whitehead and Perry concluded that "The No. 1 commonality for people believing conspiracy theories is this: their being identified as Christian nationalists."[223]

Third, some evangelicals, like Ramsey, had assumed a sense of entitlement suggesting that to mask-up was somehow bowing to the oppression of government, The Left, The Elite. Jesus says: "Love your neighbor, consider others' needs as well as your own, die to yourself, bless your enemy." Privilege says: "I'll protect *my* rights, which are more important than *your* health."

A 2020 study of 4,245 people in eight countries, including the US, "demonstrate[d] that individuals who hold conspiracy theories about COVID-19 [were] more likely to be motivated by self-concern, even to the detriment of their neighbors. Conspiracy theorists were, in general, more likely to practice hoarding, less likely to endorse vaccination, and less concerned with the welfare of those close to them."[224]

Fourth, many evangelicals were being fed fear daily by right-wing radio and TV folks who fueled conspiracy theories to boost ratings and make them more money. No fear, no followers.

Finally, a lot of evangelicals didn't seem willing to expose themselves to any "outside ideas" that challenged their own.

That's precisely why I was purposely talking to others—including, shortly after the election, my own pastor: to discern what was true.

"I just feel so discombobulated," I said, "like all I've been taught as a Christian suddenly doesn't really matter."

He listened. He encouraged me. And as I heard about his struggling to keep the church afloat—some parishioners felt the mask requirements too stringent, others not stringent enough—I was reminded how difficult his already-tough job had gotten.

Amid my own challenges—losing a friend, losing a mother, and contracting COVID—I had, in some ways, lost sight of the pain of others. And plenty of sold-out-to-Jesus pastors, mine among them, were feeling plenty of it.

When we listen, we learn and consider the needs of others. When we don't, we stay tethered to ourselves in fear and defiance. As David French said: "In the arena of law and culture, all too many Christians are adopting a posture that declares 'Don't tell me what to do' far more than it asks, 'How can I serve you?'"[225]

A reader responded to French with this:

> I'm a conservative … who is on staff (part-time) at a predominately white evangelical church. I'm mentally and spiritually exhausted after … Trump and one year of a pandemic.
>
> I'm tired of explaining to the leadership why I won't put my toddler in the nursery. I'm tired of asking people to wear their masks when they talk to me or explaining why I reject their hugs or handshakes. I'm tired of patiently explaining why I don't support an immoral, incompetent, and immature man (what I'm really defending is my allegiance to Christ—if I don't support Trump my salvation is in question).
>
> I'm not giving up on the church, but I am tired of feeling like an outcast at the place where I should feel at home. It's an odd thing to be so disconnected from the "reality" of your friends and family yet be so close in proximity.[226]

Responded French:

> If you'd told me five years ago that politically conservative Christians would be one of the American populations most resistant to basic public health measures in the worst pandemic in a century, I would have accused you of anti-Christian bigotry. Yet here we are.[227]

And the man's reply:

> I would have said the same thing five years ago. These are the same people who brought me food when I was sick or comforted me through painful times. The disconnect between their current and past behavior is disorienting.[228]

Reading that exchange was discouraging to me but weirdly affirming. It suggested I wasn't alone in my feeling of disconnectedness. What differentiated my situation from the responder to French was that I never felt snubbed by friends or church members.

Because of COVID, Sally and I rarely saw people from our church, and when we did, we never talked politics; I hunkered down, edited books for clients, and continued to write the marriage-coaching curriculum.

No, my sense that I was somehow betraying The Tribe came from evangelical leaders who labeled conservatives not supporting Trump as "almost demonic" (Graham),[229] "absolutely spineless morons" (Jeffress),[230] "human scum" (Stephanie Grisham, Trump's former press secretary),[231] and "scumbags" who are "betraying" God and country (Illinois evangelical pastor Chris McDonald) [232]

ON MY HIKES, I had begun listening to a few podcasts that dared to drill into issues such as race, Christian nationalism, and immigration, including Bob Roberts' "Bold Love," Veggie Tales founder Phil Vischer's "Holy Post," and French's "The Dispatch" podcast. I was like a lake with a handful of inlet streams but no outlet, taking in information but not offering anybody thoughts of my own.

But after Dobson planted a hazy conspiracy theory—the threat of a civil war instigated by Democrats—to urge voters to back Trump in 2020, I couldn't stay silent on social media anymore. Though I had dutifully laid low on Facebook for four years, on Twitter I began retweeting, with comments of my own, occasional posts that galled my Christian soul; twelve such retweets, it would turn out, before the November 2020 election.

The first was posted on the day in June 2020, Trump had defied protestors with a Bible in his hand after people were wringing their hands over the post-George-Floyd-death riots.

> Easy to decry the looting; harder to read a book and better understand the roots of anger among blacks. Nothing good comes easy.

On August 28, 2020, a Texas pastor, Jack Graham, tweeted about pastors who'd attended an event at the invitation of Trump in Washington, D.C., and been heckled by protesters afterward.

> About 150 faith leaders were invited to the President's speech and

afterwords [sic] we were confronted by Marxist, leftists, thugs ... filthy blasphemous infidels. We saw with our own eyes and up close the evil of the anarchists and anti-Christ lawlessness. The insanity has to stop.

My response:

> And as a fellow believer I ask: given Jesus's propensity to care for the disenfranchised, are you equally angered by the deaths of young black men? Does that insanity, too, need to stop? Or is it just when [white] pastors are screamed at and flipped-off?

My retweets, of course, were like shooting spit wads at an oncoming tank. With a relatively small Twitter following at the time—1,500 people—I rarely got much response; in fact, I couldn't remember a time when my opinions triggered even a single ongoing discussion. But it felt good to finally say how I felt.

Because, as French so succinctly put it, "here we are."

My Hope for the Future

That we might see ourselves as victors, not victims

IN THE "Ted Lasso" TV series, Ted, a football-turned-soccer coach in England, goes to see the team therapist to help him deal with pain from his past. After he hesitates to open up about his "father wound"—the man took his life when Ted was a boy—the therapist tells him, "The truth will set you free, but first it will piss you off."

It's a raw comment, to be sure, in what can be a raw show, but embodies truth that we evangelicals should heed: instead of staying comfortably ignorant of ourselves, we need the courage to look in the mirror, even when—*especially* when—it's uncomfortable. Or makes us angry.

Far-right leaders have foisted a political dynamic on evangelicals that is good for the party but bad for our witness: the idea that, as evangelicals, we are victims. That's not Bible-based, that's Tribe-based. Over decades of time, the Moral Majority, Rush Limbaugh, and Fox News loaded the bases with "we're oppressed" rhetoric and Trump, as the cleanup hitter, brought everybody home with a grand slam. Only it was a false home. One that might satisfy us but works against a god whose Word suggests we're to prioritize justice for others over justice for ourselves.

"No sin is worse than the sin of self-pity," wrote Oswald

Chambers, "because it obliterates God and puts self-interest upon the throne. It opens our mouths to spit out murmurings and our lives become craving spiritual sponges; there is nothing lovely or generous about them."[1]

Going forward, Christians need to choose self-examination over self-pity, introspection of ourselves over bitterness toward others.

"The real question is not whether evangelicals experience an interplay between theology and culture (we all do); rather, it is whether evangelicals are willing to be self-critical enough to recognize that there may be significant cultural blind-spots that are hindering the advancement of the Gospel itself," wrote Sean Michael Lucas, senior pastor of Independent Presbyterian Church in Memphis.[2]

We can count on being persecuted regardless of how righteous or unrighteous we act; Jesus said so himself. But He was maligned for his compassion, love, association with sinners, and rebuking the powerful and self-righteous. Today, evangelicals are often chastised for being intolerant, arrogant, mean, and condemning.

Two different things. Many of today's Christians aren't being maligned because they emulate Jesus, but because they *don't*. Today, many evangelicals believe they face more discrimination than African Americans or Muslims, in large part because The Tribe teaches a sense of victimhood that the Bible does not. It's about grievances, not grace.

"If the world rejects us because of Christ and him crucified, so much the worse for the world," wrote Russell Moore. "If the world rejects us because they think Christ is just a mascot for what we would already be supporting or doing if Jesus were still dead, God have mercy on us."[3]

As children of God, we were uniquely created for His glory. We've been granted eternal life. We are forgiven of our sins.

And God has promised to be with us every step of the way. So, why, then, do so many evangelicals live as if we are oppressed? Because it fits the far-right narrative that's been spoon-fed them since the Moral Majority in 1979; victimhood justifies our anger.

In the parable of the Good Samaritan (Luke 10:25-37), a Levite and a priest walk by a man on the side of the road who's been beaten. The two share Jesus's religion and ethnicity but they don't stop to help. However, the Samaritan, a religious and ethnic outsider, does. He helps the man. Takes a risk. "Go and do likewise," said Jesus.

The Good Samaritan defied The Tribe to, instead, be "the hands and feet of God."

"The teaching of the Sermon on the Mount is not—Do your duty, but—Do what is *not* your duty," wrote Chambers. [Italics mine.] "It is not your duty to go the second mile, to turn the other cheek, but Jesus says if we are His disciples we shall always do these things ... Every time I insist upon my right, I hurt the Son of God, whereas I can prevent Jesus from being hurt if I take the blow myself ... Never look for the right in the other man, but never cease to be right yourself ... We are always looking for justice; the teaching of the Sermon on the Mount is—Never look for justice, but never cease to give it."

19.

Line in the Sand

I long for a world of Traverse-City grace, but Trump remains defiant. I can't taste or smell a thing, but I can sense danger.

Much sheer effort goes into avoiding truth: left to itself, it sweeps in like the tide.

—Fay Weldon, *The Rules of Life*

Salad, fish, cheese, orange juice. It didn't matter what I ate or drank, it all tasted the same: like nothing. Deodorant, sweat, candles, ocean breezes. It didn't matter what I took a whiff of, it all smelled the same: like nothing.

Day after day. Week after week. Not tasting or smelling anything because of COVID was getting old.

I had no idea how I'd gotten the virus in late October 2020; I got eye rolls because I nearly always wore a mask. In the two weeks prior to feeling my first symptom, my only trips beyond to the grocery store were two golf outings—an activity deemed safe by the state of Oregon's Department of Health. None of the guys I played golf with tested positive, so it wasn't from them. In short, I was clueless where I'd gotten "tagged."

Because Sally tested negative, we needed to try to keep it that way. County health officials recommended I quarantine for fourteen days. We basically divided the house in two; I got my office, the main bathroom, and a TV in our living room. Sally got everything else. When I was through with my fourteen-day quarantine, she served her sentence. Crazy times, but she never got COVID.

Once clear, I kept interviewing folks in parking lots: people from church, Mukhtar and Hayfa, a Catholic friend who told me he honestly didn't believe "our country could take another four years with Trump in the White House," people who believed Trump was our country's only hope, and a close evangelical friend who, over a cheeseburger, cautioned me that swapping out conservatism for liberalism was false security—was still trusting in a man-made "ism" instead of the things of God.

"In the end," he said, "neither man-made party is going to cut it. But Jesus isn't man-made."

ON SEPTEMBER 21, in his last debate with Biden, Trump tipped his hand regarding how he might react should he lose the November 3, 2020, election. Moderator Chris Wallace asked Trump if he would, in such a case, condemn white supremacists and tell them to refrain from violence. Trump refused to answer. Instead, he referenced the Proud Boys, a far-right, neo-fascist, and exclusively white male organization that promotes political violence.

"Proud Boys, stand back and stand by," he said as if speaking directly to them, not the nation. "I'll tell you what, somebody's got to do something about Antifa and The Left."

Did the president of the United States just say what I thought he'd said?

It sounded like a veiled threat of violence—against the citizens he had vowed, by oath, to protect. Wallace, I think, wondered the same, which is why he gave Trump a second chance to back down what clearly sounded like "fighting words." He asked Trump if he would "urge his supporters to stay calm" and "pledge tonight that you will not declare victory until the election has been independently certified."

Trump wouldn't do so, *couldn't* do so, not in the framework of his "I-must-win-at-all-cost" mindset. Instead, he called on his followers to "watch very carefully" because "bad things" were already happening at the polls, the inference being that the fix was already in. In other words, depending on the outcome, independently certified election results weren't going to be good enough for Donald Trump.

Lots of smoke, no fire. Lots of suggestions that the election was rigged; no actual evidence to back up the claim. That had always been the Trump way: strike fear in the hearts of his followers with bold, if unsubstantiated, accusations. And obscure the truth with worrisome—and fabricated—"they're-out-to-get-us" rhetoric. "If you tell a lie big enough and keep repeating it," said Hitler propogandist Joseph Goebbels, "people will eventually come to believe it."[233]

For any other candidate in US history, Wallace's questions would have been softball pitches prompting automatic responses; Trump was simply being asked if he would affirm baseline principles of American democracy. But assuaging the American public had never been Trump's style; inciting it *had*. How else could you explain the countless times interviewers had given him chances to own something, apologize, and move on—and he'd chosen instead to double down? He could not accept defeat.

"The president," wrote Zack Beauchamp of *Vox*, "seems to be actively stoking violent conflict surrounding American elections."[234]

I began getting concerned.

IN HALF A CENTURY of sermons I'd heard, pastors had often reminded me that how we react to the small stuff is a predictor of how we'll react to the big stuff; if we cheated on our mileage-expense form at work, we'd be more likely to cheat on our spouses. For that reason, I read

Rick Reilly's *Commander in Cheat,* a book about how Trump the golfer cheated often, onerously, and indiscriminately. [235]

"He kicks the ball out of the rough so many times the caddies call him Pelé," wrote Reilly.[236]

This, by the way, is not par for the course with golfers I know. I've had friends dutifully take double-digit scores—in a simple two-man round of golf with nothing on the line; I'm proud, as a believer, and ashamed, as a golfer, to say I've done the same.

Trump, meanwhile, said he won club championships in which he didn't even play. After errant drives, he'd drive ahead with his cart—like he was doing now with the election, getting ahead of the game with hints of fraud—and play his opponent's ball because his own was in the woods. All well documented. All so he could win. Laughable on one hand, but worrisome if he carried the same kind of attitude—*I will stop at nothing to win*—to a national election.[237]

Whenever Trump even sensed he might lose, he began building a narrative to avoid doing so. He had done so after the Iowa Caucus in February 2016 when he charged winner Ted Cruz with fraud.[238] And he had done it eight months later, after a debate with Hillary Clinton in which he refused to confirm that he'd accept the outcome of the election. "I will totally accept the results of this great historical presidential election," he said. "If I win."

That's not leadership, not democracy, not acquiescing to the Constitution upon which our country rests and to which a president gives an oath to uphold; that's cowardice. Betrayal to a pledge. Greed shoving aside responsibility.

A cluster of GOP congressmen, in the days before their backbones would turn to Jell-O, condemned Trump for such obstinance. "If he loses," Sen. Lindsey Graham, R-SC, told the media during the 2016 primaries, "it will not be because the system is 'rigged' but because he failed as a candidate."[239]

"Peaceful transfer of power & acceptance of election results is fundamental to our democracy & Constitution," tweeted another Republican, Rep. Carlos Curbelo, R-Fla. "This cannot be undermined ever."[240]

But Trump would try.

THE DAY BEFORE the November 3 election, I may have been one of the few people on the planet to see the irony in Trump holding his final rally in Traverse City, Michigan, a town whose name triggers in me Christ-based forgiveness at its best. In his 1997 book, *What's So Amazing About Grace?* Philip Yancey shares a story, based in Traverse City, about a "prodigal daughter" who runs away from home to the big city, seeking her fortune. Years later, leveled by the cold world of prostitution, she decides to return home.[241]

She's lost, lonely, empty. Before hopping on the bus, she calls her parents three times. No answer. She leaves a message that she'll be home the next night at midnight, but gets on the bus filled with the fear of further rejection, particularly from her father.

The bus arrives in Traverse City on time—and, as she feared, nobody is outside the terminal this late. But …

> … there, in the concrete-walls-and-plastic-chairs bus terminal in Traverse City, Michigan, stands a group of forty brothers and sisters and great-aunts and uncles and cousins and a grandmother and a great-grandmother to boot. They're all wearing goofy party hats and blowing noise-makers, and taped across the entire wall of the terminal is a computer-generated banner that reads "Welcome home!"
>
> Out of the crowd of well-wishers breaks her Dad. She stares out through the tears quivering in her eyes like hot mercury and begins the memorized speech, "Dad I'm sorry. I know …"
>
> He interrupts her. "Hush, child. We've got no time for that. No time for apologies. You'll be late for the party. A banquet's waiting for you at home."[242]

THAT NIGHT, as results were coming in, I re-read this modern-day version of the Prodigal Son story that's found in Luke 15:11-32. As always, it touched me deeply. Afterward, I felt wistful for a time when Christians were known for that kind of grace. I knew it was still out there, sprinkled in the Traverse Cities across the country, Christians showing God's grace in the quiet beyond the cacophony of "Build the Wall!" rallies, "Go Home!" t-shirts, and cat fights on Facebook.

But it had come to this: When we as evangelicals should have been offering the world the grace of Traverse City, many were determined to return a man to the White House who didn't understand grace in the least. What kind of man, without cause, fires the head of the FBI without telling him, then insists the fired director pay for his flight home from government business in LA? A man devoid of grace. The man America elected to the most honored position in the land.

"Be careful of the friends you make," I'd heard pastors preach. "Either you will make them more like you or they will make you more like them." As a friend to evangelicals, Trump hadn't changed a bit; but as a friend to Trump, plenty of evangelicals seemed to have—at least among the "spotlight" crowd. They were rougher and tougher; less grace-filled, more greedy; less Christ-like, and—how else can it be said?—more Trump-like.

Said G.K. Beale in *We Become What We Worship*, "We resemble what we revere, either for ruin or restoration."[243]

A FEW DAYS after the election, I was relieved to learn Joe Biden and Kamala Harris had been declared the winners. Frankly, my reaction had little to do with my having voted for that ticket—or, for that matter, with politics per se.

I was relieved because America would soon have a leader who, if nothing else, saw beyond himself, listened to others, respected the truth, and governed with at least a glint of grace. I'd read Harris's biography and admired her nowhere-to-somewhere climb. But mine was admittedly a defensive vote—less *for* Biden, whose health worried me, than *against* Trump. I simply believed the Democrats had a better chance to stabilize a country that had endured a chaotic regime threatening to get worse.

"It's like Biden is this 'trusted grandfather' figure," said one of my few evangelical friends—a guy from Houston—who'd voted for him. "For now, we just need someone with some common sense who can get us back on track with some sense of normalcy."

Still, I'd read enough history to know what would happen now: The Left, suddenly granted cart-blanch power, would overreach. Indeed, it began canceling The Right; some Trump supporters had their social media accounts shut down, were blackballed for jobs, and were ridiculed mercilessly on social media. It was just another indication that we're naïve to place our trust in people, regardless of their political affiliations.

"One problem with democracy as it plays in our country is that the majority rules so hard," wrote novelist Barbara Kingsolver in *Small Wonder*. "We seem bent on dividing all things into a contest of Win and Lose, and declaring the losers are *losers*. Nearly half of us are routinely asked to disappear while the slim majority works its will. But the playing field is the planet earth, and I for one have no place else to go."[244]

Kingsolver, a Democrat, wrote this soon after George W. Bush had become president in 2001, but her wisdom works both ways—and *now* as well as *then*. Still, I didn't believe for a nanosecond that the Far Right was going to slink off to a corner of that "planet earth," lick its wounds, and stay silent. It would fight to grab back that power. And the game would go on—a game, frankly, that would never have a winner.

As I've said before, from my evangelical perspective, the core problem was never Trump per se, but a latent, pride-fueled "Christians-first" attitude that he excused, encouraged, and emboldened among evangelicals. So, no, while I thought the Democrats' victory would stabilize a government that was becoming unhinged, I expected Biden would make mistakes—and he did, our military's bloody withdraw from Afghanistan in August 2021 foremost among them.

I also thought the Republican loss had the potential to make far-right evangelicals retreat deeper into their fog of skewed vision regarding what Scripture commands us to be about: love, not fear; others, not self; Jesus, not idols.

For now, I breathed a sigh of relief, forgetting a lesson I should have learned long ago.

Never underestimate Donald Trump.

20.

Denial

**As millions of Republicans refuse to
accept the results of a fair election, I find hope
in a strange place: the eyes of two Muslims.**

Truth ... is the first casualty of tyranny.

—Barbara Grizzuti Harrison

To few people's surprise, Trump was not conceding the election. He fired tweets as if from a machine gun—"fraudulent," "rigged," "stolen." In Colorado, a church posted a sign: "Trump won/Dems cheated. Keep the faith and brace yourself." In Tennessee, a pro-Trump pastor in front of his church laughed with eerie sarcasm, "Biden won! Biden won! Biden won!" he repeated like a pull-string doll.

Trump, like a king whose kingdom was crumbling, leaned on his troops to defend him. Had his priority truly been *America*, he would have conceded with the dignity of fellow Republican McCain, who in his ten-minute concession speech to Obama in 2008 not only congratulated and commended the victor, but when his backers started booing the President-elect, shook his head to quell the uproar. "Please," he said, "I urge all Americans who supported me to join me in not just congratulating him but offering our next president our goodwill and earnest effort to find ways to come together ... Whatever our differences, we are fellow Americans."[245] In 2016, Hillary Clinton congratulated Trump, offering to "work with him on behalf of our country. I hope that he will be a successful president for all Americans."[246]

Alas, if Trump had any such "better angels" to call on, he was keeping them grounded in the halo hanger. Instead, in the wake of Biden being confirmed the winner on November 7, 2020, Trump deployed a fleet of attorneys to file more than sixty lawsuits.[247] He mounted a campaign to pressure Republican governors, secretaries of state, and Republican-controlled state legislatures to nullify results by replacing slates of Biden electors with those declared to Trump, or manufacturing evidence of fraud.[248] He verbally attacked Senate Majority Leader Mitch McConnell for congratulating Biden and Harris on their victory, arguing that he, Trump, couldn't have lost because, as he tweeted, he got "75,000,000 VOTES, a record for a sitting President (by a lot)." And, in a brazen act of political coercion, he demanded that Georgia Secretary of State Brad Raffensperger, a Republican, find him "11,780 votes," saying it was "not possible" that he lost to Biden in that state.[249] (Three recounts suggested otherwise.)[250]

Democracies don't run like this. They try things in court, based on *evidence*. They run police, FBI, or Department of Justice investigations, based on *evidence*. In terms of the environment, they make conclusions, based on scientific *evidence*. But when you build your life on winning, as Trump did, evidence couldn't get in the way of your finding a way to prevail; if you can claim you won a golf tournament in which you didn't even play, you're not about to concede a presidential election despite getting 74 fewer electoral-college votes than the winner.

On the day after the election, Trump's spiritual advisor, Paula White, appeared in a Facebook live stream in which she conducted a prayer service to secure Trump's reelection, repeatedly calling on "angelic reinforcement" from angels out of Africa and South America as well as "an abundance of rain."[251]

Finally, I thought, *the time has come.* This was crazy. This was still America, where the common good embodied in our Constitution would rise above the pettiness of this political soap opera, right? Trump's tweets had become the stuff of a ten-year-old crying "foul" when his Monopoly race car had been beaten by the top hat. Surely his followers would finally say "enough." Surely, all but the most loyal passengers on the Trump train would finally get off at this stop, right?

Wrong. Like Trump when cornered with defeat, many Trump backers doubled down. Despite no substantial evidence to support their stances, 72 percent of Republicans surveyed on December 22, 2020 said they believed it "very likely" that the Democrats had "stolen the election."[252] This despite virtually every Trump lawsuit having been denied, dismissed, settled, or withdrawn—some by Trump-appointed Republican judges. Despite every state's chief election official, in many cases Republicans, certifying the victory for Biden-Harris. And despite the Trump-appointed Attorney General William Barr saying there was "no evidence" of fraud. But Trump's followers sided with him, not the evidence.

Why, amid the lies, do people cling so strongly to bully leaders like Trump? In *Christianity Today's* exceptional podcast series, "The Rise and Fall of Mars Hill," *CT* offered an answer to how blindly Indiana basketball fans clung to Coach Bobby Knight, who threw chairs, choked a player, embarrassed the university with snarky comments to the media, but won lots of basketball games. *CT's* series was on Mark Driscoll, pastor of a Mars Hill church in Seattle whose meteoric rise imploded when Driscoll was drummed out of leadership after he seemed to have gotten bigger than the church.

"Outside observers will often ask why insiders don't stand up to abusive leaders and bullies—and the answer is abusers are almost never standing on their own," said *CT*. "Knight acted with impunity not simply because he was tolerated by the university but because they were invested in his status as a legend and icon for their own brand."[253]

This, I had come to believe, was a big part of the staying power Trump had with evangelicals: What he did for "the brand" justified any and all bully methods he used to fortify that brand. Never mind that this approach clashed with Scripture; the end justified the means.

"An organization becomes so identified with an individual that they are determined to protect and insulate them, no matter what the cost," said *CT's* Mike Cosper. "Because the benefit of that protection, whether it's about money or image or power, our mission is deemed to be more important than the negative effect it might have on other people."[254]

IN THE DAYS after the election, Trump tweeted that "this was the most corrupt election in the history of our Country." The Cybersecurity and Infrastructure Security Agency, directed by a Trump appointee, said the election was "the most secure in American history ... there is no evidence that any voting system deleted or lost votes, changed votes, or was in any way compromised."[255] Trump's response? He fired the agency's director, Christopher Krebs, for defending the integrity of the election.[256]

Not all evangelicals cried foul. When picking up some firewood from farmers north of Eugene, I listened as an evangelical couple I knew explained why they'd voted for Trump. They liked his willingness to defend conservatives like them who, they felt, had been ignored or attacked during the Obama years. Liked his patriotism theme. And liked his concern for the borders.

"But we're not like some of these people who thought he was divinely appointed by God," the woman said. "And now that Biden is president I can say, 'He's my president,' even though I didn't vote for him."

She and her husband were exceptions, not the rule. Everywhere, evangelicals bristled with a sense of indignation, as if it were noble and patriotic to dispute the results of a free and fair election. Wrote a high school classmate of mine, an evangelical, on Facebook: "I ... *know* the vote count was manipulated by outside forces." [Italics mine.] Or, like many, had she so desperately wanted Trump to win that she had simply *convinced herself that she knew*?" After all, if this was purely about electoral justice, not "our guy winning," would she have been just as certain the outcome had been rigged had Trump won by the same margin and Biden been the one claiming fraud—despite presenting no evidence to support such a claim? And did she find it odd that Trump only challenged states in which he'd lost?

Let's be honest, this wasn't about electoral justice—what was true and fair and right—but about the home team winning. Facts didn't matter; Trump mattered. Forget "consider-the-source" thinking. In their unwillingness to connect the dots regarding objective rulings from courts to election officials to the attorney general, many evangelicals were willing to trust the only player in this game who had a long history of *unabashed untrustworthiness*: Trump. He was their Bobby Knight, a guy who bettered the brand.

Forget the One who said "the truth shall set you free." "When [Trump] says this election was rigged or stolen, I tend to believe him," tweeted Franklin Graham.

As with COVID information, only Trump could be trusted. The more objective election experts, the courts, the people with firsthand information—and no reason to be biased—could *not* be trusted. Hard as it was to accept, I had determined that among many of Trump's evangelical loyalists, their love for the man was simply unconditional.

"When people feel naked and alone, they revert to tribe," wrote David Brooks, a conservative *New York Times* columnist. "Their radius of trust shrinks, and they only trust their own kind. Donald Trump is the great emblem of an age of distrust—a man unable to love, unable to trust. When many Americans see Trump's distrust, they see a man who looks at the world as they do."[257]

In the final results, Biden received 81.3 million votes to Trump's 74.2 million, a 51.3-percent-to-46.8-percent victory and a 306-232 win in the bottom-line Electoral College. But the evangelical elite was having nothing to do with such results.

The Family Research Council's Perkins, the guy who'd dismissed the turn-the-other-cheek command of Jesus, signed a letter in December 2020 urging state legislatures to override the election results and to appoint their own electors, claiming, with no evidence whatsoever,

"There is *no doubt* President Donald J. Trump is the *lawful winner* of the presidential election. [Italics mine.] Joe Biden is not president-elect." (It was like a losing football coach asking fans, after a 32-23 defeat, to harass the officials until they changed the outcome.)[258]

A week before the Electoral College convened, Pat Robertson had told viewers of his *700 Club*—yeah, the one I'd been on—that the results would be overturned and Trump would prevail. "We must declare that God Almighty is not going to let this great nation of ours be taken over by fraud … the Lord Himself will intervene before this country turns into something socialist."[259] (But, wait, what about all that Romans 13:1 stuff about there being "no authority except that which God has established?" Was Robertson suggesting God got it wrong, that His authority had a Republican-only clause to it?)

Newly elected Congresswoman Marjorie Taylor Greene of Georgia, an evangelical Christian, appeared at a rally in a "stop the steal" mask, saying the state's "election should be decertified!" (Asked by a reporter if that also applied to *her* election on the same ballot, in which she'd won by a landslide, she said, "We're just talking about the President's race.")

Secretary of State Mike Pompeo, an evangelical Christian, refused to acknowledge President-elect Biden's victory, declaring on November 9 that "there will be a smooth transition to a second Trump administration." (Countries whose governments attempt to override certified election results are totalitarian states run by fascist governments. That's not America.)

Author Eric Metaxas, an evangelical talk-show host, Harvard grad, and author of a splendid book on Dietrich Bonhoeffer, *boinged* like a Jack-in-the-Box after the election. In an interview with fellow conservative Charlie Kirk, he said, "It's like stealing the heart and soul of America. It's like holding a rusty knife to the throat of Lady Liberty." (No, it's like in 2016 when Trump won because he got more Electoral College votes than Clinton and like in 2020 when Biden got more such votes than Trump.)

"This is evil," Metaxas said. "It's like somebody has been raped or murdered—this is like that times a thousand."[260] (No, murder and rape *are* evil. This was a fairly decided election. Big difference.)

The "stolen election" reaction of Metaxas and other evangelicals drew me back to a book called *The Case for Christ* by Lee Strobel. A former atheist and former *Chicago Tribune* reporter, Strobel was a Yale Law School grad with whom I'd had lunch while in Chicago on a book tour. What impressed me about the book was this: he laid out a case, step by step, for why he believed Christ was who He said he was. He didn't base his beliefs on "people who have heard from God" or conspiracy theories or on what was politically convenient or on what he hoped might be true. He based his case on evidence, which, in the new evangelical world order, no longer mattered to many.

Given Metaxas's Harvard background, his suggestion that to defend your party you can simply "wave off" the judicial system, ignore substantiated facts, and bully forward with your own set of rules was essentially a buttoned-down form of anarchy. That he could promote this as an avowed Christian was doubly troubling. I may be convinced that red lights aren't intended for me—and that the tools in my neighbors' garage *are*—but that doesn't mean it's OK to ignore traffic signals or steal Brad's reciprocating saw.

Metaxas's ignore-the-facts thinking brought to mind a phone interview I'd done with a leader of the Rajneeshpuram commune when I was Sunday editor of *The Bulletin* in Bend, Oregon, in 1982.[261] I can't remember the particular issue I'd asked her about, but Ma Anand Sheela, secretary to Rajneesh commune founder Bhagwan Shree Rajneesh, had offered me an answer that was just the opposite of what she'd said the previous week.

"That," I told her, "sounds like a contradiction to what you said earlier."

"But, Bob," she said with a laugh. "Life itself is a contradiction!"

The unspoken bridge on which she built her stance was as indefensible as it was flimsy: if truth can be rationalized away, if "right" and "wrong" no longer matter, then, hey, anything goes; it's open season on lawlessness.

Evangelical churches had been teaching against such situational ethics as long as I'd been attending them. I remembered a Sunday school class in Bend on the subject, how as Christians we needed to stand firm on God's truth instead of "bowing to moral relativism." Now, that's exactly what was happening among the evangelical power bloc. Taking a cue from Trump, people such as Metaxas were walking, talking contradictions of the very faith they promoted.

I wasn't only bothered by such hypocrisy, I was worried about where such thinking could lead; when our loyalties ignore basic truths and we bow to the feet of tribalism, we are at the whim of the masses, not the Master. As I was writing this book, I was finishing another, *Saving My Enemy,* about an American soldier and German soldier who tried to kill each other in World War II and yet became close friends late in life. I was stunned at how, in the late 1930s, the German people remained loyal to Hitler, even after he orchestrated a raid on the Jews (*Kristallnacht*) in 1938—in essence, began killing his own people. But watching a pro-Hitler parade, one member of Hitler Youth echoed Metaxas's overboard passion when he said, "I longed to hurl myself into this current. I wanted to belong to these people for whom it was a matter of life and death."[262]

Ultimately, that kind of blind obedience can lead to all sorts of danger, including violence. In the case of Rajneeshpuram, what was founded as a feel-good hippy commune morphed into a cultish band of red-clad bullies whose aim ultimately swung from enlightenment of the masses to power for the few. And those who got in the way of "the movement" became enemies who had to be dealt with, often harshly.

Soon, choppers were flying above the commune with machine gunners crouched in their open bays. Oregon's state attorney general, the late David Frohnmayer—one of the most honorable, ethical, and gracious leaders I've known—had been among those placed on their hit list. And the Rajneeshees had contaminated a salad bar in The Dalles to cut down on the number of voters who could potentially work against the commune's best interests.[263]

Now, nearly forty years later, Metaxas and others were echoing sentiments that were eerily similar: "We need to fight to the death, to the last drop of blood, because it's worth it," he said.[264]

Rod Dreher—an evangelical, a writer for *The American Conservative,* and a friend of the man—was incredulous with how unwilling Metaxas was to face reality.

> There is no way around it, and it grieves me to say it: Eric Metaxas is calling for violent bloodshed to defend Donald Trump's presidency, and he doesn't care that Trump's lawyers have not been able to prove in court that Trump had the election stolen from him. ... he is willing to kill or be killed for a political cause *for which there is not enough evidence to advance a court case, even among friendly judges.*
>
> This is fanaticism. But according to Eric, to disagree with him is to be under the sway of the Devil.[265]

I wouldn't last a single round in a political argument with either man; out of my league, both. And, as I said, I'd never thought politics was "the answer." But in fall 2016 I had told my letter-writing friend Marley that evangelicals' zeal for Trump sometimes came with a hidden suggestion that, as believers, we had to take things into our own hands because God couldn't handle it if Trump lost. "Christians are panicking about America (see 'idol worship') instead of trusting the God of the universe."

True to form, Graham, Perkins, Robertson, Metaxas—most of the upper-echelon evangelical leaders—were not running *from* Trump to God, but from God *to* Trump, as if Dobson's "end-of-western-civilization" panic was justified.

AT THANKSGIVING 2020, Sally and I bowed our heads and thanked God for our blessings—at a dining-room table around which were the smiling, un-masked faces of our two sons, two daughters-in-law, and five grandchildren. Only not in person; instead, life-sized photographs of their heads, affixed to poster boards and taped, on the back, to unopened pop cans to prop them up. It was our way of feeling the warmth of family and keeping COVID-safe.

We hated not gathering in person, particularly because this was our first Thanksgiving without my mother and because our kids lived only ten minutes away. But I still had COVID and the vaccine was still months away from release.

We've had better Thanksgivings. Not having the kids, grandkids, and Mom at our table diluted the experience. So did my inability to taste or smell my turkey and gravy, though it was satisfyingly hot and well-textured.

That night, I had just reminded myself that "this too shall pass" when I noticed, in the darkness from my office window, a car pull up in front and two people get outside. I had no clue who they were but the silhouettes in the streetlight didn't look familiar. When I stepped onto the porch, I realized these strangers in the dark were actually friends: Mukhtar and Hayfa.

I had gotten to know them a bit over coffee. Both had been born in America. He was thirty-five and Hayfa thirty-four. Muslims, they had been physicians at a medical center in Tunisia who had come to America—Hayfa had relatives in Eugene—to learn English so they could get their medical licenses here. Not an easy undertaking. She studied much of the day. He delivered pizzas and pumped gas, then studied whenever he could.

A week after we'd had them over for Thanksgiving the year before, there'd been a knock at the door. Mukhtar had come bearing cookies that Hayfa had baked for us, with a "Merry Christmas" card that said:

> Family isn't always blood. It's the people in your life who want you in theirs; the ones who accept you for who you are. The ones who would do anything to see you smile & who LOVE YOU no matter what.

On the card was a handwritten note:

> Thank you for the [$123] present and the moment that you and your grandchildren gave to me. I felt in my hometown and [with my own] family.
> —Mukhtar (Domino's pizza guy).

Now, eleven months later, the two were back—with more cookies. I had never seen Hayfa's full face because, per Muslim custom, she covered it. And with his COVID mask, Mukhtar's face, too, was hidden. But even in the darkness, their eyes danced with the joy of human connection.

Among Whitehead and Perry's findings regarding evangelicals was that "So intense is [the] fear of Muslims that we found it was the third strongest predictor of voting for Donald Trump behind only 'Republican affiliation' and 'identification with political conservatism.'"[266]

This episode in my front yard didn't stoke any such fear in me. The cookies were not laced with poison and the note did not threaten our lives. "To say thank you again," it said, "for last Thanksgiving."

After they left, I slowly shook my head in wonder and, for the first time in a while, felt a little hope for the world.

My Hope for the Future

That we might stop bowing to celebrity 'leaders'

WHEN A FEBRUARY 2021 snow and ice storm left millions of Texans without power, Sen. Ted Cruz, R-Texas, an evangelical, booked a flight to Cancun—during a pandemic—to join his family on vacation. Meanwhile, Shaza Alshaara, a Syrian refugee, cooked 600 meals—two straight days in the kitchen—for those who were sheltered in the Dallas Convention Center.[1]

But who do we, as evangelicals, value more?

A month after Cruz's vacation, his backers—most undoubtedly evangelicals—lavished him with $5.3 million in donations for first-quarter 2021. Meanwhile, two-thirds of white evangelicals do not believe the US should accept refugees such as Shaza Alshaara.

"This is incredible," said Bob Roberts Jr., an evangelical pastor in Texas with a heart for refugees. "We've built such false caricatures of refugees and immigrants to our own detriment."

We've bought into a "celebrity culture" that encourages us to place unwarranted value on people because of position, power, wealth, and prestige, not because of their spiritual integrity and character. Why? Because politics, not faith, has become the bottom line for too many Christians. How else can you explain that, with Trump in power, those white Americans identifying as evangelicals increased from 25 percent to 29 percent during his four years as president? David French attributes it to "the near-culmination of decades-long transformation of white evangelicalism from a mainly religious movement into a Republican political cause."[2]

We follow a "carpenter" who never owned a house, went to college, or pined for attention. But too many of us revere those who are just the opposite: the powerful, the prestigious, the wealthy. We fund them to protect us instead of, like Shaza Alshaara, serving those in need.

"To be the salt and light of the world does not require a person to do extraordinary acts or amass spectacular influence," wrote Jethani in *What If Jesus Was Serious?* "The world does not need more ambitious Christians. Rather, salt and light are the outcomes of ordinary lives lived in rich communion with God. Our world desperately needs more of those."[3]

IN A YEAR of doing research for this book, I discovered much of the wisdom I valued deepest came not from big-name evangelicals in the spotlight but from people in the shadows—everyday people I knew from church or the community—who valued their faith above their political party.

Moving forward, it's time we stopped taking our cues from celebrity "leaders" whose lives often don't meet the "consider-the-source" test for trust.

"If a man attracts by his personality, his appeal is along that line," wrote Chambers. "If he is identified with his Lord's personality, then the appeal is along the line of what Jesus Christ can do. The danger is to glory in men; Jesus says we are to lift *Him* up."[4]

Long ago, I needed to make ten shelf braces the same size so I cut a pattern out of paper that I planned to trace onto wood for each cut. But once I got going I got lazy and thought:

forget the pattern, just use the last piece of wood cut as my template. Bad idea, really bad idea. Each time I made a new brace, my cut would be slightly off, meaning each brace was slightly *more* off. By the time I got my tenth cut, the braces I was making hardly resembled the original pattern.

Some evangelicals no longer resemble the original pattern—Jesus. Instead, we more closely resemble our ever-changing and flawed templates. As Beth Moore puts it: "Jesus isn't simply a big 'us.' He's the master. He's perfection. He's the template to which we need to conform."

"What if the underlying malady afflicting Christians today isn't that we take Jesus too seriously but that we've failed to take Him seriously enough?" wrote Jethani. "What if much of the culture's judgment of Christians isn't the result of obeying Jesus, but the result of Christians ignoring him?"[5]

As evangelicals, we need to wake up. "The American church is not being persecuted from the outside," says Jethani. "It's been perverted from the inside."[6]

In May 2021, Congresswoman Taylor Greene disagreed with House Speaker Nancy Pelosi's request that lawmakers prove they've been vaccinated against COVID in order to drop the mask-wearing rule in the chamber by saying: "We can look back at a time in history where people were told to wear a gold star, and they were definitely treated like second-class citizens so much so that they were put in trains and taken to gas chambers in Nazi Germany. And this is exactly the type of abuse that Nancy Pelosi is talking about."[6]

Seriously? An evangelical Christian was equating having to wear a cloth mask to protect others from COVID to being forced into cattle cars and ultimately murdered along with millions of others? It was a perverse and distorted view of "oppression," an afront to families who'd lost ancestors in the Holocaust, and another sign that at least some evangelicals simply couldn't get over themselves as victims.

Though Taylor Greene, an unabashed conspiracy theorist, ultimately apologized, she also had won her largely evangelical district with 75 percent of the vote. That's absolutely frightening.

In my Prologue, I suggested I'd assumed that wherever the motorcycle of faith ventured, the sidecar of "Christian Far Right" had to come along, too. Now, I'd come to believe we, as evangelicals, had switched places—our faith had been relegated to the sidecar. Hard-right politics, hands revving the engine, was driving the beast. And we act helpless to do anything but hang on and follow.

Wrong.

We need to resist The Tribe and its celebrity "leaders." We need to embrace the Savior. We need to forget the motorcycle, take up our crosses, and follow Jesus.

2021

21.

Capitol Offense

After the attack, I wince when Graham aims his anger not at rioters but at the 10 Republicans who, he said, betrayed Trump like Judas betrayed Jesus.

Be careful, lest in fighting the dragon you become the dragon.
   —Nietzche

On Monday, January 4, 2021, I walked into the post office to get my mail when, out of the blue, a fellow customer said to me: "In two years, this post office will not be here."

I furrowed my brow. "Excuse me?"

"When Biden is declared president, this country will become socialist."

I paused. "As I recall, that was said shortly before Obama took over in 2009 and look, we all survived, didn't we? We didn't become a socialist country. The sky didn't fall."

"This will be different," he said, then walked off.

The exchange was the kind of thing that wouldn't have taken place in the pre-Trump era. Now, in a place where people used to say "Mornin'" or, before a game, "Go Ducks," you had people trying to spread far-right fear. Mutual respect was out, suspicion was in.

Not that I had handled the conversation particularly well. In retrospect, I realize that in my zeal to make sense of the Trump years I'd developed an edge that sometimes suggested "you're wrong" more than "God's right." I didn't see the guy at the post office like Jesus had seen the woman at the well: as someone made in God's image but who was struggling, confused, and searching for answers. I saw him as a political enemy. What was this man's story and how had he come to believe what he believed? Instead of asking such questions—instead of being curious, as Jesus would have—I had defaulted to the same "must-win" mode that I decried in others, my motives fueled more by pride or negligence than by compassion.

Think bigger, Welch. I doubled-down on my listening, the camp chairs getting lots of use in the next few weeks. I met with an agnostic, pro-Biden Democrat who had a deep curiosity about evangelicals. Had hot chocolate with an evangelical Christian who had an incredible ministry to prisoners. (In 2016, his wife voted for Trump; he could not.) And spoke for an hour on the phone with a former president of a Christian college in California who'd been such an encouragement to me in my younger days.

"Anytime religion gets in bed with politics," said Dick Foth, "everyone loses. It never works. In this case, people seem willing to settle for a smaller kingdom: this administration, the Republican Party, the Tea Party—what's the good news about that? It's a little like selling your birthright for a bowl of soup."

ON WEDNESDAY, January 6, the day Congress was expected to certify the Biden-Harris win, Trump remained defiant. By the time I crawled out of bed at 7 a.m. Pacific Standard Time, he was still leaning on Vice President Mike Pence to decertify the outcome by sending the results back to the states. "All Mike Pence has to do is send them back to the States. AND WE WIN. Do it, Mike, this is the time for extreme courage." (Actually, the vice president's authority, under the 12th Amendment and the Electoral Control Act, is confined to opening envelopes with the results from each state and announcing the finally tally. Nothing more.)[267]

"You need to see this," said Sally, who'd been watching TV next to a flickering fire.

A CNN reporter was talking while the camera showed a mob of people on the steps of the Capitol trying to force themselves beyond a paltry police barricade. Inside, Congress was meeting to decide whether to confirm the Biden-Harris victory.

Outside, American flags, Confederate flags, and Trump banners waved above the crowd of thousands. A sprinkling of what's-wrong-with-this-picture stuff: A wooden cross. A man holding a noose. A "Christ is King" sign. A Nazi placard.

"Unbelievable," I said.

The mob forced its way beyond the outer barricades, then worked its way up the steps to the building itself. Near the doors to the Capitol, a rioter appeared to be beating a police officer with an American flag.[268]

"Give it up if you believe in Jesus!" a man yelled. People cheered. "Give it up if you believe in Donald Trump!" People cheered louder.[269]

HOW HAD this all started? Later, I learned the play-by-play: A "Save America March" had begun about 9 a.m. Eastern Standard Time just south of the White House.

"Today is the day American patriots start taking down names and kicking ass," said Rep. Mo Brooks, R-Ala., an evangelical Christian, as the first speaker. Later, he asked the crowd of thousands: "Are you willing to do what it takes to fight for America? Louder! Will you fight for America?"[270]

Shortly thereafter, Trump attorney Rudy Giuliani repeated conspiracy theories that voting machines used in the election were "crooked"— such remarks would later get him sued by the maker of said machines, which, evidence showed, had worked just fine—and at 10:50 a.m. EST called for "trial by combat." Eight minutes later, a Proud Boys contingent left the rally and marched toward the Capitol Building.[271]

From the podium, Donald Trump Jr. told Republican lawmakers tempted to vote to validate the Biden win: "If you're gonna be the zero and not the hero, we're coming for you!"[272]

When "Senior" took the podium and began talking, the crowd began chanting, "We love you! We love you! We love you!"[273]

"Something's really wrong," Trump said. "[It] can't have happened.' And we fight. We fight like Hell and if you don't fight like Hell, you're not going to have a country anymore ... we're going to walk down—and I'll be there with you—we're going to walk down ... to the Capitol and we're going to cheer on our brave senators and congressmen and women."[274]

"Take the Capitol!" chanted the crowd during his talk. "Storm the Capitol!" And "Fight for Trump!"[275]

Before Trump had finished speaking at 1:12 p.m., an estimated eight thousand supporters had begun moving up the National Mall toward the Capitol. Trump either lied about going with the crowd to the Capitol as he'd just promised—or changed his mind. Instead, he went back to the White House and watched on TV.[276]

Shortly after 2 p.m. a swarm of rioters dragged three D.C. Metro police officers out of formation and down a set of stairs, trapped them in a crowd, and assaulted them with improvised weapons, including hockey sticks, crutches, flags, poles, sticks, and stolen police shields. About ten minutes later, a window was shattered by a piece of lumber and rioters began climbing into the Capitol, one proudly waving a large Confederate flag.[277]

On his phone, Trump reached Sen. Tommy Tuberville, R-Ala., but said nothing about quelling the riot; instead, he instructed the senator to do more to block the counting of Biden's electoral votes.

At 2:24 p.m., Trump tweeted that Pence "didn't have the courage to do what should have been done." Some Trump followers immediately began tweeting for Pence to be hunted down; the mob began chanting "Hang Mike Pence!"[278]

The rioters entered, ransacking, and looting offices, photographing themselves, urinating, defecating, and praying. One asked God for "the evil of Congress [to] be brought to an end."[279]

After the Senate chambers had been evacuated, the mob briefly took control of the room, posing for photos with raised fists and praying aloud on the Senate dais that Pence had left only minutes earlier.[280]

Trump was "delighted" to hear rioters had entered the Capitol, Sen. Ben Sasse, R-Nebraska, later said, based on what he'd heard from White House officials.[281]

At 2:47p.m., as his supporters violently clashed with police, Trump tweeted, "Please support our Capitol Police and Law Enforcement. They are truly on the side of our Country." He added, "Stay peaceful," though the *Washington Post* later reported he had resisted doing so, only following through at the insistence of his staff.[282]

By 3:25p.m., Trump tweeted, "I am asking for everyone at the US Capitol to remain peaceful. No violence! Remember, WE are the Party of Law & Order—respect the Law and our great men and women in Blue."[283]

It was a tad late for that; by now, a handful of people were dead and dozens injured. House Minority Leader Kevin McCarthy, R-Calif., later said that he had phoned Trump to ask him to "calm individuals down" but that Trump had defended the rioters, telling him, "Well, Kevin, I guess these people are more upset about the election than you are."[284]

Sixteen minutes later, Trump issued a video message on social media that said, "This was a fraudulent election, but we can't play into the hands of these people. We have to have peace. So go home. We love you. You're very special."[285]

At 6:25 p.m., Trump tweeted: "These are the things and events that happen when a sacred landslide election victory is so unceremoniously & viciously stripped away from great patriots who have been badly & unfairly treated for so long," then, "Remember this day forever!"[286]

A "sacred landslide election victory?" "You're very special?" "Remember this day?" Trump was deluded, his words detached from reality, though true to who he was as a leader. "For the mouth speaks what the heart is full of," says Matthew 12:34. People had died and he had a hand in inciting the violence, though he later called his remarks "totally appropriate," blaming the Democrats for causing "tremendous anger" with their impeachment effort.[287]

The day will go down as one of the saddest in US history. In the early hours of the next morning, 3:41 a.m. to be exact, Congress confirmed the outcome of the Electoral College vote, Biden's 306 votes to Trump's 232. Pence declared that Biden and Harris would take office on January 20, 2021.[288]

IT SHOULD never have come to this—Congress having to certify the vote in the middle of the night amid the rubble of a riot. With a single statement Trump could likely have saved at least nine lives, more than a hundred law-enforcement people from being injured, and at least $30 million in money needed to repair the Capitol.[289] All he needed to have said was what every losing president in history had managed to say: *I concede. And now it's time to help ensure a smooth transition for the good of the country.* But, remember, Trump couldn't lose.

Just as Nero fiddled while Rome burned, Trump tweeted while the Capitol was trashed. Tweeted while five people died. (Four officers, wracked by emotional anguish in the attack's aftermath, would later kill themselves.) Tweeted while at least 138 police officers were being injured, some beaten with lead pipes and trampled, one zapped six times with a stun gun, one losing an eye, one stabbed with a metal fence stake.

Why? Because character, it turned out, *did* matter. And a lack of it proved deadly.

In the aftermath, a few evangelicals—unlike Trump—were bold and brave. "We must repent for making the person who occupies the White House more important than the one who occupies our hearts," Samuel Rodriguez, the lead pastor at New Season Church in Sacramento, California—and a Trump insider—told his congregation on the Sunday after the attack.[290]

"If you can defend this, you can defend *anything*," wrote Russell Moore. "If you can wave this away with 'well, what about . . .' then where, at long last, is your limit?"[291]

When Trump was impeached, for a second time, January 11, 2021, ten Republicans had the courage to vote their consciences and not their party, including Rep. Liz Cheney, R-Wyo., the No. 3 Republican in the House.

"The president of the United States summoned this mob, assembled the mob, and lit the flame of this attack," Cheney said. "Everything that followed was his doing."[292]

But those who defy The Tribe pay a price. In May 2021, Cheney would be drummed out of her leadership role in the Republican Party. Why? Because, like Comey, Bolton, and others, she would dare to do something that had become the unwritten no-no of the GOP: refuse to lie, which sounded eerily like a modern-day manifestation of Galatians 4:16: "Have I now become your enemy by telling you the truth?" Given her ouster, apparently so.

Regarding those who downplayed the attack, Capitol Police Chief Steven Sund begged to differ. "These criminals," he said, "came prepared for war."[293]

Amid such courage to "call it what it was," however, came those who grasped at whatever straws they could to defend Trump.

"This is what happens when you mob the police," said Pastor John Hagee whose Cornerstone Church in San Antonio, Texas, would later host a QAnon-linked rally wherein hundreds would chant, "Let's go, Brandon," a far-right code phrase for, "Fu-- Joe Biden!"[294] "Wake up, America! America and democracy cannot function without the rule of law. We back the blue!"[295]

Tim Remington, a conservative Christian pastor at The Alter Church in Coeur D'Alene, Idaho, blamed the media. "I rebuke the news in the name of Jesus," he told his congregation in his message the Sunday after the attack. "We ask that this false garbage come to an end. ... It's the lies, Communism, socialism. I don't know how we've put up with it this long."[296]

Timeout. The president and his cohorts incited their followers to "trial by combat." His troops carried out the dog-whistle command. And in Hagee's eyes, a lack of support for law enforcement was the culprit here? And, in Remington's eyes, the media was to blame for reporting that America's Capitol had been attacked?

By now, I shouldn't have been surprised. Shouldn't have been surprised that folks such as former VP candidate and self-identified "Bible-believing Christian" Sarah Palin—without a shred of evidence—blamed the attack on Antifa, which, an FBI investigation showed, was not involved.

Shouldn't have been surprised that Franklin Graham condemned not Trump but the Republican members of Congress who voted to impeach a president of its own political party, going so far as to refer to Judas betraying Jesus. "Shame! … After all that he has done for our country, you would turn your back & betray him so quickly …. It makes you wonder what the thirty pieces of silver were that Speaker [of the House Nancy] Pelosi promised for this betrayal," he posted on Facebook.

Shouldn't have been surprised that Reed would canonize the former president with a sense of "fallen soldier" grandeur. "The political winds within the Republican Party have blown in the opposite direction," said Reed shortly after Biden's inauguration. "Republicans have decided that even if one believes [Trump] made mistakes after the November election and on January 6, the policies [he] championed and victories he won from judges to regulatory rollback to life to tax cuts were too great to allow the party to leave him on the battlefield."[297]

Leave him on the battlefield? Trump *started* this war and watched—with "delight," said Sasse—from the cozy confines of the White House. He left his country on that battlefield as he tweeted his anger at Pence—while people were being killed and seriously injured. That's not battlefield valor, that's cowardly delusion. That's the final act of an unhinged man. To imbue Trump with even a hint of heroism is to cheat our country's true heroes, hundreds of thousands of whom have died and shed their blood for our freedom on *real* battlefields, not on a White House sofa thumb-punching an iPhone.

But Reed's predictable defense of the president encapsulated the Trump-and-his-followers relationship perfectly: even when he worked against the very country he feigned to love and the Constitution he pretended to defend, Trump's final act as president proved himself prophetic: he *could* stand in the middle of Fifth Avenue and shoot somebody and wouldn't lose any voters.

The relationship between Trump and his most loyal supporters, I realized, could only be described as one of co-dependency—like a man who abuses his wife or girlfriend. *I can do anything to you and you will still be loyal to me*—the very thing Trump had said before he was elected in 2016. "If you can't stand Donald Trump, you think Donald Trump is the worst, you're going to vote for me. You know why? Justices of the Supreme Court."[298]

"People who are in abusive relationships have a habit of minimizing the bad behavior of their abusers," wrote Dr. Marcia Sirota, a psychiatrist and author. "They rationalize and justify the other person's behavior and it allows them to tolerate the unacceptable."[299]

And if a victim dares to *not* go along with the abuse? In what Sirota calls "crazy-making," a victim who responds to abuse with "normal and appropriate reactions"—for example, Pence's refusal to obey Trump and defy the Constitution—is labeled, by the abuser, as "bad, wrong, crazy and selfish." Witness Trump's tweets castigating Pence, a guy who, for four years, had been as loyal to the President as a cocker spaniel.

"Eventually," wrote Sirota, "the abuser convinces their victim that this is the way normal relationships operate, or at least this is the best that their victim can ever do." Indeed, Trump's behavior had become so normalized that not even his inspiring an attack on the Capitol made some evangelicals flee the house or call 911.

"The Republican Party," wrote conservative *New York Times* columnist David Brooks, "has become detached from reality."[300]

Imagine if the incumbent Obama had lost the 2012 election and asked his vice president, Biden, to defy the Constitution and overturn the election … Obama who'd said, "We fight like Hell"… Obama who'd watched thousands storming the Capitol, many of them people of color. Would evangelicals have been so quick to dismiss it? To refuse to call it was it was? Would Rep. Andrew Clyde, R-Ga., still have called the attack a "bold-faced lie" that more closely resembled a "normal tourist visit" with visitors acting in "an orderly fashion?"[301]

Lost in all this was a prophetic remark Rubio, a Republican, had made nearly five years earlier, regarding Trump's propensity to divide: "The politics of resentment against other people will not just leave us a fractured party, they will leave us a fractured nation."

ON JANUARY 20, 2021, Joe Biden was inaugurated as the forty-sixth president of the United States. "History, faith, and reason shall lead the way," he told the nation.[302]

Trump, meanwhile, had asked for the Pentagon to coordinate a military-style farewell parade for him on that day. It refused. Vice President Pence and his wife chose to attend the inauguration of Biden and Harris.

At 8:18 a.m. on Inauguration Day, Trump took the Marine One helicopter from the South Lawn to Joint Base Andrews, where Air Force One waited to take him and his family to Florida. An Air Force Band played "Hail to the Chief." Army field guns fired a twenty-one-gun salute.

"It is my greatest honor and privilege to have been your president," he told the crowd of a few hundred at the private event. "Have a good life."

Later, he said, "I wish the new administration great luck and great success."

And then, Air Force One rose into the sky. After four years as president, Trump was gone.

There was a sense of grandeur to it all. Nobility. Boldness. As if to say: "Mission accomplished!" Trump had orchestrated the private ceremony himself, even asking for the plane to take flight just as Frank Sinatra's "I Did It My Way" played.

A less subjective read of Trump's presidency would have suggested a more appropriate image to sum up his impact on America: a moment that occurred at about 4 a.m., the day after the attack. It was a photo taken of Rep. Andy Kim, D-NY, who was leaving in the early hours following the vote to certify Biden's victory. It had been taken not far from where a photo was snapped the previous day of Rep. Josh Hawley, R-Mo., an evangelical Christian, offering a "great job!" fist-pump to the remains of the mob that had stormed the Capitol.

On his way out, Kim had noticed officers cleaning up debris from the previous day's storming of the Capitol. Never mind the trauma of having been whisked out of the House chambers as hundreds stormed the building. Never mind that he'd been up for nearly twenty-four hours and probably wanted to get back to his worried family. Never mind that this wasn't his job. Leaders, as my pastor had taught me long ago, step up and take responsibility for the benefit of others.

And so it was that the congressman—garbage bag in hand, mask on to protect others—did what his conscience compelled him to do: began helping clean up the mess that Donald Trump had left behind.[303]

My Hope for the Future

That we might find the courage to change

SOON AFTER the 2020 election, I was talking with a farm couple I know, traditionalists whose pastures look the same now as they did three decades ago, set-in-their-ways folks for whom change doesn't come easily. As an elder in his church, the man admitted that the race-sensitivity training his pastor had the staff take was challenging. But he and his wife were trying to be open-minded, in part because their daughter, after a divorce, married an African American man.

"We love him and he's broadening our world," she said. "He drives a Mercedes and works for Nike and gets pulled over *all* the time."

When her daughter invited her to Portland in the summer of 2020, the woman was surprised at what she found in the suburban neighborhood: a sprinkling of Black Lives Matter protests, peaceful but heartfelt. "Done in honor of my son-in-law," she said. "So, there I was, a farmer standing in a suburban neighborhood with my 'Black Lives Matter' sign."

The woman was *willing to change* her perspective. And that's the essence of our faith, isn't it? The old will become new, the lame will walk, the blind will see. Those who were lost will be found. Those who have fallen will soar like eagles.

Change.

It's not the church's job to make America great again, it's the church's job to glorify God—and not with the "bless-our-little-attack" prayers that some offered in the Capitol January 6, 2021. As long as the political right—or the political *anything*—becomes our passion as Christians, it's "game-over." Jesus transcends Right, Left, everything in between, and everything beyond.

"Every so often," said a local evangelical pastor who watched the number of attendees dip as he spoke more on white advantage, "I think the church needs to rebuild, reboot, start over. And this is one of those times."

■ **First, change must begin with us getting out of our evangelical cocoons and engaging with—not railing at—the world around us.** We would be wise to stop loathing The Left, start listening to the "least of these," and dare to lament how we've fallen short as image-bearers of God. Owning our shortcomings doesn't mean wallowing in guilt. It means allowing the Holy Spirit to enlighten us, to remake us, to teach us—as I'd done after facing my self-righteousness regarding the little girl at the library and my selfishness regarding the classmate who'd committed suicide.

"How do we end systemic racism in our society?" asked Former President George W. Bush after the George Floyd shooting. "The only way to see ourselves in a true light is to listen to the voices of so many who are hurting and grieving."

As a journalist, one of the most insightful afternoons I've spent was with Myrlie Evers-Williams, the widow of Civil Rights activist Medgar Evers, who, in 1963, was gunned down in the family's driveway at age thirty-seven, leaving behind three small children. (See the movie *Mississippi Burning*.) What struck me most deeply was Myrlie's utter lack of bitterness, despite her husband having been murdered by a bigoted white man. Late in the day, she sat down at her piano and played a song, Debussy's "Claire de Lune," that I will never forget.

As evangelicals, I fear, too many of us have grown bitter. It's hard to hate someone when you learn their story. But you can't learn their story if you believe it's your goal to fortify the wall between The Right and The Left instead of helping tear it down. Abraham Lincoln had the right perspective. "I don't like that man," he said. "I must get to know him better."

How we regard others is how we regard Christ. "As you did it to one of the least of these my brothers, you did it to me," Jesus says in Matthew 25:40.

"Jesus fraternized with a broad spectrum of people," wrote Tom Hovestol in *Extreme Righteousness: Seeing Ourselves in the Pharisees*. "He built relationships with the 'pious' and the pariahs, the rich and the poor, male and female, the learned and the common, the 'churched' and those who wouldn't darken its door."[1]

In writing *Saving My Enemy*, I was interested to note that the post-war version of Don Malarkey, an arch-conservative, had hung out at a pool hall with a Japanese American who'd been interned during WWII, a Chinese American, and a liberal Mennonite. But here's the thing: the men cared enough about each other to joke about their differences. That was two decades ago; the thought of an evangelical having such an eclectic group of friends today is almost laughable. Likewise, I can hardly imagine an evangelical church, as ours did in 1994, being willing to hold a memorial service for the son of a newspaper editor—part of the Trump-labeled "enemy of the people."

In the end, we need to realize that we aren't as different from The Enemy as we might think: we're all insecure, we're all broken, and we're looking all for hope and assurance that things are going to be OK. In Erich Maria Remarques *All Quiet on the Western Front*, he tells of a World War I infantryman who kills an enemy soldier, then looks at him—really looks at him. "But now, for the first time, I see you are a man like me. I thought of your hand-grenades, of your bayonet, of your rifle; now I see your face and our fellowship. Forgive me, comrade. If we threw away these rifles and these uniforms you could be my brother . . . ."[2]

- **Second, change must begin with broadening our info sources.** As it is, America has split into two camps regarding news, one that unabashedly promotes The Right and one that at least aspires to be objective, even if liberal bias is inevitable. We need to be more selective about where we get our news, resisting the urge to let the chief criteria be "whoever reinforces my beliefs." In a single year, I discovered a handful of Bible-based podcasts that did wonders in helping me understand how to better play out my faith in a world that's resorted to political tribalism as its be-all-end-all.

"The longer we live in separate media worlds, the deeper and broader our divisions will become," wrote Timothy Dalrymple of *Christianity Today*. "The longer we give ourselves to media gluttony, skimping on the deeper nourishment that cultivates Christ within us, the less we will have in common."[3]

We live in well-fortified bubbles. Forty-four percent of Republicans who get their news through the "mainstream" believe the 2020 "election was stolen" from Trump. That alone is incredible, given the numerous checks and balances—often involving Republicans—that certified Biden's victory. But here's what's even more troubling: 86 percent of Republicans who get their news from Fox believe the same thing.[4] Too often, people whose main source of information is Fox News aren't seeing the world as it is, they're seeing the world as Fox News *wants* them to see it. Instead, some ignore the James 1:19 call to be "quick to listen," refusing to even entertain the possibility that they might have skewed vision.

As a country, we've always had disagreements between

political factions but the two sides at least began with a fact-based sense of reality. Under Trump, that eroded so severely that an election deemed fair by all those who did their jobs to ensure such fairness—during a Republican administration—cried foul when the evidence unquestionably said "fair."

"More and more Americans are effectively living in a self-created political reality," wrote Peter Wehner. "It's now possible to isolate oneself in an information space that entirely confirms one's preexisting views and biases."[5]

In November 2021, The Dispatch, a center-right online magazine that was a longtime contributor to Fox News, severed its relationship with the network because "the voices of the responsible are being drowned out by the irresponsible." The last straw was the Tucker Carlson-hosted *Patriot Purge*, which The Dispatch said was "a collection of incoherent conspiracy-mongering, riddled with factual inaccuracies, half-truths, deceptive imagery, and damning omissions. And its message is clear: The U.S. government is targeting patriotic Americans in the same manner—and with the same tools—that it used to target al Qaeda ... This is not happening. And we think it's dangerous to pretend it is. If a person with such a platform shares such misinformation loud enough, there are Americans who believe—and act upon—it."[6]

On the Right and Left, there can be no significant hope for a better world if our default format includes no sliver of space for the ideas that (a), as humans, we are all flawed and (b) it's not about us but the common good.

For believers, I like Timothy Keller's encouragement to live "distinctively Christian." "It's not about walling ourselves off from The Enemy or embedding on their side. It's not about pulling away from the culture, and not trying to take it over ... It's about an attitude of service, uncompromising in our beliefs, but not withdrawing and not trying to dominate."[7]

And it's about a whole lot more than who you voted for as

president. "The goal is not to have all Christians share the same exact politics but to have all Christians think *Christianly* about politics," say the three authors of *Compassion (&) Conviction.*

We've been conditioned to make everything a Right/Left debate. We need to get beyond that tired paradigm.

I was encouraged to hear of an evangelical church in our community that, prior to the 2020 election, held a symposium on how to vote from a Christian perspective. Not on *who to vote for*, but on what to consider when you do. In times of controversy, too many churches turn inward instead of upward and outward. We need to think more broadly and let go of the "we-always-vote-this-way" line of thinking. Our goal should not be to stay cozy in The Tribe; our goal should be to glorify God. The Tribe and God serve two distinctly different purposes.

- **Third, change must begin with a better understanding of why we value what we value.** *The Righteous Mind* author Jonathan Haidt talks about how *intuition* is the elephant and *reason* the rider of the elephant. "Reason," he wrote, "is the servant of the intuition."[9]

We need less intuition, more reason. "Many of us believe that we follow an inner moral compass," wrote Haidt, "but the history of social psychology richly demonstrates that other people exert a powerful force, able to make cruelty seem acceptable ... ."[10]

"Your elephant knows which way to lean in response to such terms such as *pro-life*, and as your elephant sways back and forth throughout the day, you find yourself liking and trusting the people around you who sway in sync with you."[11]

The good news? "The elephant is far more powerful than the rider, but it is not an absolute dictator."

So, when does the elephant listen to reason?

"The main way that we change our minds on moral issues is by interacting with other people," wrote Haidt. "We are terrible at seeking evidence that challenges our own beliefs, but other people do us this favor, just as we are quite good at finding errors in other people's beliefs. When discussions are hostile, the odds of change are slight. The elephant leads away from the opponent, and the rider works frantically to rebut the opponent's charges.

"But if there is affection, admiration, or a desire to please the other person, then the elephant leans *toward* that person and the rider tries to find the truth in the other person's arguments."[12]

Remember my reference to a local pastor who took a bold stand against racism? He'd spent his entire life *not* doing so. What changed him? A face-to-face encounter with a black parishioner who enlightened him regarding the verbal abuse she'd taken from people at church. He chose empathy instead of apathy.

As evangelicals, we need to quit letting the elephant call the shots and listen, instead, to the intuition that is the Holy Spirit.

■ **Finally, change must begin with the courage to think more broadly.**

After the Trump years, "I am more committed now to listen to people who are different from me," a young woman in our church told me. "I have discovered so much value in that, and I am so grateful for it. We may disagree in the end, but it changes us when we practice listening and humility—with the intent to understand instead of digging in our heels on what we think we know. The more I know, the more I realize what I don't know."

She had much to "unlearn." But was willing to change.

The rise of the Christian Far Right left her "slower to trust what I have always believed to be true or what I was told to believe, especially as it relates to the 'us' and 'them' narrative I'd been taught," she said. "And here's what I was taught: All Democrats are demonic. Black people are lazy, vengeful, and violent. Things like that."

We talked about her upbringing at a private Christian school in 1990s Texas—a school that had begun as an answer to desegregation. She talked about the time a teacher ridiculed a student because the student's parents voted for a Democrat; "in Texas, church and politics are one and the same," she said. And she talked about how the parents of her best friend, who was black, had transferred their daughter to a public school in the late 1990s because of what they saw as false teaching in the private school—that slaves happily boarded the ships for America and that the Bible's "don't-be-unequally-yoked" verse (2 Corinthians 6:14) refers to interracial dating.

"You obviously think broader," I said to her. "What triggered that?"

"That incident was part of it. As a middle schooler, I didn't know how to fully process it, but that just didn't seem right to me. Why would a public school be a safer, more honest place for a black student than a private Christian school? I didn't see 'Jesus' much in our school."

She read a book called *God's Politics* by Jim Wallis, a Christian who founded *Sojourners* magazine.

"It shifted my thinking," she said. "I realized there was a whole other side to things."

"Going forward," I asked her, "what do we need to do as believers?"

"The best thing for America is having within her borders a Church that seeks peace and prosperity with unwavering fidelity to Jesus as the King, not a political party, and seeks first *His* Kingdom, not shallow Christendom. We are in a post-Christian culture; the sooner Christians accept that and begin to live as exiles instead of the wanna-be ruling class, the better."

This might be the most profound statement in my book, and it comes not from a spotlight evangelical—they're too busy defending The Tribe—but a young woman in our church whose eyes and heart are well-focused.

Change.

"Christian culture simply doesn't lend itself to change, and change isn't easy within religious environments that value uniformity from birth until death," wrote Stephen Mattson in *The Great Awakening*. "Institutionalized Christianity expects you to learn, keep, and maintain the same theological doctrines for life."[13]

BUT CHANGE should be the essence of our lives in Christ; if it's not, why are we sitting through sermon after sermon, attending Bible study after Bible study? What's the point of learning if not to see how we've been wrong and to be inspired to get it right? If not to be inspired to change? Isn't the Church, by God's design, predicated on the idea that we should learn and grow and refuse to be the people we once were? Isn't that what the mainstay of our faith—repentance—is all about?

A year after I got in the face of the basketball coach of the Christian school—anger justified, approach and temperament *not*—we were playing the same team. Recognizing me, the school's other coach came up to me before the game.

"You're the guy who ripped us last year because of our lack of sportsmanship, right?" he said.

I nodded. "Not my finest moment. Sorry."

He extended a hand to shake. "We needed to hear that."

A teacher at the school, he invited me to speak to his class about how my faith played out in my job as a journalist. I did so, using the opportunity to tell the story of how we'd met—and to honor him in front of his students for the grace he'd accorded me.

We both looked in the mirror, saw our shortcomings, took risks, changed, and grew because of it; the result, I think, was glory for God, passed on to twenty-five students, some of whom may have paid it forward to others.

Change.

A pastor friend who went from a Trump backer to a Trump

doubter said he pivoted when he started listening not to people who agreed with him, but to those who didn't. "I began to look at the world differently," he said.

Case in point, he said, was the video of MacArthur telling Beth Moore to "go home!" "Three things scared me about that. First, the arrogance and narrow-mindedness of what MacArthur said. Second, the response from the crowd—claps of approval. And, third, that a decade ago I would have been one of those people applauding. Recognizing that brought me a sense of shame, a sense of humility, and a sense of necessary repentance."

Change.

My Texas friends adopted an African American baby and left their evangelical megachurch for a predominantly black church. That's courage—daring to leave comfort for the uncomfortable. Their old church, they said, would never begin to acknowledge racism; "it was always, 'Oh, *they're* just always complaining.'"

Change.

It begins by returning to the One who's been overlooked in all the rancor and rage, Jesus. The One who I saw so clearly years ago in a couple I interviewed about their homespun ministry to the homeless. The couple—let's call them Mary and Joseph—reminded me that the Church must build itself back from the ground up, through love, and not from the top down, through fear. To that end, each week the two prepared and served sandwiches and coffee to the poor in their neighborhood.

As I interviewed them, I will never forget a life-in-a-shopping-cart guy who asked a question whose answer we, as evangelicals, would be wise to contemplate. Accepting his free sandwich and coffee, the homeless man said, "So, like why you doin' this, dude?"

Joseph shrugged. "Just doin' what we think Jesus would be doin'."

The homeless guy nodded his head and smiled a bit.

"So," he said, "you guys are, like, *real* Christians, huh?"

I thought of Trump's suits-and-ties team of evangelical pastors surrounding him, smiling large for the "I-got-invited-to-the-table" photo that would hang on their office walls back home—ostensibly to remind everyone, most notably themselves, that they were doing God's work. And I thought about the in-the-shadows folks like Mary and Joseph who seem to be quiet difference-makers.

Alas, later, while I was helping at an outdoor lunch for the homeless and organized by the couple, I began worrying if perhaps I'd misjudged Joseph. Perhaps he'd deceived me. Perhaps I was learning that the powerful have no lock on pride and hypocrisy.

To wit, I was puzzled to note that as dozens of homeless lined up for the just-prepared meal, it was Joseph who was first in line—and was heaping huge mounds of food on his plate. If this event was being done in the name of the same Jesus who washed His disciples' feet, wasn't it a bit self-serving for the leader to go first? Whatever happened to leadership as taking responsibility for the benefit of others?

Curious, I stepped closer. My new perspective—and that's the key in this whole Trump-evangelical story, a willingness to change our perspectives—helped me see a bigger picture. There, behind Joseph, was a tattered homeless man in a wheelchair.

The heaping plate, it turned out, was for him.

Afterword

**Going forward, I realize, it's
partly about "what happened"
but mainly about how I respond to it.**

If only there were evil people somewhere insidiously committing evil deeds, and if it were necessary only to separate them from the rest of us and destroy them! But the line dividing good and evil cuts through the heart of every human being . . . .
—Alexander Solzhenitsyn

In Boston, I once had a speaking engagement about ninety minutes from downtown. My instinct was to trust Mapquest—Interstate 90 to Interstate 95—but my conscience and Sally's whispered: "take the map's squiggly lines."

We did so. And, lo and behold, came cross author Henry David Thoreau's Walden Pond. We had accidentally stumbled upon one of the meccas of American literature.

Suffice it to say this book was a squiggly-lines experience.

When I began the project, I knew the general direction I wanted to travel but purposely left the specific destination undecided to allow for the guiding of the Holy Spirit. I can attest that German philosopher Martin Buber was right when he said, "Every journey has a secret destination of which the traveler is unaware." My willingness to question Trump, far-right conservatism, evangelicals, and myself brought me to a place I hadn't planned on reaching: a deeper, richer, more authentic Christian faith than I had when I began.

Between politics, the pandemic, and the deaths of a mother and a friend, 2020 would seem to have been a convenient time for me to exit the freeway of faith. And, in a way, I suppose I did, since the freeway represents a sort of pedal-to-the-metal pointing of my vehicle in one direction and simply going the same way I'd gone for half a century. Instead, I arrived at what seems to be purer faith—by taking back roads I'd never known existed.

The freeway is the easy way, the comfortable way, but often *not* the most enriching, enlightening, or inspiring way. Nor the way Jesus traveled. "If anyone would come after me, he must deny himself and take up his cross and follow me," Jesus said in Matthew 16:25.

That doesn't sound easy, which is exactly the point: my journey reminded me how comfortable my faith had gotten, how significant comfort is to flying with the flock, and yet how being uncomfortable leads to change and growth.

WHAT I'VE tried to do is realign evangelicals to the Scripture-based blueprints, a process that stretched me immeasurably. Why? Because in my attempt to encourage others, I had to face my own shortcomings. And because, beyond sinking myself deeper into Scripture, I had to shut up and listen to people who knew far more than I did.

I learned a wealth of nuances I would have otherwise missed; in short, how incredibly diverse people are regarding politics and faith. I sometimes disagreed with the people across from me, but the experience always broadened my vision. Just because someone doesn't see the world as I do doesn't make them bad, and just because I think I'm right doesn't make me good. Or, for that matter, *right*. All I've offered on these pages is one man's experience, one man's opinion, one man's hope for the future based on my understanding of Scripture. Nothing more.

Some of the best lessons came from editors who I asked, in essence, to criticize me and who politely obliged. Other lessons came from people I asked to share their views on Trump, the Far Right, and faith.

Once, two hours after I'd had a spirited conversation with a friend—my departure from the evangelical status quo seemed to unsettle him—the guy showed up unannounced at my house. Not to berate me. But to talk further. He wasn't out to convince me how right he was and how wrong I was; he was, I realized, out to listen and share and learn and grow. I loved it. As I did when, after returning to church, I learned that a group of people had begun meeting to read about, and discuss, trying to bridge the racial divide. Sally and I were quick to join them.

If nothing else, I hope this book says: Let's stop ignoring the elephant in the room and stop beating each other to death on Facebook. Let's pull out a couple of parking-lot chairs and listen to each other. We are all flawed—we all have, in essence, "pre-existing conditions"—and that may be profitable common ground on which to begin.

Beyond my parking-lot interviews, I discovered an array of refreshing voices of evangelicalism, people such as David French, Phil Vischer, Skye Jethani, Christian Taylor, Beth Moore, Bob Roberts, Kaitlyn Schiess, Russell Moore, and *Christianity Today*'s Mike Cosper, whose "The Rise and Fall of Mars Hill" series so eerily echoed nuances of Trump and the Far Right. All helped me see deeper, wider, and more "Christianly."

THE INFLUENCE of Trump and the Far Right are not going away. Any hope that the GOP would return to a common-good Republicanism—the kind of honorable politics that drove conservatives such as Sen. John McCain and former Secretary of State Colin Powell—ended in February 2021. That's when the Conservative Political Action Conference gave Trump an approval rating of 97 percent and, in a gesture that amplified his idolatrous Old Testament hold on some evangelicals, flaunted an aux-bronze golden statue of him.[304]

This, then, is a time of reckoning for evangelical churches. How Christians respond going forward may well determine whether evangelicalism returns to what it was originally intended to be—a vibrant faith that gives hope to all—or sinks deeper into a Christian nationalism that prioritizes benefits for the self-chosen few.

At stake are younger generations wondering if, amid the political darkness, there is still a reason to believe. At stake, frankly, is the evangelical church, period.

If we're going to have any positive influence on the world, it won't be accomplished by getting "down and dirtier" to regain lost political power but by being more authentic followers of Jesus. By fulfilling the Great Commandment: to love God and others. Otherwise, we're destined to win the battle but lose the war—claiming victories for The Tribe but forgoing any hope of changing hearts for His glory.

"The way we are with each other is the truest test of our faith," wrote Brennan Manning. "How I treat a brother or sister from day to day, how I react to the sin-scarred wino on the street, how I respond to interruptions from people I dislike … ."[305]

WRITING A MEMOIR is both enlightening and incriminating, enlightening because with each sentence you craft, you're forced to examine your heart, incriminating for the same reason. If I'm wiser than I was when I began this project, I'm also wary of my imperfection. In fighting the dragon, have I become the dragon? In calling on evangelicals to reach higher, am I doing so myself?

As Anglo-American poet W.H. Auden put it: "How do I learn how to love my crooked neighbor with my crooked heart?" And, given my book's topic, what do I do with all those "love-thy-neighbor" sermons where pastors reminded me that *everyone* is our neighbor, in this case even Donald Trump. Can I forgive him? Can I wish for him good things? Can I pray that he might find the humility to allow God and others to matter to him more than himself?

I hope so.

LIKE ALICE in Wonderland, we all went down a rabbit hole during the Trump/COVID years and few returned where they started. For me, returning to church, for example, was awkward; beyond COVID-created tension—who knew masks could be so controversial?—the Trump years had emboldened many of us, though often in opposite ways. Some people were more entrenched in twining God, country, and the Far Right; others awakening to the sense that Trump's influence was pulling us apart from, not drawing us nearer to, the heart of God.

Engaging my closest friends in conversation was difficult at best, painful at worst. Some of that was on me; I waited too long—if at all—to share with them about the book I was writing. Some were hurt, assuming I didn't value their opinions. Not the case. It wasn't that I didn't value their perspectives, different from mine though they might have been.

In part, it was because I didn't want to draw them into something that they had no obligation to "join." And in part because, like putting off making a dental appointment, I avoided the get-togethers to avoid uncomfortable situations. In doing so, I now realize I violated one of the very principles I further in this book: at its deepest, love can be—*must* be—uncomfortable, but it's in that discomfort, that willingness to engage others rather than retreat, that we honor the bond and each other.

"What do you do when you feel you're losing the people you love to a false reality?" asks *Christianity Today's* Dalrymple. "What do you do with the humbling truth that they have precisely the same fear about you?"[306]

To that end, I am encouraged by a line in one of my favorite books and movies, Norman MacLean's *A River Runs Through It*: "You can love completely," he wrote, "without complete understanding." I'm uncertain what that meant to MacLean, but to me it teems with God's grace and unconditional love.

My friends may never completely understand why I see things as I do and I may never completely understand why they see things as they do, but our friendships are not predicated on agreement. Instead, they're predicated on deeper things. Disagreeing with one another does not mean having to hate one another; if anyone understands that, it should be Christians, who are the beneficiaries of the greatest undeserved love on the planet: God's grace.

SINCE I PRAYED that prayer for a job and my Trump journey began, I'm all the more convinced that Jesus—not the Church, the country, or The Tribe—must be where I place my hope. I'm less convinced that the Church, as a whole, is courageous enough to confront the faith-politics issue, racism, COVID, and the like. And less convinced that "evangelical" is how I want to be defined. But in the end, I'm reminded that it's less important how others define me than how He defines me: worthy despite my weakness.

I've come to realize that despite all I learned on my journey, I still have more questions than answers. Like many, I'm ensconced in uncertainty about the future. Politics? Church? Friends? COVID? I have no idea what the way forward means for me, where I belong anymore—other than in His grip.

But I'm strangely OK with that, too. I'm less worried about where I fit than quietly content with realizing where I *don't*. And I'm humbled that I can answer Nouwen's question—"To whom do I belong, to God or to the world?"—with greater confidence now than in 2015.

That's not smugness speaking; that's simply insight from someone who took a hard look at himself and the Christian culture he swam in. And, in the process, was reminded that this Earth will never be my home—and no president will ever be my savior.

In Scripture, Peter refers to Christ followers as "strangers and pilgrims" (1 Peter 2:11, KJV). For me, at journey's end, that feels right, as if I've come full circle in my half-century of faith, back to my sense that I'm "just another beggar looking for a piece of bread."

Back to the teenage days of Young Life, when we sang—and unsullied by the world, truly believed—that, "They will know we are Christians by our love /Yes, they will know we are Christians by our love."

Epilogue

In February 2021, at the Conservative Political Action Conference in Orlando, attendees prioritized eight issues for the future. "Election integrity" was by far the top choice (62 percent), followed by Constitutional Rights (48 percent) and Immigration/Border Wall (35 percent). "Dignity/Pro-Life," the issue that many thought explained the evangelical surge to Trump, finished last at 16 percent.[307]

- On February 17, 2021, Rush Limbaugh died from complications of lung cancer. He was seventy.
- On February 28, 2021, I met with Marley for the coffee I had promised him three years earlier. We had a great talk. The next day he emailed: "I wish to say something to you, my good friend: You've

converted me. And I have now seen that I have to join you in your views. Yes, you've won me over. I'm convinced. I remember when Joseph was presumed dead and Jacob said, 'I'm convinced' when he realized Joseph was alive. Bob, you held on long enough to break through, to get me to that 'convinced' moment."

- In March 2021, Beth Moore announced she was no longer a Southern Baptist and was parting ways with the denomination's publishing arm. "I am still a Baptist, but I can no longer identify with Southern Baptists," she said.

- In April 2021, a Hennepin County (Minn.) jury convicted Derek Chauvin in the murder of George Floyd. He was later sentenced to 22.5 years in prison. Out of an estimated 15,000 police killings since 2005, he was the seventh on-duty officer to be convicted of murder.

- In May 2021, Russell Moore, who headed up the public-policy arm of the Southern Baptist Convention, left to join *Christianity Today*. "My family and I have faced constant threats from white nationals and white supremacists, including within our convention," he wrote in a February 2020 letter that was reported by Religion News Service.

- In August 2021, Jerry Falwell Jr. resigned as president of Liberty University after Reuters reported he'd been involved in sexual indiscretions. Falwell sued Liberty University for damaging his reputation, later dropping the suit. Later, Liberty University sued Falwell for $10 million for breach of contract and fiduciary duty. The suit also alleged that Falwell failed to disclose to the university's board of trustees his affair and "personal impairment by alcohol."[308]

- The same month, the National Religious Broadcasters abruptly fired its senior vice president of communication, Daniel Darling, after he appeared on MSNBC to discuss why he chose to get vaccinated against COVID.[309]

- On October 1, 2021, a poll was released by the University of Virginia's Center for Politics showing that 52% of Trump voters and 41% of Biden voters at least somewhat agree that it's time to split the country, favoring blue/red states seceding from the union.

- On November 24, 2021, a jury in Glynn County, Georgia, found three men—Gregory McMichael, his son Travis McMichael, and their neighbor William "Roddie" Bryan Jr.—guilty on multiple counts of murder for the killing of Ahmaud Arbery.

■ At Thanksgiving 2021, after having undergone aromatherapy to try and restore my smell and taste, I was able to enjoy most of my turkey and gravy—my first almost-full-flavor bites in thirteen months.

■ On December 19, 2021, Trump, at the invitation of Senior Pastor Robert Jeffress, offered what was billed as the "Christmas message" at Dallas First Baptist Church's Sunday morning service. He mentioned immigration, "the border," and the need to "make America great again," but nothing about Christmas.

"I think our nation is in great trouble," said Trump. "There's a lot of clouds hanging over our country right now. Very dark clouds. But we will come back bigger, better and stronger than ever. I'm telling you that."

He received a standing ovation from the crowd of 4,000. People lifted their hands high in the air, not in praise of Jesus but to get cellphone photos of Trump.

To contact the author

Email
bobwelch@bobwelchwriter.com

Web
bobwelchwriter.com

Snail Mail
PO Box 70785
Springfield, OR 97475

Twitter
@bob_welch23

Further Exploration

BOOKS TO READ

On love and grace

A Gentle Answer: Our Secret Weapon in an Age of Us Against Them by Scott Sauls. (Nashville, Thomas Nelson, 2020).

Love Over Fear: Facing Monsters, Befriending Enemies, and Healing Our Polarized World by Dan White Jr. (Chicago: Moody Publishers, 2019).

The Ragamuffin Gospel by Brennan Manning. (Sisters, Oregon: Multnomah Books, 1990).

What's So Amazing About Grace? by Philp Yancey. (Grand Rapids, Michigan: HarperCollins Zondervan, 1997).

What If Jesus Was Serious? by Skye Jethani. (Chicago: Moody, 2020).

The Return of the Prodigal Son: A Story of Homecoming by Henri J.M.

Nouwen, (New York: Image Books, Doubleday, 1992.)

On America and politics

The Myth of the Christian Nation by Gregory A. Boyd. (Grand Rapids, Michigan: Zondervan, 2005).

A People's History of the United States by Howard Zinn. (New York: Perennial Classics, 2001).

On Trump

Too Much and Never Enough: How My Family Created the World's Most Dangerous Man by Mary L. Trump. (New York: Simon & Schuster, 2020).

The Death of Politics: How to Heal Our Frayed Republic after Trump by Peter Wehner. (New York: HarperOne, 2019).

On the Religious Right

Taking American Back for God by Andrew Whitehead and Samuel L. Perry. (New York: Oxford University Press, 2020).

Jesus and John Wayne by Kristen Kobes du Mez, (New York: Liveright Publishing Corporation, 2020).

On narcissists and leadership

When Narcissism Comes to Church by Chuck DeGroat. (Downers Grove, Illinois: InterVarsity Press, 2020).

Necessary Endings by Henry Cloud. (New York: Harper Business, 2010).

On race

White Awake: An honest look at what it means to be white by Daniel Hill. (Downers Grove, Illinois: IVP Books, 2017).

Caste: The Origins of Our Discontent, Isabel Wilkerson. (New York: Random House, 2020).

PODCASTS TO CHECK OUT

- "The Holy Post." Veggie Tales founder Phil Vischer joins author and former pastor Skye Jethani for a fast-paced and often funny conversation about theology, media, pop culture, and living a thoughtful Christian life. *www.holypost.com*
- "Bold Love." Pastor Bob Roberts, Jr. explores building friendships outside the church without compromising your beliefs. *https://bobrobertsjr.com/podcast/*
- "The Dispatch." David French joins Sarah Isgur and Jonah Goldberg in providing fact-based reporting and commentary on politics, policy and culture—informed by conservative principles. *https://podcast.thedispatch.com/*
- "Quick to Listen." A podcast by *Christianity Today* that encourages gentle dialogue over contemporary issues. *https://www.christianitytoday.com/ct/podcasts/quick-to-listen/*

WEBSITES TO VISIT

- BioLogos invites the church and the world to see the harmony between science and biblical faith as it presents an evolutionary understanding of God's creation. Founded by Francis Collins, a Christian and longtime director of the National Institutes of Health. *biologos.org*
- "Be the Bridge." A Bible-based effort to respond to the racial brokenness and systemic injustice in our world. *https://bethebridge.com/building-bridges/*

MOVIES/DOCUMENTERIES/VIDEOS TO WATCH

- *13th*. A 2016 American documentary film by director Ava DuVernay that explores the "intersection of race, justice, and mass incarceration in the United States."
- *Four Hours at the Capitol*. A 2021 documentary that chronicles the January 6, 2021, attack on the U.S. Capitol.

- *The Social Dilemma.* A 2020 Netflix documentary on the insidious nature of social media to influence our opinions.
- *What is an Evangelical?* Holy Post's Phil Vischer helps answer the question. https://bit.ly/3nGGrOi
- *"But What About Abortion ... ?"* Vischer and Jethani on a controversial topic. https://www.holypost.com/post/but-what-about-abortion
- *Race in America.* Vischer offers a 17-minute historic overview. *https://www.youtube.com/watch?v=AGUwcs9qJXY*

FACT-CHECKING SERVICES TO CONSIDER

Fact-check stories that originate from an array of sources and with all different political leanings at:

- Snopes, a fact-checking website that's been described as a "well-regarded reference for sorting out myths and rumors" on the Internet. *snopes.com*
- Politico, a political journalism company based in Arlington County, Virginia, that covers politics and policy in the United States. *politico.com*

Readers' Group

Discussion Questions

■ 1. You have the chance to dine with any three people mentioned in this book. Which three would you choose and why?

■ 2. The author interspersed ten "My Hope for the Future" sections in the book. If you could only choose one as necessary for refocusing evangelicals, which would you choose and why?

■ 3. In researching the book, the author discovers two false summits—"Trump as the problem" and "evangelicals' undying loyalty to the Far Right as the problem"—before realizing that there's a frightening peak he still had to climb. What is that third peak and why might it be such a scary ascent?

■ 4. Choose one point the author made that you vehemently disagree with. Why do you think it is wrong? What do you base your reasoning on?

■ 5. What are some of the ways the author suggests patriotism—a love of one's country—is different from Christian nationalism?

■ 6. Among the author's early Christian influences were author Brennan Manning and singer Rich Mullins. How were their lives and perspectives on faith different from some of the "spotlight evangelicals" Welch referred to?

■ 7. Of all the topics Welch discussed with dozens of people he interviewed, race, he wrote, was the one most incendiary. Why might that be? What's to lose from talking about race? What's to gain?

■ 8. If you're an evangelical Christian, how many meaningful relationships have you had with non-believers? If you're not a believer, how many such relationships have you had with evangelicals? What's the value of being able to talk with those who look at the world differently than we do? What's the risk? Does the benefit outweigh the risk?

■ 9. The author tells of a time when he was offended by a college administrator who told him "I didn't realize you were one of us"—and later admits he thought the same thing about a little girl singing at the library. In analyzing the two incidents, what did he suggest was his "bottom-line sin?"

■ 10. Welch asserts that following Christ means an ongoing willingness to change, look at things differently, and, on occasion, repent. What's one topic you've changed your mind about in the last decade? What led to your being willing to rethink that topic? And if you haven't changed your mind on anything, what was it that prevented you from doing so?

■ 11. Discuss Henri Nouwen's quote, "To whom do I belong? To God or to the world?" Where do you belong? Why does it matter?

■ 12. What's the best lesson you took away from the

Trump-as-president years? The worst?

■ 13. Welch tells of a former journalism instructor who taught him to "consider the source" when it came to trusting someone. What does he mean? Why does it matter where we get our information? What should we be wary about regarding who we trust?

■ 14. The author quotes a therapist from the TV Show "Ted Lasso" who says, "The truth will set you free—but first it will piss you off." What do you think she meant? Why does truth matter?

■ 15. Welch wrote, "I had come to believe that the difference between how people lived out their faith was related to how each of us regarded the concept of grace, God's willingness to love us despite our sin." As Christians, why should grace be a priority? What can get in the way of us giving grace to others?

■ 16. In assessing the way Beth Moore was treated by some evangelicals, Welch wonders if some believers are locked in what he called "Opposite Day" behavior. What do you think he meant by that? Do you see that happening, too, or is he exaggerating?

■ 17. Welch wrote: "Some far-right evangelicals have assumed that the world they want is the world God would want." How do you think these two worlds might differ?

■ 18. What do you think the author meant when he wrote: "I have to consciously accept discomfort to broaden my world?"

■ 19. Did this book cause you to change your perspective on anything? If so, what?

■ 20. The author references a line from Norman MacLean's *A River Runs Through It*: "You can love completely without complete understanding." What does this mean to you? How can you apply it to your life?

Acknowledgments

To Dan Roberts, whose nagging me to come to a Fellowship of Christian Athletes meeting in 1970 changed my life,
Thank you, Dandy, for thinking me worthy of being nagged.

To pastors who taught me along the way, Keith Thompson, Mark Webster, Ken Hutcherson, Dwight Englund, Greg Scandrett, Rick Taylor, Ernie Mathes, Steve Hill, and Tracy Sims,
Thank you for walking the talk, and teaching me—no, showing me—that true leaders are humble.

To mentors who've huddled with me over the decades, offering hot-chocolate wisdom on life: Dean Rea, Stan Blinkhorn, Dave Weinkauf, Dick Foth, and Sandy and Vicki Silverthorne,
Thank you for the insight and inspiration but, mainly, for listening to my

sometimes-troubled heart.

To *Register-Guard* editors Jim Godbold and Jack Wilson,
Thank you for believing in me—and, between the two of you, hiring me for four different jobs.

To the fellow University of Oregon student who placed the "lilies of the field" verse in the window of your Young-Earl dorm room in the rainy winter of 1973-74,
Thank you for lifting my spirits each morning and reminding me I wasn't alone. Your inspiration helped keep me afloat in a time when I was sinking.

To Tom Penix,
Thank you for "surf-rider" wisdom found in our common affection for Oswald "Ozzie" Chambers—and for being such a supportive friend.

To Don Mack and Chris Mack,
Thank you for the last-minute rescue.

To Tom Boubel, John Woodman, Jay Locey, Nancy (Grosjaques) Farris, Kathy "Kink" Kingsbury, Carolyn McCready, Faris Cassell, Karen Zacharias, and Brad Bills,
Thank you for the encouragement on the book.

To Clarice Wilsey, passionate Episcopalian and fellow author who believed in this project from Day One,
Thank you for your prayers, words, and editing.

To "Marley,"
Thank you for sharpening me in our email exchanges and for daring to look at the world differently.

To: Mukhtar, the "Domino Pizza Guy," and Hayfa,
Thank you for broadening our family's world—and for the cookies!

To: Ashley Banks,
Thank you for wisdom beyond your years.

To the dozens who pulled up parking-lot chairs with me or talked with me over the phone, sharing your spiritual and political views.
Thank you for insight, honesty, and, of course, social-distancing.

To those who edited one of the three not-ready-for-prime-time versions of the book: Dave Bemis, Clarice Wilsey, Eric Fuller, Ken Carson, Nancy Farris, Kevin Miller, Jane Kirkpatrick, Dave Kayfes, Steve Kuhn, Kelly Fenley, Tom Penix, Jack Wilson, Sydney Koh, and Kink.

Thank you for taking the time to help me find a truer north.

To copy editor Lisa Crossley, the quiet hero of *The Register-Guard* features department back in our glory days,

Thank you for saving me from myself, though any remaining errors—and I'm sure there will be some—are on me, not you.

To the two other members of The Three Amigos, Shane Ryder and Steve Temple,

Thank you for sharpening me in our early-morning meetings in the Olive Garden parking lot, over the sound of that incessantly annoying leaf blower.

To the three Texans—Eve Wiley, and Michael and Caitlin Fechner—and to Pastor Ben Cross,

Thank you for the courage to follow your convictions.

To Mike Hawley,

Thank you for convincing me to not quit when I was ready to.

To the late Jimmy Bartko,

Thank you for teaching me what real courage looks like. Sorry we never got to play that round of golf. See you on the back nine.

To my father-in-law, Harold,

Thank you for demonstrating unconditional love to me.

To my late mother, Marolyn,

Thank you for showing me the value of being curious about, and caring for, other people.

To Ryan, Susan, Jason, and Deena,

Thank you for simply being who you are: passionate, independent, and loving difference-makers to those around you. You are blessings in my life.

And, finally, to Sally Jean,

Thank you for challenging me to check my biases, for inspiring me with your own expanding vision, and for being OK with me hunkering down at the coast so often to write. I'll love you till the cows come home.

Bibliography

Bartko, Jim, with Bob Welch. *Boy in the Mirror: An athletic director's struggle to survive sexual abuse as a child.* (Eugene, Oregon: DAJ Publishers, 2020).

Bolton, John. *The Room Where It Happened.* (New York: Simon & Schuster, 2020).

Burchett, Dave. *When Bad Things Happen to Good People.* (Colorado Springs, Colorado: Waterbrook Press, 2002).

Carlson Evans, Diane, with Bob Welch. *Healing Wounds: A Vietnam Combat Nurse's 10-Year Fight to Honor Women in Washington, D.C.* (Brentwood, Tennessee; Permuted Press, 2020.

Chambers, Oswald. *The Quotable Oswald Chambers*. (Grand Rapids, Michigan: Discovery House, 2008).

Cloud, Henry. *Necessary Endings*. (New York: Harper Business, 2010).

Comey, James. *A Higher Loyalty.* (New York: Flatiron Books, 2018).

DeGroat, Chuck. *When Narcissism Comes to Church*. (Downers Grove, Illinois: InterVaristy Press, 2020).

Denker, Angela. *Red State Christians: Understanding the Voters Who Elected Donald Trump*. (Minneapolis: Fortress Press, 2019).

Diangelo, Robin. *White Fragility: Why It's So Hard for White People to Talk About Racism*. (Boston: Beacon Press, 2018).

Farley, Andrew. *The Naked Gospel*. (Grand Rapids, Michigan: Zondervan, 2009).

Fitch, David E. *The Church of Us vs. Them*. (Grand Rapids, Michigan: BrazosPress, 2019).

French, David. *Divided We Fall: America's Secession Threat and How to Restore Our Nation*. (New York: St. Martin's Press, 2020).

Gordon, Ernest. *To End All Wars*. (Grand Rapids, Michigan: Zondervan, 1963).

Graham, Billy. *Just as I Am*. (New York: HarperCollins, 1997).

Haidt, Jonathan. *The Righteous Mind: Why Good People Are Divided by Politics and Religion*. (New York: Vintage Books/Random House, 2012).

Hatfield, Mark. *Between a Rock and Hard Place*. (Waco, Texas: Word, 1976).

Hedges, Chris. *War Is a Force That Gives Us Meaning*. (New York: Anchor Books, 2002).

Hugo, Victor. *Les Misérables*. (New York: Signet Classic, 1987).

Frame, Randall L., and Alan Tharpe, *How Right is the Right?* (Grand Rapids, Michigan: Zondervan, 1996).

Jones, Robert T. *White Too Long.* (New York: Simon & Schuster, 2020).

Kahnke, Patrick.

MAGA SEDUCTION: Resisting the Debasement of the Christian Conscience. (St. Paul, Minnesota, 2020).

Keillor, Garrison. *Homegrown Democrat: A Few Plain Thoughts from the Heart of America.* (New York: Viking, 2004).

Kingsolver, Barbara. *Small Wonders.* (New York: Harper Collins, 2002).

Kinnaman, David. *unchristian: What a New Generation Really Thinks of Christianity.* (Grand Rapids, Michigan: Baker Books, 2007).

Kobez du Mez, Kristen. *Jesus and John Wayne.* (New York: Liveright Publishing Corporation, 2020).

Kristof, Nicholas D., and Sheryl WuDunn, *Tightrope: Americans Reaching for Hope.* (New York: Alfred A. Knopf, 2020).

Lakoff, George. *Moral Politics.* (Chicago: University of Chicago Press, 2002).

Manning, Brennan. *The Ragamuffin Gospel.* (Sisters, Oregon: Multnomah Books, 1990).

Mattson, Stephen. *The Great Reckoning: Serving a Christianity That Looks Nothing Like Christ.* (Harrisonburg, Virginia: Herald Press, 2018).

Nouwen, Henri J.M. *The Return of the Prodigal Son: A Story of Homecoming.* (New York: Image Books, Doubleday, 1992).

Posner, Sarah. *Unholy: How Christian Nationalists Powered the Trump Presidency, and the Devastating Legacy They Left Behind.* (New York: Random House, 2021).

Reed, Ralph. *For God and Country.* (Washington, D.C.: Salem Media, 2020).

Sauls, Scott. *A Gentle Answer: Our Secret Weapon in an Age of Us Against Them.* (Nashville, Thomas Nelson, 2020).

Schumann, Taylor. *When Thoughts and Prayers Aren't Enough: A Shooting*

Survivor's Journey into the Reality of Gun Violence. (Downers Grove, Illinois: InterVarsity Press, 2021).

Schiess, Kaitlyn. *The Liturgy of Politics.* (Downers Grove, Illinois: InterVarsity Press, 2020).

Shorris, Earl. *The Politics of Heaven: America in Fearful Times.* (New York: W.W. Norton & Company, Inc., 2007).

Trump, Mary L. *Too Much and Never Enough: How My Family Created the World's Most Dangerous Man.* (New York: Simon & Schuster, 2020).

Thirty Evangelical Christians, *The Spiritual Danger of Donald Trump.* (Eugene, Oregon: Cascade Books, 2020).

Tyson, Jon. *Beautiful Resistance: The Joy of Conviction in a Culture of Compromise.* (Colorado Springs: Multnomah, 2020).

Wehner, Peter. *The Death of Politics: How to Heal Our Frayed Republic after Trump.* (New York: HarperOne, 2019).

Welch, Bob. *Saving My Enemy: How Two World War II Soldiers Fought Against Each Other and Later Forged a Friendship That Saved Each Other's Life."* (Washington, D.C.: Regnery History, 2021).

Welch, Bob. *The Wizard of Foz: Dick Fosbury's One-Man High-Jump Revolution.* (New York: Skyhorse Publishing, 2018).

White Jr., Dan. *Love Over Fear: Facing Monsters, Befriending Enemies, and Healing Our Polarized World.* (Chicago: Moody Publishers, 2019).

Whitehead, Andrew, and Samuel L. Perry, *Taking American Back for God.* (New York: Oxford University Press, 2020).

Woodward, Bob. *Fear: Trump in the White House.* (New York: Simon & Schuster, 2018).

Yancey, Philp. *What's So Amazing About Grace?* (Grand Rapids, Michigan: HarperCollins Zondervan, 1997).

Reference notes

Prologue

1. Peter Wehner, "Are Trump's Critics Demonically Possessed?" *The Atlantic*, Nov. 25, 2019.
2. Henri J.M. Nouwen, *The Return of the Prodigal Son: A Story of Homecoming*. (New York: Image Books, Doubleday, 1992, 42.
3. https://www.barna.com/research/friends-loneliness/
4. https://bit.ly/2MzKxsj
5. The editor was Brenda Copeland of Simon & Schuster's Atria Books, the book *American Nightingale*.
6. Culture & Media in Faith & Christianity, "White Evangelicals Have Become Less Motivated to Address Racial Injustice," September 15, 2020.

1. The Prayer

7. David Masci and Gregory A. Smith, "5 Facts About U.S. evangelical Protestants," *Pew Research Center,* March 1, 2018.

8. Ibid.

9. "The 2020 Census of American Religion," Public Religion Research Institute, July 8, 2021.

10. https://www.nae.org/what-is-an-evangelical/

11. Nicholas Kristof, "Can Trump Help Us Bridge the 'God Gulf?'" *The New York Times,* October 22, 2016.

12. Nicholas Kristof, "Can Trump Help Us Bridge the 'God Gulf?'" *The New York Times,* October 22, 2016.

13. Nick Penzenstadler, and Susan Page, "Exclusive: Trump's 3,500 lawsuits unprecedented for a presidential nominee," June 1, 2016.

14. Marc Heatherington and Jonathan M. Ladd. "Destroying trust in the media, science, and government has left America vulnerable to disaster." *Brookings.* May 1, 2020.

2. The Past

15. Mark Hatfield, *Between a Rock and Hard Place.* (Waco, Texas: Word, 1976), 13-4.

16. Randall Balmer, "The Real Origins of the Religious Right," *Politico,* May 27, 2014.

17. In 1983, the U.S. Supreme Court upheld the IRS's decision.

18. Randall Balmer, "The Real Origins of the Religious Right," *Politico,* May 27, 2014.

19. https://politi.co/3wgWq9v

20. http://kairos2.com/quotations.htm

21. Billy Graham, *Just as I Am.* (New York: HarperCollins, 1997), 452.

22. Sarah Posner, *Unholy: How Christian Nationalists Powered the Trump Presidency, and the Devastating Legacy They Left Behind.* (New York: Random House, 2021), 107.

23. Chris Hedges, *War Is a Force That Gives Us Meaning.* (New York: Anchor Books, 2002), 15.

24. Sean Flynn, "The Sins of Ralph Reed," *GQ,* July 12, 2006. https://bit.ly/3bsAs9t

25. Ibid.

26. Joel C. Rosenberg, "Rush Limbaugh gave his life to Jesus Christ a few years ago & it gave him tremendous hope as he faced his toughest fight," *allisrael news,* February 19, 2021.

27. Dan White Jr., *Love Over Fear: Facing Monsters, Befriending Enemies, and Healing Our Polarized World.* (Chicago: Moody Publishers, 2019), 22-3.

28. Joel C. Rosenberg, "Rush Limbaugh gave his life to Jesus Christ a few years ago & it gave him tremendous hope as he faced his toughest fight," *allisrael news,* February 19, 2021.

29. Kristen Kobes du Mez, "No, Rush Limbaugh Did Not Hijack Your Parents' Christianity," *Religion Dispatches,* February 22, 2021. https://bit.ly/3kffOxw

30. Phyllis Schlafly, "Will We Allow Clinton to Redefine the Presidency?" *Eagle Forum,* February 11, 1998.

31. James Dobson, "An Evangelical Response to Bill Clinton," 1997, in *The Columbia Documentary History of Religion in American Since 1945,* ed. Paul Harvey and Philip Goff (New York: Columbia

University Press, 2007), 303-307.

32. Ryan Smith, "Pat Robertson: Haiti 'Cursed' after 'Pact with Devil,'" CBS News, January 13, 2010.

33. Philp Yancey, *What's So Amazing About Grace?* (Grand Rapids, Michigan: HarperCollins Zondervan, 1997), 15.

34. https://bit.ly/30QyKNM

Hope for the future:
Remember our mission

1. Oswald Chambers, My Utmost for His Highest. (Westwood, New Jersey: Barbour and Company, Inc., 1963), 100-101.

2. https://pewrsr.ch/3kPeCT6

3. Saving Grace

35. https://en.wikipedia.org/wiki/Rich_Mullins

36. Brennan Manning, *The Ragamuffin Gospel.* (Sisters, Oregon: Multnomah Books, 1990), 11-12.

37. https://bit.ly/3wl4Qg8

38. Ernest Gordon, *To End All Wars.* (Grand Rapids, Michigan: Zondervan, 1963), 115.

39. Andrew Farley, *The Naked Gospel.* (Grand Rapids, Michigan: Zondervan, 2009), 32.

40. Garrison Keillor, *Homegrown Democrat: A Few Plain Thoughts from the Heart of America.* (New York: Viking, 2004), 209.

41. David Kinnaman, *unchristian: What a New Generation Really Thinks of Christianity.* (Grand Rapids, Michigan: Baker Books, 2007), 177.

42. Lloyd Grove, "Marrying shock-jock bravado with incendiary right-wing rhetoric, Limbaugh became AM radio's most popular talk-show host and took an entire political party with him," *Daily Beast,* February 17, 2021.

4. The Perfect Storm

43. Rebecca Kaplan, "Trump: McCain only a war hero because he was captured," July 18, 2015.

44. Amber Phillips, "'They're rapists.' President Trump's campaign launch speech two years later, annotated," *The Washington Post,* June 16, 2017.

45. "Trump criticized for comments on Muslim mother of fallen US soldier," *Fox News Live,* July 30, 2016.

46. Chris Moody and Kristen Holmes, "Donald Trump's History of Suggesting Obama Is a Muslim," *CNN online,* September 18, 2015.

47. Neetzan Zimmerman, "Trump mocks Fiorina's physical appearance: 'Look at that face!'" *The Hill,* September 9, 2015.

48. Madison Peace, "'Theologian Wayne Grudem Is Wrong About Trump Being a Morally Good

Choice," *The Federalist*, August 8, 2016.

49. Ralph Reed, *For God and Country.* (Washington, D.C.: Salem Media, 2020), 95.

50. https://bit.ly/34cVfur

51. Chuck DeGroat, *When Narcissism Comes to Church.* (Downers Grove, Illinois: InterVarsity Press, 2020), 23.

52. Chris Hedges, *War Is a Force That Gives Us Meaning.* (New York: Anchor Books, 2002), 15.

53. Ibid., 11.

54. John Hanson, "President Trump Says You Can Thank Him for Bringing 'Merry Christmas' Back," *The Political Insider*, December 21, 2020.

55. David E. Fitch, *The Church of Us vs. Them.* (Grand Rapids, Michigan: BrazosPress, 2019), 34-6.

56. Ralph Reed, *For God and Country.* (Washington, D.C.: Salem Media, 2020), 56.

57. Morgan Lee, "Christian Nationalism Is Worse Than You Think," *Christianity Today,* January 13, 2021. https://bit.ly/37F0lSj

58. Elizabeth Dias, "Exclusive: Evangelical Leaders Plan Meeting to Test Donald Trump's Values." *Time,* May 20, 2016.

59. Thirty Evangelical Christians, *The Spiritual Danger of Donald Trump,* (Eugene, Oregon: Cascade Books, 2020).

60. David Campbell and Geoffrey Layman, "How Trump has changed white evangelicals' views about morality," *The Washington Post,* April 25, 2019.

61. Mark Galli, "Political Exegesis: On Mulligans and Turning Cheeks," *Christianity Today,* January 25, 2018.

62. Ibid.

63. William Saletan, "Trump's Christian Apologists Are Unchristian," *Slate,* November 25, 2018.

64. "'All we get is a lousy hat': Mitt Romney blasts Donald Trump's career & candidacy," *RT,* March 3, 2018.

65. "Trump's Approval Slips Where He Can't Afford to Lose It: Among Evangelicals," *ReportGlobalNews,* June 5, 2020.

66. Deborah Fikes, "A Challenge to My Fellow Evangelicals," *The New York Times,* August 19, 2016.

67. Nicholas D. Kristof and Sheryl WuDunn, *Tightrope: Americans Reaching for Hope.* (New York: Alfred A. Knopf, 2020), 102.

68. Christine Dunn, "Author speaking in Providence, says housing crisis worse than a decade ago," *Providence Journal,* September 14, 2016.

69. "Transcript: Marco Rubio: 'I ask the American people: Do not give in to the fear,' *Los Angeles Times,* March 15, 2016.

70. Paul Miller, "We Knew," *The Dispatch,* Jan. 14, 2021.

71. Rick Reilly, *Commander in Cheat: How Golf Explains Trump.* (New York: Hatchette Books 2020).

Hope for the Future:
Love One Another

1. Scott Sauls, A Gentle Answer: Our Secret Weapon in an Age of Us Against Them. (Nashville, Thomas Nelson, 2020), 29.

2. Carol Kuruvilla, "Billy Graham's Granddaughter: Evangelicals' Excuses for Trump Hurt Their Reputation," Huffington Post, October 21, 2020.

3. Dan White Jr., Love Over Fear: Facing Monsters, Befriending Enemies, and Healing Our Polarized World. (Chicago: Moody Publishers, 2019), 29.

5. Marley & Me

72. https://bit.ly/3yCke8v

73. David E. Fitch, *The Church of Us vs. Them.* (Grand Rapids, Michigan: BrazosPress, 2019), 135.

74. David French, *Divided We Fall: America's Secession Threat and How to Restore Our Nation.* (New York: St. Martin's Press, 2020), 2.

74. Elliot Aronson and Carol Tavris, "The Role of Cognitive Dissonance in the Pandemic," *The Atlantic,* July 12, 2020.

75. Ibid.

6. Trials & Triumph

75. "Along the Trail: An undesirable decision," *The Register-Guard,* Eugene, Oregon, August 26, 2016, A3.

76. Angela Denker, *Red State Christians: Understanding the Voters Who Elected Donald Trump.* (Minneapolis: Fortress Press, 2019), 73.

77. Katie Reilly, "Read Hillary Clinton's 'Basket of Deplorables' Remarks About Donald Trump Supporters," *Time,* September 10, 2016.

78. Associated Press, "Trump says he can't recall using insults, then attacks Kelly," *MSNBC,* August 7, 2015.

79. Jose A. Del Real and Anne Gearan, "Trump: If Clinton 'were a man, I don't think she'd get 5 percent of the vote," *The Washington Post,* April 26, 2016.

80. Jane C. Timm, "Trump on Hot Mic: 'When You Are a Star You Can Do Anything to Women,'" *NBC News,* October 7, 2016.

81. Alex Isenstadt, "Republicans panic as outrage with Trump boils over," *Politico,* April 9, 2020.

82. James Dobson, "An Evangelical Response to Bill Clinton," 1997, in *The Columbia Documentary History of Religion in American Since 1945,* ed. Paul Harvey and Philip Goff (New York: Columbia University Press, 2007), 303-307.

83. "The Power Issue: Beth Moore is Forcing Evangelical Christianity to Get Woke," *Texas Monthly,* December 2018.

84. https://www.theguardian.com/us-news/2016/oct/10/debate-donald-trump-threatens-to-jail-hillary-clinton

85. "Christians by political party," Pew Research Center: Religion & Public Life. https://pewrsr.ch/2P8sKtJ

86. Thirty Evangelical Christians, The Spiritual Danger of Donald Trump, (Eugene, Oregon: Cascade Books, 2020), 9.

87. Sarah Pulliam Bailey, "The Trump effect? A stunning number of evangelicals will now accept politicians' 'immoral acts,'" *Washington Post,* October 19, 2016.

88. Kristen Kobes du Mez, *Jesus and John Wayne.* (New York: Liveright Publishing Corporation, 2020), 271.

89. Randall L. Frame and Alan Tharpe, *How Right is the Right?* (Grand Rapids, Michigan:

Zondervan, 1996), 77.

90. Jemar Tisby and Tyler Burns, "Interview: Andy Crouch," *Pass the Mic* podcast, January 3, 2017.

91. Diane Landberg, "Narcissism and the System it Breeds," lecture for the Forum of Christian Leaders, video, 1:05:52, published May 5, 2016, www.youtube.com/watch?v=4BU3pwBa0qU.

92. Stephen Mattson, *The Great Reckoning: Serving a Christianity That Looks Nothing Like Christ.* (Harrisonburg, Virginia: Herald Press, 2018), 139.

93. Oswald Chambers, *The Quotable Oswald Chambers.* (Grand Rapids, Michigan: Discovery House, 2008), 188.

94. … back in the days when motors were allowed on Waldo. The Oregon State Marine Board banned the use of internal combustion motors on Waldo Lake in 2010 in response to a long and sustained effort by environmental organizations and other citizen groups to preserve the unique water purity of the lake.

95. Patrick Kahnke, *MAGA SEDUCTION: Resisting the Debasement of the Christian Conscience.* (St. Paul, Minnesota),

96. Mary L. Trump, *Too Much and Never Enough: How My Family Created the World's Most Dangerous Man.* (New York: Simon & Schuster, 2020), 15.

Hope for the future:
Replace pride with humility

1. Dave Burchett, When Bad Christians Happen to Good People. (Colorado Springs: Waterbrook Press, 2002), 1.

2. Donald Miller, Blue Like Jazz. (Nashville: Thomas Nelson Publishers, 2003), 118.

7. The New President

97. Mary L. Trump, *Too Much and Never Enough: How My Family Created the World's Most Dangerous Man.* (New York: Simon & Schuster, 2020), 43.

98. Ibid, xx.

99. Sarah Pulliam Bailey, "How a book about evangelicals, Trump and militant masculinity became a surprise bestseller," *Washington Post,* July 16, 2021.

100. Peter Wehner, *The Death of Politics: How to Heal Our Frayed Republic after Trump.* (New York: HarperOne, 2019), 11.

101. Angela Denker, *Red State Christians: Understanding the Voters Who Elected Donald Trump.* (Minneapolis: Fortress Press, 2019), 84.

102. Nicholas Kristof, "Stereotyping Trump voters is shortsighted," *The Register-Guard,* Eugene, Oregon, February 25, 2017.

103. Earl Shorris, *The Politics of Heaven: America in Fearful Times.* (New York: W.W. Norton & Company, Inc., 2007), 217.

104. Jonathan Haidt, *The Righteous Mind: Why Good People Are Divided by Politics and Religion.* (New York: Vintage Books/Random House, 2012), 103.

105. Ibid.

106. David French, *Divided We Fall: America's Secession Threat and How to Restore Our Nation.* (New York: St. Martin's Press, 2020), 82.

107. Dan White Jr., *Love Over Fear: Facing Monsters, Befriending Enemies, and Healing Our Polarized World.* (Chicago: Moody Publishers, 2019), 28.

108. Kevin Batts, "0.00000001% Chance of Being Killed by an Illegal Immigrant," *The Libertarian Republic,* September 18, 2016.

109. Sojourners staff, "Finding Our Way in a Post-Trump America," *Sojourners,* January 2021.

110. Kristen Kobes du Mez, *Jesus and John Wayne.* (New York: Liveright Publishing Corporation, 2020), 4.

111. Scott Sauls, *A Gentle Answer: Our Secret Weapon in an Age of Us Against Them.* (Nashville, Thomas Nelson, 2020), 78.

112. Ulrike Elisabeth Stockhausen, "Evangelicals and Immigration: A Conflicted History," *Process: a blog for American history,* March 18, 2019.

113. Ryan P. Burge, "For White Evangelical Republicans, Approval of Trump is About Immigration More Than Abortion," *Religion in Public.* https://bit.ly/2ZGK4Is

114. David French, "The Cultural Consequences of Very, Very Republican Christianity, *The Dispatch,* November 15, 2020. https://bit.ly/2NROHfO

115. Henri J.M. Nouwen, *The Return of the Prodigal Son: A Story of Homecoming.* (New York: Image Books, Doubleday, 1992, 42.

116. Anna Campoy, "Data from Texas shows that US-born Americans commit more rape and murder than immigrants." *Quartz,* March 14, 2018. https://bit.ly/2ZFCxcH

117. Gustavo Arellano, "Donald Trump's Wrong. Mexicans Aren't Going to Rape you." *Politico Magazine,* July 8, 2015. https://politi.co/3dDFmTG

118. Uri Friedman, "Where America's Terrorists Actually Come From." *The Atlantic,* January 30, 2017. https://bit.ly/3by5Mn9

8. Lilies of the Field

119. Bob Woodward, *Fear: Trump in the White House.* (New York: Simon & Schuster, 2018), 246.

120. Ibid., 244.

121. Ibid., 252.

122. King James Version; couldn't resist that wonderful "ye of little faith" phrase.

Hope for the future:
Find the courage to live beyond fear

1. Ralph Reed, *For God and Country.* (Washington, D.C.: Salem Media, 2020), 95.

9. 'Fire the SOB'

123. Nikhil Sonnad, "The NFL's racial divide, in one chart." Quartz, May 24, 2018. https://bit.ly/3urgcxD

124. Ian Thomsen, "The Research is Clear: White People are Not More Likely Than Black People to be Killed by Police," *News@Northeastern,* July 16, 2020.

125. Ian Schwartz, "Trump: NFL Owners Should Fire the 'Son of a Bitch' Player Who 'Disrespects Our Flag' By Kneeling," *RealClear Politics,* September 23, 2017.

126. Bob Welch. *The Wizard of Foz: Dick Fosbury's One-Man High-Jump Revolution.* (New York: Skyhorse Publishing), 2018.

127. Isabelle Wilkerson, *Caste: The Origins of Our Discontent,* . (New York: Random House, 2020), 186-87.

128. Ibid..

129. Robert T. Jones, *White Too Long.* (New York: Simon & Schuster, 2020), 175.

10. 'One of Us'

130. Ali Vitali, Kasie Hunt and Frank Thorp V, "Trump referred to Hait and African nations as 'shithole' countries," *NBC News,* January 10, 2018.

131. Emma Green, "The Tiny Blond Bible Teacher Taking on the Evangelical Political Machine, *Atlantic Monthly,* October 2018. https://bit.ly/2O5dA7S

132. All Sides, "GOP Sen. Sasse says Trump 'kisses dictators' butts' and mocks evangelicals, October 15, 2020.

133. *Relevant,* "Report: Trump Makes Fun of His Evangelical Supporters When They're Not Around," September 29, 2020.

134. Diane Carlson Evans, with Bob Welch. *Healing Wounds: A Vietnam Combat Nurse's 10-Year Fight to Honor Women in Washington, D.C.* (Brentwood, Tennessee; Permuted Press, 2020.

Hope for the Future:
That We Would Welcome In Instead of Wall Off

1. Gregory A. Boyd, The Myth of the Christian Nation. (Grand Rapids, Michigan: Zondervan, 2005), 53.

2. Cal Thomas and Ed Dobson, Blinded by Might: Can the Religious Right Save America? (Grand Rapids, Michigan: HarperCollins Zondervan, 1999), 23.

3. Steve Bence, 1972: Oregon track, Nike shoes, and my life with both. (Beaverton, Oregon: SB 4 Press, 2021).

4. Patrick Woodhouse, *Etty Hillesum: A Life Transformed.* (Grand Rapids, Michigan: Eerdmans, 2002), 145.

11. Wise Men & Folly

134. Anne Applebaum, "The Facts Just Aren't Getting Through," *The Atlantic,* August 9, 2020.

136. Elizabeth Baker, "My Evangelical Church Is Gaslighting Me, But I Refuse to Fall For It Anymore," *Huffington Post,* January 14, 2021.

137. Elizabeth Baker, "My Evangelical Church Is Gaslighting Me, But I Refuse to Fall For It Anymore," *Huffington Post,* January 14, 2021.

138. Chris Buskirk, "Yes, Christians Can Support Trump Without Risk to Their Witness," *Center for American Greatness,* May 8, 2018. https://bit.ly/3q3ggR3

139. Andrea Jefferson, "Trump Says He's a Christian, But That He 'Doesn't Need to Ask for Forgiveness' for His Sins," *Political Flare,* December 24, 2019.

140. Mara Konnikova, "Trump's Lies vs. Your Brain," *Politico Magazine,* January/February 2017. https://politi.co/3pUlcHF

141. Katie Rogers and Nicholas Fandos, "Trump Tells Congresswomen to 'Go Back' to the Countries They Came From," *The New York Times,* July `4, 2019.

142. Henry Cloud, *Necessary Endings.* (New York: Harper Business, 2010), 126-143

143. Ibid., 126-143

144. Ibid. 126-143

145. James Comey, *A Higher Loyalty.* (New York: Flatiron Books, 2018), 228-29.

146. Ibid., 236-37.

147. Ibid., 236-37.

148. Ibid., 243.

149. Ibid., 263.

150. Ibid., 267.

151. Ibid., 276.

12. Opposite Day

152. https://bit.ly/3bmwAIn

153. Bob Smietana, "Saddleback Church just ordained three women as pastors. The Southern Baptist Convention says only men should be," *The Washington Post,* May 11, 2021.

154. Jay Childs, "John MacArthur and Beth Moore: What's All the Hubbub About?" *Grace Unlimited,* October 31, 2019.

155. Philp Yancey, *What's So Amazing About Grace.* (Grand Rapids, Michigan: HarperCollins Zondervan, 1997), 15.

156. Bess Levin, "As Sarah Sanders Signs Off, A Look Back at Her Biggest Lies," *Vanity Fair,* June 13, 2019.

157. "Defeating Hillary is Not Worth Sacrificing Our Witness," *The Roys Report,* October 10, 2016.

158. Andrew Solender, "Trump Praises Drivers That Biden Campaign Says Tried to Run Bus 'Off the Road,'" *Forbes,* October 31, 2020.

159. Jemar Tisby, "The Biggest Threat to Christianity in the US," *Footnotes by Jemar Tisby,* December 22, 2020.

160. Oswald Chambers, *My Utmost for His Highest,* (Westwood, New Jersey: Barbour and Company, Inc., 1963), 61.

Hope for the Future:
That We Might Value Character Over Comfort

1. Nilay Saiya, "Proof That Political Privilege Is Harmful for Christianity," Christianity Today, May 6, 2021.

2. Ibid.

3. Philip Yancey, Soul Survivor: How Thirteen Unlikely Mentors Helped My Faith Survive the Church. (New York: Galilee Doubleday, 2003, 110.

4. C.S. Lewis, The Four Loves. (New York: Harcourt Brace Jovanovich, Inc., 1960, 168.

13. Flags & Crosses

161. David French, "Discerning the Difference Between Christian Nationalism and Christian Patriotism," *The French Press,* January 31, 2021.

162. Ibid..

163. Paul LeBlanc "Ex-Trump adviser Michael Flynn's call for 'one religion' in the US garners swift condemnation," *CNN Politics,* November 15, 2021.

164. Anugrah Kumar, "Majority of White Evangelicals Believe You Have to Be Christian to Be Truly American," *Christian Post,* February 4, 2017.

165. Quarterly.gospelinlife.com

166. In terms of Christian nationalism, Perry and Whitehead based their "who qualifies" criteria on whether the people in the survey agreed with the following statements: 1. "The federal government should declare the United States a Christian nation"; 2. "The federal government should enforce strict separate of church and state"; 3. "The federal government should allow the display of religious symbols in public spaces"; 4. "The success of the United States is part of God's plan." 5. "The federal government should allow prayer in public schools." The two funneled survey responders into four groups, in regard to whether they embrace Christian nationalism or don't: "rejecters" (21.5 percent), who disagree or strongly disagree on the statements; "resisters" (26.6 percent), middle-of-the-roaders; "accommodators" (32.1 percent), base-level Christian nationalists; and "ambassadors" (19.8 percent), those who are "all in."

167. Ibid., 58-9.

168. Kristen Kobes du Mez, *Jesus and John Wayne.* (New York: Liveright Publishing Corporation, 2020).

169. Ibid., 61-2.

170. Kirsten Weir, "Politics is personal," *American Psychological Association,* November 1, 2019.

171. Andrew Whitehead and Samuel L. Perry, *Taking American Back for God.* (New York: Oxford University Press, 2020), 20.

172. Ibid., 62.

173. Andrew Whitehead and Samuel L. Perry, *Taking American Back for God.* (New York: Oxford University Press, 2020), 86.

174. Taylor Schumann, *When Thoughts and Prayers Aren't Enough: A Shooting Survivor's Journeye into the Reality of Gun Violence.* (Downers Grove, Illinois: InterVarsity Press, 2021).

175. Stephen Mattson, *The Great Reckoning: Serving a Christianity That Looks Nothing Like Christ.* (Harrisonburg, Virginia: Herald Press, 2018), 144.

176. Ibid., 20.

177. David French, "Why Do They Hate Us?" *The French Press,* December 20, 2020.

178. John Bolton, *The Room Where It Happened.* (New York: Simon & Schuster, 2020), 2.

179. https://bit.ly/3dJtIoU

14. Death & Deception

180. Aki Peritz, "The intelligence community got the pandemic right. Then politicians botched it." *The Washington Post,* September 11, 2020.

181. Ibid.

182. Herb Scribner, "'This is deadly stuff,': President Trump played down coronavirus to stop panic, new book says, *Deseret News,* September 9, 2020.

183. Robin Abcarian, "Why did Trump lie about the COVID-19 when he knew how serious it was?" *Los Angeles Times,* September 12, 2020.

184. Scottie Andrew, "The US has 4% of the world's population but 25% of its coronavirus cases," *CNN,* June 30, 2020.

185. Mark Galli, "Trump Should be Removed from Office, *Christianity Today,* December 19, 2019.

186. Ibid.

187. Ibid.

188. Tom Gjelten, "Survey: White Evangelicals See Trump as 'Honest' and 'Morally Upstanding,'" March 12, 2020.

15. COVID Nation

189. Jim Bartko, with Bob Welch. *Boy in the Mirror: An athletic director's struggle to survive sexual abuse as a child.* (Eugene, Oregon: DAJ Publishers, 2020), 24.

190. David Bauder, "Trump uses daily coronavirus briefing to attack reporter," *ABC News,* March 20, 2020.

191. Kriston McIntosh, Emily Moss, Ryan Nunn, and Jay Shambaugh, "Examining the White Black Wealth Gap," *Brookings,* February 27, 20202.

192. David French, "Structural Racism Isn't Wokeness, It's Reality," *The Dispatch,* July 25, 2021.

193. George W. Bush, "Statement by President George W. Bush," *George W. Bush Presidential Center*, June 2, 2020.

194. Culture & Media in Faith & Christianity, "White Evangelicals Have Become Less Motivated to Address Racial Injustice," September 15, 2020.

195. George Lakoff, *Moral Politics.* (Chicago: University of Chicago Press, 2002), 114-15.

196. James Crawley, "George Floyd's Death Considered Murder by 64 percent of Blacks, 28 percent of White in America: Poll, *Newsweek,* March 10, 2021.

197. Robin Diangelo, *White Fragility: Why It's So Hard for White People to Talk About Racism.* (Boston: Beacon Press, 2018), 42.

198. Daniel Hill, *White Awake: An honest look at what it means to be white.* (Downers Grove, Illinois: IVP Books, 2017), 129-131.

199. https://bit.ly/3mzaAjb

200. David Callahan, "How the G.I. Bill left out African Americans," *Demos,* November 11, 2013.

16. The Decision

201. Mary L. Trump, *Too Much and Never Enough: How My Family Created the World's Most*

Dangerous Man. (New York: Simon & Schuster, 2020), 207.\

Hope for the future:
That we might rededicate ourselves to the Truth

1. Holly Meyer, "NIH director Francis Collins urges Christians to look for truth about COVID-19 vaccines, not conspiracy theories and misinformation," *The (Nashville) Tennessean*, December 3, 2020.

2. Glenn Kessler, Salvador Rizzo, and Meg Kelly. "Trump's false or misleading claims total 30,573 over 4 years," *The Washington Post,* January 24, 2021.

17. Choosing Sides

202. Kashmira Gander, "Trump Says Coronavirus 'Affects Virtually Nobody,' as US Has World's Highest Death Toll," *Newsweek,* September 22, 2020.

203. "Dave Ramsey, COVID Conspiracy Theorist, Insults Low Wage Earners," *The Wartburg Watch 2021,* December 21, 2020.

204. Cassandra Stephenson, "Personal finance guru Dave Ramsey lists Franklin mansion for $15.45 million," *Nashville Tennessean,* February 23, 2021.

205. RNS Staff, "Full Ramsey Solutions Response," *Religion News Service,* January 15, 2021.

206. Ibid.

207. Shane Claiborne, "The New American Revival: Christian Nationalism's 'Delta Variant,'" August 31, 2021.

208. David French, "The Spiritual Problem at the Heart of Christian Vaccine Refusal," *The Dispatch,* March 7, 2021.

209. Hannah Sparks, "Atheists are more likely to get vaccinated, survey finds," *New York Post,* March 9, 2021.

210. Matt Perez, "Trump Rages Over Simple Question: 'I'd Say That You're a Terrible Reporter,'" *Forbes,* March 20, 2020.

211. Sarah Enselein, "John MacArthur Admits prior Church COVID Outbreak, Own Illness," *The Roys Report,* August 30, 2021.

212. Janelle Griffith, "Louisiana pastor charged with defying coronavirus order against large gatherings." *CBS News,* March 31, 2020.

18. Consider the Source

https://edition.cnn.com/videos/health/2021/10/09/francis-collins-nih-covid-vaccine-evangelical-christians-acosta-nr-vpx.cnn

213. "McEnany says President Trump 'never downplayed the virus,'" *CNN,* September 9, 2020.

214. Mandy Armitage, MD, "How Do COVID-19's Annual Deaths and Morality Rates Compare to the Flu's?" *Good Rx,* August 27, 2020.

215. "What Are Americans' Views on the Coronavirus Pandemic?" *The Commonwealth Fund,* March 20, 2020.

216. Kristen V. Brown and Justin Sink, "Trump's Comments on Disinfectants Prompts Exerts to Warn Against Inhaling Bleach to Kill Coronavirus," *Time,* April 24, 2020.

217. Bryan Metzger, "'Trump counties' had over 3 times more COVID deaths than 'Biden counties' in October, according to a new report, *Yahoo! News,* November 8, 2021.

218. Brandon Gage, "Donald Trump's Superspreader Events Have Killed Hundreds and Infected Tens of Thousands, New Study Shows," *Hillreporter.com,* October 31, 2020.

219. 'All we get is a lousy hat': Mitt Romney blasts Donald Trump's career & candidacy," *RT,* March 3, 2018.

220. Daniel A. Cox, "Rise of conspiracies reveals an evangelical divide in the GOP," *Survey Center of American Life,* February 12, 2021.

221. Natalie Colarossi, "White Evangelicals Are More Likely to Believe in QAnon Than Any Other Faith Group," *Newsweek,* February 11, 2021.

222. Steve Benen, "South Dakota's Noem hopes to capitalize on her COVID failures," MSNBC, July 23, 2021.

223. Andrew Whitehead and Samuel L. Perry, *Taking American Back for God.* (New York: Oxford University Press, 2020).

224. Christian Rigg, "Belief in COVID-19 conspiracy theories linked to greater egotism," *PsyPost,* May 15, 2021.

225. David French, "The Spiritual Problem at the Heart of Christian Vaccine Refusal," *The Dispatch,* March 7, 2021.

226. Ibid.

227. Ibid.

228. Ibid.

229. Peter Wehner, "Are Trump's Critics Demonically Possessed?" *The Atlantic,* Nov. 25, 2019.

230. Carol Kuruville, "Pastor Calls Evangelical Christians Who Don't Support Trump 'Morons,'" *Huffington Post,* February 15, 2019.

231. Julia Musto, "Press Secretary Grisham on Trump's 'human scrum' tweet: Those working against him are just that," *Fox News,* October 24, 2019.)

232. Kyle Mantyla, "Chris McDonald: Christians Who Criticize Trump are Betraying God," August 28, 2019.

Hope for the Future:
That We Might See Ourselves as Victors not Victims

1. Oswald Chambers, My Utmost for His Highest, (Westwood, New Jersey: Barbour and Company, Inc., 1963), 99.

2. https://bit.ly/3bW67kE

3. Russell Moore, "The Roman Road from Insurrection," www.russellmoore.com, January 11, 2021.

19. Line in the Sand

233. "How Liars Create the Illusion of Truth," *Association for Psychological Science,* November 9, 2016.

234. Zack Beauchamp, "The emergency is happening right now," *Vox,* September 30, 2020.

235. Rick Reilly, *Commander in Cheat: How Golf Explains Trump.* (New York: Hatchette Books, 2020).

236. David Moye, "Donald Trump Cheats at Golf In Some Really Ridiculous Ways: Sports Writer," *The Huffington Post,* April 2, 2019.

237. Ibid.

238. "When Donald Trump lost the Iowa caucus in 2016, 'he immediately cried that Cruz cheated.'" *Politifact,* November 18, 2020.

239. Elizabeth Chuck, "GOP Slams Trump: Not Accepting Election Results Would Be 'Beyond the Pale,'" *NBC News,* October 20, 2016.

240. Ibid.

241. Philp Yancey, *What's So Amazing About Grace?* (Grand Rapids, Michigan: HarperCollins Zondervan, 1997), 49.

242. Ibid.

243. Jon Tyson, *Beautiful Resistance: The Joy of Conviction in a Culture of Compromise.* (Colorado Springs: Multnomah, 2020), 23.

244. Barbara Kingsolver, *Small Wonders.* (New York: Harper Collins, 2002), 18.

20. Denial

242. Carmine Gallo, "John McCain's 10-Minute Concession Speech Reminds Americans That Words Can Unite and Inspire," *Forbes,* November 7, 2020.

246. "Hillary Clinton's concession speech (full text)," *CNN,* November 9, 2016.

247. Pete Williams and Nicole Via y Rada, "Trump's election fight includes over 50 lawsuits. It's not going well." *Decision 2020,* November 23, 2020.

248. https://bit.ly/3fim2fS

249. Jack Durschlag, "Audio released of Trump call to Raffensperger," *Fox News,* January 4, 2021.

250. Christina A. Cassidy and Anthony Izaguirre, "Explainer: Election claims, and why it's clear Biden won," *The Associated Press,* January 19, 2021.

251. John Owen Nwachukwu, "US election 2020: How Trump's Spiritual Adviser assured him of angels from Africa, South America to give him victory," November 7, 2020.

252. Elizabeth C. Connors, "Do Republicans really believe the election was stolen—or are they just saying that?" *The Washington Post,* December 22, 2020.

253. Mike Cosper, "The Bobby Knight Problem," *The Rise and Fall of Mars Hill* podcast, *Christianity Today,* September 21, 2021.

254. Ibid.

255. Jason Lemon, "Chris Christie Condemns Republicans Still Lying About Election: 'It's Shameful,'" *Newsweek,* January 24, 2001.

256. Kevin Collier, Katy Tur, Julia Ainsley, and Ken Dilanian, "Trump fires head of election cybersecurity who debunked conspiracy theories," *NBC News,* November 17, 2020. *The Washington Post,* December 22, 2020.

257. David Brooks, "America Is Having a Moral Convulsion," *The Atlantic,* October 5, 2020.

258. Adam Russell Taylor, "When Christian Media Peddle Lies," *Sojourners,* February 11, 2021.

259. Ibid.

260. Rod Dreher, "Eric Metaxas's American Apocalypse," *The American Conservative,* December 10, 2020.

261. Rajneeshpuram was built in north-central Oregon beginning in 1981. For a deeper understanding of it, the *Wild Wild Country* documentary offers one of those truth-as-stranger-than-fiction looks: https://www.imdb.com/title/tt7768848/

262. Bob Welch, *Saving My Enemy: How Two World War II Soldiers Fought Against Each Other and Later Forged a Friendship That Saved Each Other's Life."* (Washington, D.C.: Regnery History, 2021), 37.

263. Frohnmayer, who went on to become the president of my alma mater, the University of Oregon, died of cancer in 2015. He was 74.

264. Rod Dreher, "Eric Metaxas's American Apocalypse," *The American Conservative,* December 10, 2020.

265. Ibid.

Hope for the Future:
That We Might Stop Bowing to Celebrity 'Leaders'

1. Kristen Kobes du Mez, Jesus and John Wayne. (New York: Liveright Publishing Corporation, 2020), 4.

2. David French, "Did Donald Trump Make the Church Great Again?" The Dispatch, September 19, 2021.

3. Skye Jethani, What If Jesus Was Serious? (Chicago: Moody, 2020), 43.

4. Oswald Chambers, My Utmost for His Highest. (Westwood, New Jersey: Barbour and Company, Inc., 1963), 233.

5. Skye Jethani, What If Jesus Was Serious? (Chicago: Moody, 2020), 10.

6. Ibid.

7. Khaleda Rahman, "Every Republican to Speak Out Against Marjorie Taylor Greene's Holocaust Remarks,"*Newsweek,* May 26, 2021.

21. Capitol Offense

266. Andrew Whitehead and Samuel L. Perry, *Taking American Back for God.* (New York: Oxford University Press, 2020), 109.

267. Kyley Schultz, "Verify: Here's what the role of the vice president is during the Electoral College certification votes," *MSN,* January 6, 2021.

268. https://bit.ly/2XghvTW

269. Gina Ciliberto, Stephanie Russell-Kraft, "They Invaded the Capitol, Saying Jesus is My Savior, Trump is My President," *Sojourners,* January 7, 2021.

270. https://bit.ly/2XghvTW

271. Ibid.

272. Ibid.

273. Ibid.

274. Ibid.

275. Ibid.

276. Ibid.

277. Ibid.

278. Ibid.

279. Ibid.

280. Ibid.

281. Lexi Lonas, "Sasse says Trump was 'delighted' and 'excited' by reports of Capitol riot."The Hill, (January 8, 2021.

282. "Associated Press Timeline of events at the Capitol, 4 dead", Associated Press, January 6, 2021.

283. https://bit.ly/2XghvTW

284. Jamie Gangel, Kevin Liptak, Michael Warren, Marshall Cohen, CNN, February 12, 2021.

285. Ibid.

286. Ibid.

287. Justin Sink, "Pence Won't Act to Remove Trump, Says Nation Needs Healing," Bloomberg, January 12, 2021.

288. Ibid.

289. Rebecca Kaplan, "More than $30 million needed for Capitol repairs and new security after assault, officials, say," *CBS News*, February 24, 2021.

290. Mariam Fam, Elana Schor, and David Crary, "What Trump-Supporting Pastors Preached After the Capitol Attack," Christianity Today, January 11, 2021.

291. Russell Moore, "The Roman Road from Insurrection," www.russellmoore.com, January 11, 2021.

292. Justin Sink, "Pence Won't Act to Remove Trump, Says Nation Needs Healing," Bloomberg, January 12, 2021.

293. "These criminals came prepared for war," *Next NewsHour*, February 25, 2021.

294. Ewan Palmer, "'Let's go Brandon' Chanted at QAnon-Linked Church Event in Texas," *Newsweek*, November 15, 2021.

295. Mariam Fam, Elana Schor, and David Crary, "What Trump-Supporting Pastors Preached After the Capitol Attack," *Christianity Today*, January 11, 2021.

296. Ibid.

297. Steve Peoples, Jill Colvin, "GOP signals unwillingness to part with Trump after riot," *Chicago Tribune*, January 27, 2021.

298. Madison Peace, "Theologian Wayne Grudem Is Wrong About Trump Being a Morally Good Choice, *The Federalist*, August 8, 2016.

299. Dr. Marcia Sirota, "When Victims of Abuse Justify Their Abuser's Behavior," *Dr. Marcia Sirota, M.D.*, https://bit.ly/3cuTJZP

300. David Brooks, "The rotting Republican mind," *The Register-Guard*, Eugene, Oregon.

301. Adam Edelman and Garrett Haake, "Republican loyal to Trump claims Capitol riot looked more like 'normal tourist visit,'" *NBC*, May 12, 2021.

302. "Full Text: Joe Biden's inauguration speech transcript," *Politico*, January 20, 2021.

303. Brian Ke, "NJ Congressman Andy Kim Helps Clean Up Capitol Building Following Riot," *Yahoo! News*, January 8, 2021.

Hope for the Future:
That We Might Be Willing to Change

1. Tom Hovestol, Extreme Righteousness. (Chicago: Moody Press, 1997), 147.

2. Erich Maria Remarque, All Quiet on the Western Front. (New York: Little, Brown and Company, 1929), 223.

3. Timothy Dalrymple, "The Splintering of the Evangelical Soul," Christianity Today, April 16, 2021.

4. PRRI, "The 'Big Lie': Most Republicans Believe the 2020 Election was Stolen," May 12, 2021.

5. Peter Wehner, The Death of Politics: How to Heal Our Frayed Republic after Trump. (New York: HarperOne, 2019), 121.

6. Steve Hayes and Jonah Goldberg, "We We are Leaving Fox News," *The Dispatch*, November 21, 2021.

7. Justin Giboney, Michael Wear, and Chris Butler. Compassion (&) Conviction: The AND Campaign's Guide to Faithful Civic. Engagement. (Downers Grove, Illinois: InterVarsity Press, 2020), 38.

8. Sen-ts'an, Hsin hsin ming. In Conze 1954.

9. Jonathan Haidt in The Righteous Mind: Why Good People Are Divided by Politics and Religion. (New York: Vintage Books/Random House, 2012), 54.

10. Ibid., 56.

11. David E. Fitch, The Church of Us vs. Them. (Grand Rapids, Michigan: BrazosPress, 2019), 139.

12. Ibid., 79.

13. Stephen Mattson, *The Great Reckoning: Serving a Christianity That Looks Nothing Like Christ*. (Harrisonburg, Virginia: Herald Press, 2018), 257.

Afterword

304. Justin Coleman, "Trump wins CPAC straw poll with 55 percent," *The Hill*, February 28, 2021.

305. Brennan Manning, *The Ragamuffin Gospel*. (Sisters, Oregon: Multnomah Books, 1990), 140.

306. Timothy Dalrymple, "The Splintering of the Evangelical Soul," *Christianity Today*, April 16, 2021.

Epilogue

307. Justin Coleman, "Trump wins CPAC straw poll with 55 percent," *The Hill*, February 28, 2021.

308. https://bit.ly/3mRvoTq

309. Nicole Acevedo, "National Religious Broadcasters spokesperson fired after pro-vaccine remarks on 'Morning Joe," NBC News, August 28, 2021.

Index

A

Abignale, Frank, 88
abortion, 38, 40-42, 77-78, 82, 94, 125, 192, 198, 212. *See also* Pro-Life movement
"Access Hollywood" video, 95-97, 156
Alshaara, Shaza, 282-283
Antifa, 139, 210, 264, 294
Arbery, Ahmaud, 229-30, 317

B

Bader Ginsburg, Ruth, 219
Bailey, George, 31
Balmer, Randall, 40
Baker, Elizabeth, 172
Bakker, Jim, 43

Barna Group, 24, 80, 222
Bartko, Jimmy, 154, 175-176, 213-215, 217, 236
Barr, William, 273
Bauer, Gary, 76-77, 96
Beachside Writers Workshop, 187, 236
Bence, Steve, 166
Berlet, Chip, 90
Bhagwan Shree Rajneesh, 277
Bible
    "Do unto others" and, 224, 244
    The Great Commandment and, 15, 312
    The Great Commission and, 16
    faithfulness to God and, 236
    "Greater love has no one ..." and,

245
"Fruit of the Spirit" and, 200-201
as a "lamp unto my feet," 201
Lost sheep, parable of, and, 245
Biden, President Joe, 185, 205, 253, 268, 271-76, 289-90, 292, 294-98
Billy Graham Center, Wheaton College, 75, 170, 239
Black Lives Matter (organization), 227-227, 234, 300
Bob Jones University, 40
Boebert, Rep. Lauren, 185
Bolton, John, 205, 295
Bonhoeffer, Dietrich, 89, 276
Brooks, Rep. Mo, 289
Brown, Gov. Kate, 36
Browning, Robert, 134
Burchett, Dave, 107
Burns, Pastor Mark, 80
Bush, President George W., 34, 104, 129, 218, 222, 269, 301
Buskirk, Chris, 172-175

C

Canzano, John, 218
Carlos, John, 144-145
Carlson Evans, Diane, 160, 162
Carter, President Jimmy, 40
Catch Me If You Can, 88
Center for Disease Control and Prevention (CDC), 209-10, 219, 253
Chambers, Oswald, 51, 90, 101, 188, 261-62, 283
Charlottesville, 128-129
Chauvin, Derek, 221, 316
Cheney, Rep. Liz, 294-295
Christian Coalition, 42, 66, 124
Christian Far Right, 12, 13, 14
roots of, 37-46, 199.
Christian nationalism, 15, 117, 196, 255, 258, 314
definition of, 196-198
influence of, 196-204
relationship of evangelical Christians to, 197-204
relationship of politics and religion to, 197-204
traits that accompany, 197-199
Christianity Today, 77, 100-01, 211-12, 228, 273, 303, 313, 315, 318
Christians,
persecution of, 122, 124, 132, 190, 193
Civil Rights Act of 1964, 41
Clinton, President Bill, 37, 44-45, 96, 99, 212
Clinton, Hillary, 36-37, 76, 78, 80, 87, 94-95, 101, 118, 129, 129, 183, 266, 272
Cloud, Henry, 175
Clyde, Rep. Andrew, 297
CNN, 21, 301
cognitive bias, 119-121
cognitive dissonance, 91-92
Cohen, Michael, 154, 160
Collins, Francis, 240, 249
Comey, James, 154, 178-180
Commander in Cheat, 265-266
Concerned Women for America, 76
Conservative Political Action Conference, 313, 317
Corvallis High, 187, 223
Cosper, Mike, 273-274, 315
Costanza, George, 185
COVID-19, 16, 21, 23, 210-11, 213-15, 217-18, 220-21, 236,-37, 243-46, 248, 250-54, 256-57, 264, 275, 279-80, 315-16
initial discovery in China, 207
early manifestations of in US, 209, 214-215, 218-221
evangelical response to, 243-250

listed as a pandemic, 213-214
severity of, 211
Stanford study of effects following Trump events, 253
social distancing and masks related to, 211
Trump response to, 209-211, 218, 237, 251-255
Cruz, Sen. Ted, 68, 266, 282-283
Cuban, Mark, 88
Cultus Lake, 237
Curbelo, Rep. Carlos, 266

D

DACA (Deferred Action for Childhood Arrivals), 121-122
Daniels, Stormy, 154
Darling, Daniel, 316
D.C. Metro Police, 290
Deep State, 254
Democratic National Convention, 36, 80
Dillard, Annie, 236-237
Dobson, James, 42-43, 96, 115, 258
Dreher, Rob, 278-279
Driscoll, Mark, 273
Duford, Jerushah, 83-84
Durbin, Sen. Dick, 154
Duke, David, 128

E

Electoral Control Act, 291
Engelbert, Fritz, 175, 177
Engelbert, Matthias, 177
Engelbert, Volker, 177
Eugene, Oregon, 20, 33, 56-57, 61, 85, 88, 118, 125, 146-47, 149, 176, 182, 206, 213-15, 228, 230, 280
    Citizens Police Academy in, 197, 227

Equal Rights Amendment (ERA), 45
Evangelicalism
    Roots of, 39-48.
Evangelical Christians,
    Bible as authority of, 33
    "born-again" conversion and, 33
    character and, 34-35, 190-193
    COVID, response to, and, 243-250, 252, 275, 284
    definition of, 33
    good works of, 18, 24, 47
    "good news" and, 33-34
    grace and, 46, 119, 267
    gun legislation and, 43, 201
    hatred for Far Left and, 89, 131
    humility and, 104-107, 246
    Holy Spirit and, 235
    idol worship and, 33, 89, 100-01, 269, 279, 314
    Jesus, allegiance to, and, 50-52
    love and, 82-84, 194
    pride and humility of, 106-109
    pro-life values and, 83
    racism and, 229-230, 234-235
    self-examination and, 260-262
    as "strangers and pilgrims," 314
    The Tribe, loyalty to, and, 283
    Trump, loyalty to, and, 72, 76, 94, 256, 275-281
    truth and, 26, 238-242
    victimhood and, 193
    walling off or welcoming in by, 164-167
Evangelical pastors, 231-232
Evers, Medgar, 299
Evers-Williams, Myrlie, 301-302

F

Falwell, Jerry Jr., 80, 96, 129, 202, 318
Falwell, Jerry Sr., 41, 283
Family Research Council, 42

Fauci, Dr. Anthony, 210
Fellowship of Christian Athletes, 54
Fiornia, Carly, 69
Floyd, George, 24, 221-222, 227, 234, 258, 318
Focus on the Family (organization), 40
Focus on the Family (magazine), 43
Ford, President Jerry, 40
Fosbury, Dick, 144
Foth, Dick, 60-61, 290,
Fox News, 22, 44, 201, 244, 260, 303
Free Willy, 38
French, David, 196-197, 256-259
Fresno Bee, 174
Fresno State, 176
Frohnmayer, Dave, 278

G

Gandhi, Mahatma, 130
Gingrich, Newt, 46
Guiliani, Rudy, 291
Good Samaritan, The, 262
Grace Community Church, 182
Graham, Billy, 40-41, 83, 96,
Graham, Franklin, 17, 74, 95-97, 129-130, 259, 277, 280, 298
Graham, Jack, 258
Graham, Sen. Lindsey, 154, 266
Grisham, Stephanie, 258
Gulf War, The (Persian), 44

H

Hagee, Pastor John, 293
Haiti, 45, 61, 156, 195-96, 202, 224, 244
Harris, Kamala, 269, 273, 278, 294, 298
Hatch, Sen. Orrin, 129

Hatfield, Sen. Mark, R-Ore., 39
Hawley, Rep. Josh, 298
High-O-Scope, 223
Hitler, Adolf, 89, 278
Hitler Youth, 278
Holocaust, The, 128
Holt, Bertha and Harry, 125
Houston Chronicle, 182

I

immigration, 121-126
Iowa Caucus, 70
It's a Wonderful Life, 31

J

Jaballa, Hayfa, 206, 264, 280-81
Jaballa, Mukhtar, 162-63, 206, 264, 280-81
Jefferson High, 223-224
Jeffress, Pastor Robert, 71, 185
Jesus Christ
   golden rule and, 244
   grace and, 267
   humility and, 130
   as the Prince of Peace, 17
Jong-un, Kim, 154
Journal-American, 135, 209-210

K

Kaepernick, Colin, 143-146, 224
Kearns Goodwin, Doris, 114
Keillor, Garrison, 66
Keller, Kathy, 126
Keller, Pastor Tim, 126, 184, 304
Kelly, Megyn, 94
Kim, Rep. Andy, 298-299
King Nebuchadnezzar, 89
King Jr., Martin Luther, 24
Knight, Bobby, 273-74
Knight, Phil, 176

Korean War, 124
Krebs, Christopher, 274
Kristof, Nicholas, 33-35
Kristallnacht, 278

L

Lewis, C.S., 23, 107
Liberty University, 80, 129, 316
Limbaugh, Rush, 43, 47, 67, 260, 317
Locke, Pastor Greg, 246
Los Angeles Dodgers, 30
Lucado, Max, 81, 126, 183
Lucas, Pastor Michael, 261

M

Ma Anand Sheela, 277
MacArthur, Pastor John, 181-186, 249, 308-309
MacLean, Norman, 313
Malarkey, Don, 177-178, 300
Mandela, Nelson, 18
Manning, Brennan, 47, 64
"Marley," 85-90, 98-99, 118, 131-133, 171, 317-18
The Masters University, 184
Matthews, Chris, 98-99
McCain, Sen. John, 70, 95, 129, 272, 313
McCarthy, House Minority Leader Kevin, 293
McConnell, Sen. Majority Leader Mitch, 272, 293
McDonald, Pastor Chris, 258
McGeachin, Lt. Gov. Janice, 185
McMullen, Evan, 103
McNally, Marianne, 178
Meacham, Jon, 114, 139
Mendenhall Ministries, 55-56, 147
Mendenhall, Mississippi, 55-56, 147
Metaxas, Eric, 276-278

Mississippi Burning, 301
Mondale, Walter, 85-86
Moore, Beth, 96, 97, 130, 156, 181-185, 313, 318
Moore, Roy (Alabama Sen.), 130, 132
Moore, Russell (SBC), 99, 205, 261, 294, 318
Moral Majority, 16, 41-42, 89, 91, 138, 260
Mullins, Rich, 63-64
Murray, Jim, 145
Musburger, Brent, 145
Muslims, 71, 126, 199
Muslim Americans, 70, 126, 162, 197, 280-81

N

Nance, Penny, 76
narcissism in leaders, 73-74
National Association of Evangelicals, 33
National Religious Broadcasters, 318
National Lampoon's Christmas Vacation, 133
Nazi Germany, 284
Newseum, 160-61
Nixon, President Richard, 41, 139
Noem, Gov. Kristi L., 254
Nouwen, Henri, 18, 126, 316

O

Obama, President Barack, 33, 36, 70, 71, 77, 113, 121, 178, 289, 297
O'Brien, Robert, 210
"Opposite Day," 185
Oregon, University of, 30, 176, 223
Oregon State Penitentiary, 24, 166

P

Pacific Crest Trail, 30, 178, 218-219
Palin, Sarah, 295-96
Parks, Rosa, 144
Pelosi, Speaker of the House Nancy, 296
Pence, Vice President Mike, 129, 289-292, 294
Perkins, Tony, 77, 275-76
Perry, Samuel L., 198-201, 202-03, 255
J.B. Phillips, 141
Pottinger, Matthew, 210
Porter, Rob, 129
Powell, Colin, 313
Priebus, Reince, 93
Prodigal Son, 267
Pro-Life movement, 46, 245
Proud Boys, 264, 292

R

racism, 141-150, 221
   Black Lives Matter (organization) and, 227-228, 234, 300
   author's personal experiences related to, 222-224
   determining if it exists, 225-26
   George Floyd and, 221-222
   profiling drivers and, 233-34
   protests over perceived, 221-222

Raffensperger, Sec. of State Brad, 272
Rage, 210-11
Rajneeshees, 277-78
Rajneeshpuram, 277
Ramsey, David, 243-246, 255
Reagan, President Ronald, 38-39, 83, 172
Reed, Ralph, 15, 40-41, 70, 94, 137, 254, 283, 296
Register-Guard, The, 27, 29, 33-34, 54, 67, 95-96, 116, 126, 134, 151-152, 163, 215
Reilly, Rick, 86, 265
Religion News Service, 245-246
Remington, Pastor Tim, 295
Republican National Committee, 93
Republican National Convention, 34
Republicans, 252
Rickey, Branch, 28
"The Rise and Fall of Mars Hill," 273
A River Runs Through It, 316
Roberts, Bob, 258, 282, 313
Robertson, Pat, 40, 43, 278
Rodriguez, Pastor Samuel, 294
Romney, Senator Mitt, 78, 103-4
Roosevelt, President Franklin, 218
Roys, Julie, 184
Rubio, Sen. Marco, 79, 129, 297

S

Sasse, Sen. Ben, 160, 293
Satan, 76
Saving My Enemy, 175
Schiess, Kaitlyn, 315
Schlafly, Phyllis, 45
Shadrack, Meshach, and Abednego, 89
Schumman, Taylor, 202
situational ethics, 277-78
Smith, Tommie, 144-46
Southern Baptist Convention, 40, 99, 182, 318
Spell, Pastor Anthony, 249
Stearns, Rich, 121-22, 255
Stetzer, Ed, 240
Strobel, Lee, 277
Sund, Chief Steven, 295
Swaggart, Jimmy, 47-48

T

Taylor, Christian, 313
Taylor Greene, Rep. Marjorie, 185, 276, 284
Tea Party, The 46
"Three Amigos, The," 218
Tokatee Golf Club, 213
Traverse City, Michigan, 267
Tribe, The, 15, 22, 43, 47, 67, 74, 102, 118, 120-21, 150, 156-9, 172, 183, 98, 200, 204-5, 222, 225, 228, 234, 245-6, 256
Trump, Fred, 114-115
Trump, Mary L., 104, 114-115
Trump University, 75
Trump, Donald, 14, 16, 21-23, 25, 36-38, 150, 178-180, 270-281
    adolescence and, 114-115
    attack on the US Capitol, involvement in, 290-299
    bullying by, 16-17, 23, 183,-184
    cheating at golf and 265-66
    COVID, response to from, 210-211, 213, 237, 245, 251-255
    2020 election results, contesting and, 271-275
    final day as president, 298-299
    foolishness of, 172-175
    grace and, 267-268
    immigration and, 70, 121-126
    impeachment of (first), 205-206
    impeachment of (second), 211-212
    as John Wayne image, 100
    media and, 37-38
    lawsuits against, 36-37
    "Make America Great Again" and, 155, 202
    Merry Christmas," not "Happy Holidays," and, 72-74, 132
    racial incidents and, 128-129, 221-222
    sexual assault allegations of, 36
    television career of, 36
    2016 Presidential Election campaign and, 14
    2020 Presidential Election results, contesting, and, 271-274
    2020 Presidential Election results, warning of defiance if he doesn't win, 264-265
    women, treatment of, and, 94-96
Trump, Donald Jr., 292
Truth Matters Conference, 181-182
Tuberville, Sen. Tommy, 292

U

US Capitol, January 6, 2021 attack on, 291-299
US Internal Revenue Service (IRS), 40
US 2016 Presidential Election results, 103
US 2020 Presidential Election results, 275
    factors in how people voted, 117-118
U.S. political system, citizens' lack of faith in, 118
U.S. Supreme Court, 71, 95

V

Valenti, Paul, 31
Vietnam, War in, 85
Vischer, Phil, 258, 313
Voice of the Martyrs, 192-193
Voskamp, Ann, 126, 154

W

Waldo Lake, 102-103

Wallace, Chris, 264-265
Wallis, Jim, 307
Wehner, Peter, 79, 116, 304
Welch, Bob
   book tours and, 35, 65-66
   book-writing and, 17, 19, 21-24, 30
   church experiences and, 55-60
   church "implosion" and, 92
   Christian nationalism and, 199-202
   college experiences and, 135-136
   complicity with the Christian Far Right and, 17
   conversion to Christianity and, 54
   COVID and, 237-238, 263, 278
   Cross Purposes, indecision about, and motives for, writing, and, 24, 235-237
   evangelical Christian identity and, 32, 155-156
   forgiveness, and, 59, 91-92, 108-109
   friends of, 14, 23, 235-236, 264
   grandfather of, 47-48
   hypocrisy of, 158-159, 186, 288
   journalism and, 18, 121
   "Lilies of the Field" trust in God and, 135-136, 155
   literary influences of, 64-65
   major Christian influences of, 55-66
   "Marley" email exchange and, 85-90,
   media, views on, and 37-38, 98
   mentors of, 62-63
   mother of, 20, 127-128, 187, 206, 219-221
   "Mrs. A" and, 61-62
   musical influences of, 63
   as a "political hybrid," 18-20
   politics and, 32
   race-related matters and, 147-148, 222-224, 231-232
   Register-Guard experiences and, 34-35, 134-135, 153-154, 159, 160-162
   Register-Guard editorials written by, 79-80, 101-102, 129-131
   Sikh client and, 122, 238, 241
   teaching journalism and, 123
Welch, Sally, 30, 102-103, 128, 228-229, 264, 301, 311-312
Weyrich, Paul, 40
What' So Amazing About Grace?, 46 64, 267
White, Paula, 273
Whitehead, Andrew L., 197-200, 202, 255
Wilkerson, Isabel, 148-149
Wirth, Shirley, 31
Wolff, Michael, 154
Woodward, Bob, 129, 210-211, 252
World Evangelical Alliance, 78
World Health Organization (WHO), 213-214
World War II, 73, 128, 278
Wuhan, China, 206, 209-210

Y

Yamhill, Oregon, 33, 117
Yancey, George, 34
Yancey, Philip, 64, 187, 267
Young Life, 53, 314

Z

Zelensky, President Volodymyr, 205

Made in United States
Orlando, FL
01 February 2022

14306978R10221